HUSKIES
HUSKIES

Go Huskies! Beat Felix the Cat!

The Story of America's High School Athletic
Nicknames and Mascots
and What They Reveal About Who We Are

Emerson B. Houck

Bradford House

Copyright © 2003 by Emerson B. Houck

All rights reserved. No part of this book may be reproduced in any way, existing or to be created, without express permission from the publisher. For further information, contact

>BRADFORD HOUSE
>7913 Ridge Road
>Indianapolis, IN 46240

ISBN 0-9745335-0-5 (HARDCOVER)
ISBN 0-9745335-1-3 (PAPERBACK)

LIBRARY OF CONGRESS CONTROL NUMBER 2003098101

Back cover / dustjacket art by Julie Houck
Cover / dustjacket design by Steven D. Armour
Interior and text design by Sheila G. Samson, WordCrafter, Inc., Carmel, IN

This book is dedicated to the one person above all others without whom it, or any other worthwhile endeavor I have undertaken, would not have been possible—my wife, Jane. Her patient understanding and unbridled enthusiasm have sustained and nurtured me throughout our lives together.

Contents

Foreword vii
Preface ix
Acknowledgments xiii

☙

1 Let Freedom Ring 1
2 Royalty? In America? 10
3 Fun With Names 20
4 Fun With History—and the Present 33
5 Fun Groupings 40
6 Some Tough Ones 51
7 A Boy Named Sue 62
8 Antiheroes 66
9 Our Daily Bread 71
10 From the Fields and Forests 87
11 Down to the Sea in Ships 104
12 Lions and Tigers and Bears—Oh, my! 117
13 Man's Best Friend 123
14 Our Feathered Friends 129
15 More From the Animal Kingdom 137
16 Heavens Above 151
17 Location, Location, Location 162
18 The Old Country 175
19 Some States 189
20 Happy Halloween 195
21 Some Nasties 202
22 Long Gone . . . Or Never Were 206

[**Contents** *continued next page*]

23 Town and Gown 220
24 The Girls Take the Field 230
25 Indian Team Names 237
26 All the Small Schools 248
27 Other Heroes 266
28 Religious Schools 271
29 A Few More Good Ones 276
30 Nicknames, Mascots, and Symbols 281
31 American History 101 287
32 End Game 305

֍

Epilogue — A Final Thought 321
Appendix I 324
Appendix II 363

Foreword

My life has been spent in sports. I played in high school and college, coached in high school, college, and the Olympic movement; and was an administrator in college, the Olympic movement, and the professional game. I have seen the professional game turn into almost pure entertainment rather than sport, and the college game and the Olympics become so influenced by commercialism that at times it is unrecognizable. The last bastion of purity is high school athletics. The players for the most part are real students who like to play and compete against their own potential. The coaches are called by a true vocation to teach and by and large those who administrate the competitions have kept it honest and fair. Overriding all of this is pride and support of community. It is refreshing and as close to purity as exists in the world of sport today.

I believe in the purity of sport. I am also a history buff who believes in the lessons that can be learned from the past. This combination, coupled with my personal friendship and admiration for Emerson Houck made *Go Huskies! Beat Felix the Cat!* an inevitable grand slam as a read for me. This is a book written from the heart by a high school and college athlete, a swimmer no less, highly educated and accomplished, but who is a purist and one who, as an adopted Hoosier, was perhaps a bit more affected than most

Go Huskies! Beat Felix the Cat!

by the lessons, purity, and magnetism of high school athletics. He has written a wonderful book that touches every small town, school district and state in our great union. He has woven the pride of each school with the history of their area, their mascot and our country in a very personal and unique way. It is indeed interesting reading, but more than that, it is a real insight on what America is and who we are as its citizens.

David R. Gavitt
Chariman Emeritus
Basketball Hall of Fame

PREFACE

From Sea to Shining Sea

I was born and raised in Oak Park, Illinois. We were proud of many things in Oak Park and our sister village of River Forest. We were proud of Ernest Hemingway, also born and raised in Oak Park and a graduate of our high school, and of Frank Lloyd Wright, who had his studio there. The village had more of his homes than any other place in the world. Inventors, architects, Hollywood stars, Olympic Gold Medalists, prize-winning authors, all had lived in Oak Park. Perhaps the focal point of our pride, however, was our high school with its academic and athletic reputation not only in Illinois but nationally. Our colors were Navy blue and burnt orange, our fight song was to the tune of the University of Illinois' fight song. Our school mascot was the Siberian Huskie. The teams we played were variously labeled Lions, Red Devils, Indians, Mustangs, Giants, Pirates, Bulldogs, Wildcats, and Wildkits. Wildkits? Where did that come from? But more about that later.

I never thought too much about whether we were the Huskies or not, or why, until much later. After all, huskies were beautiful animals, loyal, brave, swift, strong, not to be messed with, most of the things we wanted our teams to be. At that time I was not clear on the difference between nicknames and mascots, either. All of this came to me later, as I began to appreciate the significance of these choices as they were made for schools like mine, and my wife's, all over the country.

Go Huskies! Beat Felix the Cat!

My wife attended Indianapolis Shortridge High School, and they had a mascot (something selected because it is felt to bring good luck) as well as a nickname. The mascot was Felix the Cat, and the team name was the Blue Devils, each chosen in the 1920s for interesting reasons. As we explore the most interesting mascots and nicknames among the over twenty thousand in American high schools, it is my hope that you will be at times charmed, surprised, mystified, amused and amazed—as I have been.

It was only after I retired and my wife and I had time to travel the highways and byways of America that it struck me how proud almost every place is of its local high school, and how often the mascot or nickname they have selected was indicative of something very important to them. This was often related to their history, geography, common heritage, or primary vocation. In other cases, these names spoke of what they saw as important in the greater scheme of things, their view of the country in which we are all blessed to live and its heroes, legends and values. Still others looked at the universe around us, poetry, world history, literature, or the wonders of nature for their inspiration. Some of the names derive from our wonderful sense of humor and our ability to avoid taking ourselves too seriously. These names are often whimsical, clever and downright amusing. In the pages that follow I have tried to selectively cover the breadth of this wide variety of choice.

My interest in these team names was piqued on a drive from Indianapolis to St. Louis one summer. We first came to the small town of Teutopolis and were informed it was the home of the Wooden Shoes. Then we arrived at Effingham. Home of the Flaming Hearts. Then it was the Vandalia Vandals, the Collinsville Kahoks, the Wood River Oilers, the Roxanna Shells, and, by the time we got to Centralia's Orphans on the way home I was really intrigued. What was the source of these names? What did they tell us about the history of the towns? I began jotting down the ones that struck my fancy, and before I knew it I was asking every gas station attendant or café waitress in every small town we went to what the mascot of their local high school was. And why. Then I began reading the sports

Go Huskies! Beat Felix the Cat!

pages of the newspapers and adding to my list of good ones. Finally, through the help of John Gillis of the National Federation of High Schools, now, happily, located in Indianapolis, I was able to get the names of the mascots of almost all of the nation's more than twenty thousand public, private and parochial high schools. By then I was really enjoying my task so I systematically went through them all and that is the source of many of the names I want to share with you now. But, the stories behind the names came from a variety of sources, many from pleasant visits and phone calls, others from writings found in libraries and online.

When you travel around America, get off the interstates and enjoy the countryside and the small towns. You will notice that many of them, along with their "Welcome to" signs will say HOME OF THE BRAVES—or the Jaguars, or whatever. Or, as in Westfield, Indiana, THIS IS SHAMROCK COUNTRY, or Richwood, Ohio, where paw prints on the road lead to a sign informing you that YOU ARE IN WILDCAT COUNTRY, or Monticello, Florida, where it says HOME OF THE FIGHTING TIGERS. Perhaps my favorite is in a small southern Indiana town where the entering sign reads WELCOME TO AUSTIN, WHERE EAGLES SOAR.

Frequently I am reminded of the cheer I heard so often at my daughter's high school, Indianapolis North Central, when she was a student there: "We are the Panthers, the mighty, mighty Panthers." Clearly we often see ourselves as members of a group with whom we are proud to affiliate, whose triumphs and tragedies we identify with as our own, and upon which we have placed a cohesive label. My daughter and her friends did not think they really were panthers, of course, anymore than my friends and I thought we were sled dogs. It was a proxy, with some attributes they and we admired, perhaps speed, or grace, power or beauty. But in many cases, names were chosen that truly did identify the group explicitly. Either way, the names are surely indicative of how we think, of our unique and collective histories, of what we value and admire, what we fear and respect, where and how we live, what makes us laugh.

xi

GO HUSKIES! BEAT FELIX THE CAT!

This, then, is an attempt to examine the variety and the cleverness of those team names and mascots we have selected for our high schools, and in the process to learn a great deal about who we are, from Maine to Hawaii, from Key West to Barrow. From sea to shining sea.

Go, Huskies!

Emerson B. Houck
Indianapolis, Indiana
September 2003

Acknowledgments

I have known Dave Gavitt for more than forty years, a man of deep faith, the highest character and integrity, a sportsman who always plays hard and fair, and win or lose, accepts either with grace and dignity. He is a man I would unhesitatingly select to coach my children or grandchildren. To paraphrase John Wooden, they call him coach: I am proud to call him friend and thank him for his encouragement as I was writing this book and for his Introduction to it.

Thanks also to Art Baxter of Hawthorne Book Services, who has taken an amateur manuscript from an inexperienced author and used his editorial skills to transform it into that most wondrous thing—a book. I had only the vaguest of notions when I embarked on this project what a vast difference there is between a manuscript and a book and what considerable talent is required to make the latter out of the former. Talent Art has in abundance, along with experience, wisdom, and good humor, and I am most appreciative to him for using all of these attributes in our work together.

Thanks also to Sheila Samson for her design work and ideas, to Steve Armour for the cover, and to Julie Houck for taking my photograph of an Indiana barn with a basketball goal on it and transforming it into the evocative work of art that adorns the back cover.

Thanks, aimed above, to Jim Hughes, whose interest in history and preservation of our past was of such great value in helping Reid Williamson lead the Historic Landmarks Foundation of Indiana to perform the wonders they have in our state. Jim, who shared my interest in the historic insights to be gained by understanding where many of our high school mascots came from, was taken from us too soon.

Thanks, of course, to John Gillis of the National High School Federation whose assistance in providing the data for this book has been invaluable and whose friendship has been a most pleasant by-product.

Once again, thanks to my wife, Jane, for her unending encouragement, patience, and support throughout every phase of this project.

Finally, and by necessity imprecisely, my thanks to the many hundreds of my fellow countrymen who took time from busy lives to tell me the stories behind their mascots, and to the imaginative souls before them who selected such a broad range of intriguing names. I accept all responsibility for errors if I have not gotten those stories straight or if I have passed on to you any that came to me that were not really true. I believe them all to be accurate but have absolutely no illusions concerning the extent of my own considerable fallibility.

1
LET FREEDOM RING

IN OUR QUEST to find out who we are one thing is abundantly clear—we are all Americans. Where did our shared values come from? When did they emerge? How are they honored today? A pretty good place to start is with the Declaration of Independence, July 4, 1776. Thomas Jefferson: "We hold these truths to be self-evident, that all men are created equal, that they are endowed by their Creator with certain unalienable rights, that among these are life, liberty and the pursuit of happiness." We might next look to James Madison and the Constitution of the United States and its accompanying Bill of Rights, ratified in 1789. And, although more years later than I wish it had been, to Abraham Lincoln's Emancipation Proclamation of 1863, and finally to Martin Luther King's ringing "I have a dream" speech, which I prefer to think of as his "Let freedom ring" speech. The Founding Fathers and those who followed, men and women whose struggles gave us the freedom we enjoy and hold sacred today, are remembered in the choice of names we have made for our municipalities, the schools in them and the mascots for those schools.

> *By the rude bridge that arched the flood,*
> *Their flag to April's breeze unfurled,*
> *There once the embattled farmers stood*
> *And fired the shot heard round the world.*

Go Huskies! Beat Felix the Cat!

The words are Ralph Waldo Emerson's, from his "Concord Hymn." The year was 1776. The location: Concord, Massachusetts. In Concord the Carlisle School teams are very appropriately known as the Patriots, and in nearby Lexington the high school teams are the Minutemen, the name given to those very embattled farmers. Independence High Schools in Columbus, Ohio, and San Jose, California, have selected the 76ers for the name of their teams and Independence High School in Charlotte, North Carolina, has selected Patriots for theirs. In Bethlehem, Pennsylvania, Freedom High School teams are also the Patriots, a name that has been replicated from coast to coast in some wonderfully appropriately named places: Valley Forge High School in Parma Heights, Ohio; Liberty High School in Renton, Washington; and Yorktown High School, in Arlington, Virginia, to name a few. It is also the name selected by the high school in North Pole, Alaska, a far-off bastion of American democracy.

Another reminder of our earliest beginnings of nationhood comes from Henry Wadsworth Longfellow's famous words:

> *Listen my children and you shall hear*
> *Of the midnight ride of Paul Revere . . .*

Revere, a north shore suburb of Boston, names its high school teams the Patriots. There is also a Revere High School in Richfield, Ohio. Its teams are the Minutemen. There are many other Minutemen around our nation, literally from coast to coast. There are the Minutemen representing the towns of Lexington in the states of Illinois, Missouri and Nebraska; and Concord, California; and at Bunker Hill, Illinois; and Concord High School in Elkhart, Indiana.

How about the Founding Fathers themselves? High schools and towns bearing George Washington's name are found all over the country. Some examples are the Patriots of Tacoma, Denver, and Charleston, West Virginia, Washington high schools; the Los Angeles Washington Generals; the Indianapolis Washington Continentals; and, my favorite, recalling the "I cannot tell a lie" legend, the Hatchets of Washington, Indiana.

Let Freedom Ring

Benjamin Franklin, remarkably versatile and innovative, is also well remembered. Franklin High Schools in Portland, Oregon, Rochester, New York, and Seattle are all called the Quakers. Not every school honoring Franklin chooses to do so by recognizing the religion that was so prominent in his adopted home city of Philadelphia. Some remember that he also discovered electricity, so it is said, by flying a kite during a thunderstorm. Philadelphia Franklin High School teams are called the Electrons. In a similar vein are the teams representing Franklin, Illinois, and Franklin Central, in suburban Indianapolis, who are the Flashes.

Who exemplifies patriotism more than Patrick Henry? "Is life so sweet, peace so dear that it is to be purchased at the price of chains and slavery? Forbid it, almighty God! I know not what course others may take, but as for me, give me liberty or give me death." Fittingly, there are Patriots representing the Patrick Henry High Schools in Minneapolis, San Diego, and in the Virginia cities of Ashland and Roanoke.

Thomas Jefferson, our third president, is generally credited with having written most of the stirring words of our Declaration of Independence that would command the attention of the world, inspire his fellow countrymen, and endure through the ages. He was also an accomplished architect who designed the impressive original campus, the Lawn, of the University of Virginia as well as his own beautiful home, Monticello, both in Charlottesville. Jefferson High Schools in Portland, Oregon, and Los Angeles are called the Democrats; Dallas Jefferson fields the Patriots; Joplin, Missouri, Jefferson teams are the Cavaliers, and Alexandria, Virginia, Jefferson the Colonials. My favorite Jefferson reference, however, comes from the town of Monticello, Illinois, which has selected Sages for their nickname. Their teams are thus the Sages of Monticello, just as Jefferson himself was, and their symbol is a wise owl.

James Madison is generally recognized as the Father of the United States Constitution, the insightful document that is the basis of all law and justice in our country, a document of amazing flexibility and adaptability, as vibrant today as it was more than two hundred years ago when it was written. Madison also served as our fourth president. He is honored by the

Go Huskies! Beat Felix the Cat!

Portland, Oregon, Madison High School Senators, and the Marshall, North Carolina, Madison High School Patriots, among many others.

Alexander Hamilton was our nation's first secretary of the treasury, killed in the infamous duel by Aaron Burr. Los Angeles Hamilton High School teams are known as the Yankees in his honor. Philadelphia West Catholic High School teams are called the Burrs, taking the winning half of that tragic duel for their own. I am sure they are Burrs under the saddles of their rivals on the athletic field!

None of the Founding Fathers served his country more faithfully or diligently than the often under-appreciated John Adams, our first vice president and second president. Adams was born in Braintree, Massachusetts, which split into Quincy while he lived. Both he and his son, John Quincy Adams, also a dedicated statesman and intellectual giant who served our country as its sixth president, are now claimed by Quincy. Quincy High School, appropriately enough, has selected the Presidents as their nickname. Also, Hastings, Nebraska's Adams High School teams are the Patriots.

John Marshall was the fourth chief justice of the United States Supreme Court and one of the most effective in our history. His career spanned thirty years of significant decisions and he is generally credited with establishing the doctrine of judicial review, central to the effective separation of powers of our government and of keeping the Constitution viable over the centuries. He is honored by several Marshall High Schools who have recognized his legal accomplishments in their choice of team nickname: the Jurists of Rochester, New York, the Justices of Richmond, Virginia, the Cleveland, Ohio, Lawyers, and the Los Angeles Barristers. Portland, Oregon, Marshall High School calls its teams the Minutemen. Chicago Marshall, a school that has enjoyed great success recently with its girls' basketball teams, is called the Commandos. I'm not sure they even had commandos in John Marshall's day, but somehow I think he would have been pleased by the choice of that nickname. There is, after all, a decided similarity between 1776's Minutemen and today's Commandos, to be sure.

Let Freedom Ring

James Monroe, our country's fifth president, was a neighbor and close confidant of Thomas Jefferson, who taught him Law and later designed his home, Ash Lawn, just outside of Charlottesville. He established the Monroe Doctrine, solidifying the Western Hemisphere. Monroe High School in Lindside, West Virginia, has selected Mavericks for their nickname, which, perhaps, many of Monroe's political opponents would find interesting.

John Jay was another leader of the cause for independence from Great Britain, serving his country as diplomat, president of the Continental Congress, contributor to the Federalist Papers, and first chief justice of the United States Supreme Court. John Jay High School in Hopewell Junction, New York, is named in his honor as are their teams, the Patriots.

The Green Mountain Boys, from the state of Vermont, led by Ethan Allen, were an effective and admired group of fighters during the Revolutionary War. Ethan Allen High School, in Wales, Wisconsin, fields teams known as the Green Mountain Men.

Crispus Attucks was the first American to be killed by the British in what is now called the Boston Massacre. He died on March 5, 1770. He was an African American, a runaway slave who, although reportedly treated well by his Framingham owner, valued freedom too much not to escape. Due to his own deep sentiments, he sympathized with the colonists seeking freedom from Great Britain. At great personal risk, not just from the British, but also from those colonists who would return him to slavery, he joined the citizenry in a confrontation with a platoon or so of Redcoat troops on the fateful morning of his death.

Crispus Attucks High School in Indianapolis became a fighter for freedom also. It was originally an all African-American high school, now it is an integrated middle school. For many years the wonderful athletes who attended Crispus Attucks had limited opportunity to test their skills against the white schools in the area. When, in the forties and fifties, all restrictions were lifted, fans began to realize what they had been missing. The Crispus Attucks Tigers turned out men such as Willie Gardner, Hallie Bryant, Bob Jewell, Willie Merriweather, and the incomparable Oscar Robertson.

Go Huskies! Beat Felix the Cat!

The first time I saw Oscar play was in the 1954 city tournament championship game when he made the winning basket in sudden death overtime against Shortridge at the Butler Fieldhouse in front of a packed house of over fifteen thousand fans. Attucks went on to win the state that year, the first time an Indianapolis school had done so. They won it again in 1956. Undefeated, something no Indiana school had ever accomplished before. Their coach, who turned out men as well as basketball players, was a fine gentleman named Ray Crowe. He played the coach of the opposition team in the state final game in the movie *Hoosiers*.

I knew Bob Jewell very well, as a chemist at Eli Lilly and Company, as a colleague and friend, a friend who died all too young. Bob was the first African American to win the Trester Mental Attitude Award, given for leadership, integrity, scholastic and academic performance to one player at each year's Indiana State Basketball Tournament's Final Four. He went on to the University of Michigan, and Indiana Central College (now the University of Indianapolis), then Lilly. He was a man I liked and respected immensely, soft-spoken, intelligent, and dignified, with his six-foot six-inch stature and erect bearing, his ready smile, he was truly a gentle giant. And he was certainly a Crispus Attucks Tiger, a fierce fighter for excellence.

A great naval hero was Commodore Oliver Hazard Perry, who won an important engagement with the British in the Battle of Erie in 1813. This battle represented the first time a British fleet had ever surrendered in its entirety and led to Perry's unforgettable message to William Henry Harrison: "We have met the enemy and they are ours." Perry High Schools in Lima, Ohio, and Pittsburgh, Pennsylvania are the Commodores, as is Perry County High School located in Hazard, Kentucky.

The Marquis de Lafayette was a French Naval officer whose assistance to the American cause for Independence helped achieve its success. Washington appointed him defender of Virginia near the end of the Revolutionary War. The marquis named one of his own sons George Washington Lafayette and many towns and cities in America have reciprocated, choosing Lafayette as their name. Most of them, however, have selected team names with little relevance to the man himself. An exception is Lafayette High School in Oxford, Mississippi, home of Ole Miss and of William Faulkner, two excellent reasons for a visit there. Oxford Lafayette teams are known as the Commodores.

Somewhat later in our history another naval commander of great renown, David Glasgow Farragut, spoke or yelled those immortal words "Damn the torpedoes, full speed ahead," a treasured part of American naval lore. Farragut's great victory was at the battle of Mobile Bay in 1863. The town of Farragut, Iowa, has a high school nicknamed the Admirals, as do Farragut High Schools in Chicago and Knoxville. Farragut High School in St. Petersburg, Florida, has selected the Bluejackets for their nickname, remembering the connection with the United States Navy.

Andrew Jackson of Tennessee, often referred to as "Old Hickory," was our seventh president, and the first born in a state not touching the Atlantic Ocean. His beautiful home, the Hermitage, outside of Nashville, is well worth seeing. Before he became President he was a very accomplished soldier, winning the important battle of New Orleans toward the end of the War of 1812. Andrew Jackson High School in Chalmette, Louisiana, is known as the Colonels, whereas Andrew Jackson High School in Kershaw, South Carolina, making reference to his Tennessee heritage, are the Volunteers. Andrew Jackson High School in the Borough of Queens, New York, calls its teams affectionately the Hickories.

Perhaps no single man has captured the imagination of the American people as has Abraham Lincoln. Besides preserving the Union, freeing the slaves, and delivering perhaps the most familiar speech in American history, the Gettysburg Address, Lincoln also had the foresight to envision the importance of unifying the nation from Atlantic to Pacific and to begin the construction of the transcontinental railroad, not completed until eleven years after his death. Cities, towns and schools across America have honored his memory, as would be expected. There are Railsplitters at Lincoln High Schools in Brooklyn, Philadelphia, Des Moines, Iowa, and Ypsilanti, Michigan, as well as in the towns of Lincoln Park, Michigan, and, of course, Lincoln, Illinois. The latter is actually the only town to bear his name with his consent while Lincoln himself was still alive and, since he himself christened the town with a watermelon, there is a statue of a watermelon on the town square and a Watermelon Festival is held there every summer.

Warren, Ohio, Lincoln, and Tacoma Lincoln, are the Abes, while Sioux Falls, South Dakota, Lincoln High School teams are the Patriots. Since Lincoln is so closely associated in many minds with Gettysburg, it is appropriate to mention that the Gettysburg High School athletes are known as the Warriors, and there surely were warriors on both sides of that dreadful battle.

Lincoln is not the only Civil War hero remembered by our high schools. Thomas Jonathan Jackson, a Confederate commander, received his sobriquet, "Stonewall," during the first battle of Bull Run in 1861 when, facing withering Union fire, he stood tall causing another Confederate officer to exhort his troops by saying, "Look at Jackson. He stands like a stone wall." Jackson is honored by the Generals of Miami Jackson High, and of Stonewall Jackson High School in Quicksburg, Virginia.

Robert E. Lee is widely remembered as well. In Houston, Jacksonville, Montgomery, and in Jonesville, Virginia, we find the Lee High School Generals. Bishopville, South Carolina, Robert E. Lee Academy has selected Cavaliers for their nickname and Staunton, Virginia Robert E. Lee High School teams are the Fighting Leemen. In Arlington, Virginia, home of the Lee-Custis Mansion, we are reminded of the close relationship between George Washington's wife, Martha Custis, and the Lee family. The appropriately named Washington and Lee High School in Arlington fields teams known equally appropriately, as the Generals.

Ulysses S. Grant, often identified with the lovely town of Galena, Illinois, was the top Union general before becoming the eighteenth president of the United States. Grant High Schools in Oklahoma City and Portland, Oregon, are the Generals in his honor.

William Tecumseh Sherman, from Ohio, was another top Union general whose march to the sea in Georgia is still remembered throughout the South with considerable acrimony. Milledgeville, Georgia, is a beautiful reminder of what was lost by Sherman's scorched earth policy. Milledgeville, the pre-Atlanta capital of the state, was spared by Sherman and is filled with street after street of Antebellum homes, churches, the Georgia Military Institute, and the impressive campus of the College of Georgia. The three high schools in Milledgeville all ignore these events: Baldwin High fields the Braves, Greene the Bulldogs, and John Milledge Academy teams are the Trojans. Regardless of how the South feels about him, Unioto High School in Chillicothe, Ohio, remembers him more positively: They are the Sherman Tanks.

Philip Sheridan, a colleague of Sherman's in the Union army, also from south-central Ohio, is honored by the high school in Thornville, which bears his name and calls its teams the Generals.

Theodore Roosevelt was our twenty-sixth president, and a Nobel Peace Prize recipient in 1906. He was a war hero, outdoorsman, and a blunt-speaking leader. When he led his troops, known as the Roughriders, up Cuba's San Juan Hill in the war with Spain, he created a legend that is well remembered to this day. There are Roughriders at Roosevelt High Schools all over this great nation: Kent, Ohio, Portland, Oregon, East Chicago, Indiana, Chicago, Seattle, Saint Louis, Los Angeles, Sioux Falls, and Johnstown, Colorado. Deviating a bit from the norm are the Teddies of Minneapolis Roosevelt.

2
ROYALTY? IN AMERICA?

ALTHOUGH WE FOUGHT a war to achieve our independence from a monarchy, and thirty-seven years later fought another to retain it, we still manage to incorporate royalty in many of its forms in the names we choose for the teams we love.

European Royalty

At the top of the hierarchy of royalty in Europe were the kings and queens. Today we find Kings at Lewis Cass High School in Walton, Indiana, and at Wrightstown, New Jersey, High School. The girls' teams at the latter are not, however, the Queens, but for some reason are the Lady Knights. The Kingsmen are at Kings Park, New York, High School and at Penn High School in Mishawaka, Indiana. There are also Kingsmen, appropriately enough at Rex Putnam High School in Milwaukee, Oregon.

Stockton, California, is located ninety miles from San Francisco on an important deep-water channel to the coast. It was first a base site for French trappers, known to have been there as early as 1832, and was originally called French Camp. The town was renamed in 1847 for Commodore Robert Stockton who had led an important battle somewhat earlier. It is also thought by many to be the town referred to as "Mudville" by Edward Thayer in his classically American poem "Casey at the Bat."

Royalty? In America?

O, somewhere in this favored land the sun is shining bright;
   The band is playing somewhere and somewhere hearts are light,
And somewhere men are laughing, and somewhere children shout;
   But there is no joy in Mudville, mighty Casey has struck out.

Well, there is joy in Stockton, whether or not it is really Mudville. As befits a town located on a river channel the Amos Alonzo Stagg High School in Stockton has named its athletic teams the Delta Kings.

A few hundred miles to the south, Newport Beach is located on the Pacific Coast just south of Long Beach. There is a six-mile-long beach there, and the harbor is home to more pleasure boats than anywhere else in America, some nine thousand yachts being moored in the waters around Newport Beach. Corona Del Mar, or "Crown of the Sea," is part of Newport Beach and the Corona Del Mar High School teams are wonderfully called the Sea Kings and the Sea Queens. I am told by an alumna that the junior high teams, located at the same site, are called the Sea Weeds. That may or may not be true, but it's much too good to pass up. Then there is Kingston, Pennsylvania, where the Bishop O'Reilly teams are called the Queensmen. The boys' teams at Princeville High School, in central Illinois are the Princes and the girls' teams are the Princesses.

Poolville, Texas, and Manning, South Carolina, high schools are the Monarchs. I always liked that nickname for the teams at Evansville, Indiana, Rex Mundi High School, because *rex mundi* means, after all, in Latin, king of the world. My favorite Monarchs, however, come from the town of Papillion, Nebraska, just south of Omaha. Now, as you all are well aware, *papillon* means butterfly in French. Papillion is close enough to *papillon* for me. The Papillion-LaVista High School teams, in their maroon, gold, and white uniforms, must indeed resemble the glorious monarch butterflies whose brave semiannual migrations over thousands of miles have astonished generations of observers!

The town of Napoleon is in south central North Dakota on the shores of Round Lake. Named after the Emperor of France, the high school teams are very aptly named the Imperials. Perhaps a game could be scheduled between Napoleon and Dinuba, California, High School. Dinuba, in the fertile San Joaquin Valley near Fresno, fields the Emperors. The Imperials versus the Emperors could be a most royal encounter.

Iowa City Regina High School teams are the Regals, which is queenly, as are the teams from Los Angeles Notre Dame Academy Girls High School. Both Royalton, Minnesota, and South Royalton, Vermont, are the Royals, as are the teams from Roy, Utah, and Upper Darby, Pennsylvania.

Hawaii is the only part of the United States to have had its own royal family, so it is quite fitting that Kahului High School on the beautiful island of Maui, known locally as the *Ali'i Lani*, are the Royals in English translation. So, too, are the teams from Aiea High School located near the shores of Pearl Harbor, not far at all from the somber USS *Arizona* Memorial.

A regent is someone who reigns in the absence, disability or minority of the sovereign. Thousand Oaks, California, northeast of Los Angeles was on the Great Butterfield Stage Route and the Stagecoach Inn was built there in 1876. La Reina (The Queen) High School in Thousand Oaks, as well as their neighbors at Reseda High School in the San Fernando Valley both field the Regents. Madison, Wisconsin, is not only the state capital but home to the gorgeous lakeside campus of the University of Wisconsin. Madison West High School teams are also the Regents.

Dukes are important in the hierarchy of royalty, and we find ample representation for them around our country. Yorkshire is north of London, and the cathedral city of York is a fascinating place to visit. During the fifteenth century, the War of the Roses pitted the Red Roses of Lancaster against the White Roses of York in an extended period of battles for supremacy of north central England. The Duke of York, a patron of early Colonial settlers, is well remembered in America. York, Nebraska, is on the Oregon Trail, between Grand Island and Lincoln, and was settled by Swiss and Germans who named it for the town they left in Pennsylvania. It is the home of the Panthers of York College and of the Dukes of York High School. Farther east, at York Township High School in Elmhurst, a western

Royalty? In America?

suburb of Chicago, are the Dukes and Lady Dukes. (Lady Dukes? Excuse me—how about Duchesses?)

Arthur Wellesley, the first Duke of Wellington, the general who gained undying fame for his part in defeating Napoleon Bonaparte's French army at the decisive battle of Waterloo in Belgium in 1815. There are the Dukes of Wellington, Ohio, who perhaps should be the Iron Dukes, as Wellesley was generally called with great fondness by grateful Britons.

The first Duke of Marlborough was John Churchill, one of England's greatest generals, who won fame for his victory at the Battle of Blenheim. Blenheim was the name he gave to the palace constructed near Woodstock on extensive acreage in central England and it was there that his even more famous progeny, Winston Churchill, was born of an American mother and a British father. Marlboro, New York, is on the west bank of the Hudson River, north of Newburgh and south of Poughkeepsie. Marlboro High School is also, naturally enough, represented by the Dukes.

Gloucester is both a charming Cathedral town in the west of England and a town in Virginia on the peninsula formed by the York and Rappahannock rivers. It is about ten miles from Yorktown and was once the site of the grandest mansion in Virginia, Roswell, built in the 1720s by a man called Manny Page who married a daughter of Robert "King" Carter. Carter was a good friend of Thomas Jefferson, who is known to have been a frequent visitor at Roswell. The area today is well represented by the Dukes of Gloucester High School.

Essex, a county to the north and east of London and near the rugged seacoast of the North Sea, can be cold and windswept and was once marshy wetlands, now generally reclaimed. Perhaps this landscape reminded settlers of what they saw at the south end of Saginaw Bay in Michigan. At any rate, Essexville is located there, near Bay City, and their teams are also the Dukes.

The House of Windsor is well regarded here in America. It is, of course, the ruling house in England, the family of Queen Elizabeth. Any trip to England should include a stop at the historic town of Windsor, a tour of the castle, and a visit to the sister town of Eton, a footbridge walk across the

More Dukes, Plus Barons and Knights

The royalty of early American jazz music includes such notables as Count Basie, King Cole, and, of course, the incomparable Duke Ellington. Edward Kennedy Ellington, destined to become one of America's greatest composers, was born on April 29, 1899, in Washington, D.C. Ellington High School in that city does not disappoint in its selection of a nickname. They are the Dukes, of course.

There are many Barons around, also, including those from Manheim, Pennsylvania, and from DeKalb High School, named for a German baron who fought on the side of the Colonies in the Revolutionary War, in Waterloo, Indiana.

Knights are also ubiquitous. There are Knights in the lists at Loyola Academy in New York City, and at Castlemont High School in Oakland, California. Doesn't the Knights of Castlemont sound good? That could be the title of a movie, or perhaps a lost manuscript written by Sir Walter Scott. Knights also guard the moat around Castle High School in Newburgh, Indiana. (Perhaps that is not a moat, but, rather, the Ohio River.) The Golden Knights represent Indianapolis Arlington High School, the Red Knights, Reading, Pennsylvania, and the Kamiak Knights, Kamiak High School in Molkilteo, Washington.

Royalty? In America?

Thames River, and its famous school. The Windsor School in New York City fields the Dukes; there are Knights at the Windsor Academy in Macon, Georgia; and the town of Windsor, New York, fields the Black Knights. Windsor Forest High School, in the thoroughly charming city of Savannah, also is represented on the fields of honor by the Knights.

Lumpkin, Georgia, is the home of the Royal Knights. It is also the home of Westville, a beautifully restored Old South village made possible by gifts from the Singer family, where it is, as the sign proclaims, always 1850.

My favorite knights, however, come from the high school in the east central Illinois town of Arthur, in Amish country, with beautiful farms all around, corn over your head in late summer, neatly shocked in the fall. Local citizens have not overlooked their Arthurian legends' heritage. Not only are the boys' teams the Knights, and the girls' teams the Lancers, the junior high teams are the Pages. Grandville, Michigan, Calvin Christian School teams are the Squires, as are those of DeLone Catholic High School in McSherrytown, Pennsylvania. There are also Squires at Manchester, Indiana, High School, but they are depicted more as prosperous, jolly land owners than as knights in waiting!

Manti, Utah, teams are the Templars, although this is due to the fact that one of the first Mormon Temples in the state was built there and occupies a prominent hilltop site overlooking the town. They are not the Knights Templar.

Sir Thomas More, later sanctified, was once chancellor of England during the reign of King Henry VIII. The marvelous play by Robert Bolt, *A Man for All Seasons*, chronicles the battle of wills between More and his king over the sanctity of the law. At one point in the play More states, "I would

15

give the Devil himself the benefit of law for my own sake." More is beheaded, finally, standing firm in his belief that his word, his integrity, is worth more than his very life. The St. Thomas More School in Oakdale, Connecticut, has very appropriately selected the nickname Chancellors.

Everyone who has enjoyed watching the changing of the guard at Buckingham Palace, where Christopher Robin once went down with Alice, is familiar with the brilliant red uniforms and the tall black fur hats of the Grenadier Guards, one of the Queen's Household Cavalry units. On this side of the Atlantic we have the Grenadiers of Colonial High School in Orlando, Florida; Grand Army of the Republic High School in Wilkes-Barre, Pennsylvania; and Elk Grove High School in suburban Chicago.

Prince Frederick, Maryland, in the Tidewater area of the state on the peninsula formed by Chesapeake Bay and the Pawtuxent River, was named for a son of King George the Second and is the seat of Calvert County, named for Cecilius Calvert, Second Baron Baltimore, who founded Maryland as a haven for Catholics in the new World. The Prince Frederick High School teams are the Cavaliers, named for the Royalists in England's Civil War. There are also Cavaliers at Fairfax High School in Virginia, near Washington, D.C.

LaPuente, California, is a western suburb of Los Angeles; the La Puente High School teams are known as the Nobles. The town of King and Queen Courthouse, Virginia, is represented by the Royal Tigers, while the Royal Lancers are found in Spearville, Kansas, and at Bishop McDevitt High School in Wyncote, Pennsylvania. There are also Lancers at Winston Churchill High School in Eugene, Oregon, and at Edinburgh in central Indiana, among several other places around the country.

Exotic Royalty

European royalty is not the only type chosen in America for our nicknames and school mascots. The southernmost part of Illinois is known as Little Egypt because the fertile soil between and near the juncture of the two mighty rivers, the Mississippi and the Ohio, was reminiscent of the land in Egypt itself along the banks of the Nile. Towns in Little Egypt carry names such as Cairo, Karnak, and Thebes. In Tamms, where Egyptian High School is located, the teams are known as the Pharaohs.

There are no pyramids other than the so-named sports arena in Memphis, Tennessee, and I have never seen a statue of the Sphinx there either, but the city is named for the ancient capital of Egypt. Memphis, Egypt, was about fifteen miles south of modern Cairo and was closely associated with the Great Pyramids of Giza and their constant companion the huge and enigmatic statue of the Sphinx. With appropriate recognition of its namesake city, Memphis Raleigh Egypt High School has also selected the Pharaohs as their mascot.

In Bagdad, Arizona, we find the Sultans, and also in California at Santana High in Santee and Sultana High in Hesperia. None of these towns are in areas remotely resembling the fertile crescent between the Tigris and Euphrates rivers in what is often described as the Cradle of Civilization in ancient Mesopotamia. Nor does the Arizona town spell its name the same way the capital of modern Iraq, Baghdad, does. But, then, there are no more sultans in Baghdad, either.

Go Huskies! Beat Felix the Cat!

In Indio, California, and Atwood, Illinois, reign the Rajahs, once the mighty potentates of India. There is an interesting story surrounding the choice of Rajahs for each of these two schools. Atwood got there first, way back in the 1920s when they had a longtime, highly successful football coach named Clarence Rogers whom most people called Rog. He was described by those who knew him as "A prince of a fellow." Hearing that, a sportswriter for the nearby *Champaign News Gazette* wrote "Rog is a Rajah of a fellow." The name was quickly adopted by the team and soon was the official nickname of all of the Atwood High School teams. More recently Atwood has consolidated with nearby Hammond High School, retaining the name Rajahs for the boys teams. The girls' teams are the Rajenes, which is more of a mystery because an Indian princess is actually a Rani. Nonetheless, Rajenes it is.

Indio is a much different story. Indio is located near Palm Springs in the Coachella Valley. Without irrigation from the many underground wells in the valley Indio would indeed be a desert. Thus the Coachella High School teams, located in nearby Thermal (If you think it gets hot where you are, try August in Thermal sometime!), had long been called the Arabs. Then, in 1988, Indio was to get its own high school and everyone knew that Coachella would be their main rival. So they wanted something that would put their rivals in their place. Mistakenly thinking that a rajah was an Arabian prince the eighth graders who were voting on a team nickname for the high school they would soon be entering selected Rajahs.

As far as I, or either school, know, there is no other high school in the country with the nickname Rajahs. If they were to play the feisty little scimitar wielding mascot of Hammond-Atwood High School with his rather unkempt turban and baggy

Royalty? In America?

pants—looking, actually, more like something Scherezade might have dreamed up in *The Arabian Nights*—would appear alongside the rather dignified and definitely Indian looking Sikh-like mascot of Indio High School with his tightly wound, jewel-encrusted turban, folded arms, and stern visage. Who would win? Both apparently are quite good at football, at least, with major titles having been won in their own competitions, so I won't hazard a guess. I do know one thing: It would be a Rajah, for sure!

Finally, at the famous Hollywood High in California, hardly a desert locale but with a definite touch of "Araby" to it, are the Sheiks. I think here we may have an example of inspiration derived from the motion picture industry. Could Rudolph Valentino have had anything to do with the selection of this team name?

3
Fun With Names

We are a nation blessed with a good sense of humor and we are not at all afraid to poke a little fun at ourselves.

Fun Town/School Names

The prize for most fun in combining athletic team nicknames with town names is shared by many places all around the country. Many of these names are wonderfully whimsical and charming.

Much of the Great Prairie, beginning in Indiana and flowing westward from there, is now cultivated land. There are patches of prairie left, however, and efforts are being made to revive and extend these precious lands. Anyone who has seen these prairies in bloom will not soon forget their haunting beauty. The citizens of one town in southern Minnesota certainly were aware of that when they named their town Blooming Prairie. Years later, when their high school teams needed a nickname, they kept the theme. The Blooming Prairie Blossoms, generally referred to as the "Awesome Blossoms"!

Not far from Blooming Prairie, just a bit south and east, is the even smaller town with the similarly inspired name of Grand Meadow. Their teams are the Super Larks.

Closer to Minneapolis, just across the Mississippi River to the south, is the rather large suburb of Burnsville. You have to love the nickname of Burnsville High School: the Blaze.

Fun With Names

I don't know how cold it gets down in Winters, Texas, but the high school teams are the Blizzard. They do take their nickname seriously, though: the school yearbook is *The Glacier*, a girls singing group is the "Snowflakes," and the unofficial school song is reported to be "Walking in a Winter Wonderland." The junior high teams are the Breezes. They have to grow up to become full-fledged Blizzards! I think it would be fun to see an intersectional game between the Burnsville Blaze and the Winters Blizzard sometime.

Wyoming, Ohio, a suburb of Cincinnati, is a long way from the Wild West. Still, out of deference to the Cowboy State, the Wyoming High School teams are also the Cowboys. Rootstown is in the northeastern part of Ohio, near Akron. Apparently when the settlers came there they decided to stop their roving and put down roots, for the Rootstown High School teams are the Rovers

Fair Lawn, New Jersey, has some proud homeowners with well kept yards in this town across the Hudson River from New York City. The Fair Lawn High School teams are the Cutters. Perhaps they mow down the opposition!

Aliquippa, Pennsylvania, is on the Ohio River about thirty miles downstream from Pittsburgh's Golden Triangle. If you want a good *bon mot*, or a witty rejoinder, Aliquippa is the place to find one. Their high school teams are the Quips.

Since New Orleans is located on a wide sweep of the Mississippi River the shape the curve makes is a crescent. Hence New Orleans is not only known as the "Big Easy," it is also frequently known as the Crescent City. New Orleans Cabrini High School is aware of this. Their teams are the Crescents. There are also Crescents at nearby Bay St. Louis, Mississippi, Our Lady Academy-Girls High School.

Incline Village, Nevada, crowns the north shore of beautiful Lake Tahoe, not only on the high ground but on a considerable slope as well. The Incline Village High School teams are the Highlanders.

James River High School, is located in Midlothian, Virginia, on the rushing waters of Falling Creek. The James River High School teams have the wonderful nickname of the Rapids, conveying not only the nature of the stream, but the nature of the players and competitors on their teams as well.

St. Louis, Missouri, was placed at the confluence of two of the country's greatest rivers to take advantage of the transportation opportunities afforded by both the Missouri and the Mississippi. Today one of the high schools in this great city is called Crossroads and its teams are called the Current. Wouldn't it be fun if the Current met the Rapids on the athletic field some day?

Merriam Webster defines flivver as a word of uncertain origin, circa 1910, meaning a small, cheap car, usually older. Kingsford, Michigan, is in the Upper Peninsula, right on the Wisconsin line. Henry Ford had a plant in Kingsford that produced some of his Flivvers and in the 1930s the people of Kingsford showed their good humor among the rugged beauty of their surroundings by selecting Flivvers as the nickname for their high school teams. The KingsFORD Flivvers.

Two places have me confused about the Revolutionary War. I certainly thought we fought the British because our leaders were convinced that the Thirteen Colonies were "and of right ought to be free and independent" from the mother country. If that is the case, why is the town of Britton, Michigan, represented on the fields of play by the Tories? And why has the town of Berlin, Connecticut, chosen the Redcoats for their teams? Am I missing something? Whose side are they on, anyway?

There is a town in West Virginia, not far west of Charleston, that is known as Poca. You will be pleased to know that the good folks of Poca did not let us down when selecting a nickname for their high school teams. They are the Dots. The Poca Dots. I have not seen their uniforms to know if this theme is carried to its logical conclusion.

Some people in Cleveland, Texas, and Pittsburgh, California, must have been Major League baseball fans, each with a good sense of humor. These two small towns, far from their big city namesakes, selected Indians and Pirates respectively for their team names. It would be like a World Series if they were ever to play each other.

Robin Hood and his Merry Men roamed the dark woods of Sherwood

Fun With Names

Forest, harassed by King John II and the Sheriff of Nottingham. Master archers, they used their skills to hunt, to help their countrymen in need, and to restore King Richard I (the Lion Hearted) to his throne. We find the Bowmen in the town of Sherwood, Oregon, southwest of Portland, and the Marksmen at Sherwood High School in Creighton, Missouri, a very small town southeast of Kansas City.

Frankfort, Indiana, is a charming small city, county seat, with Courthouse and market square, well kept homes, churches, a population of around fifteen thousand, and a high school gym that seats more than six thousand spectators. The gym is round, would make all but the largest of colleges proud, and was featured in the movie *Blue Chips*, which starred Nick Nolte as a beleaguered basketball coach. The Frankfort gym is named for Everett Case who coached the Frankfort basketball team to four state championships in the 1920s and '30s, then went on to even greater fame at North Carolina State University. Frankfort, however, had fun with their school's nickname. Their teams are the Hot Dogs and their mascot is a feisty little dachshund.

Logansport, Indiana, was named for a "White Indian," Major John Logan. However, those who chose the nickname for the high school decided on a less serious approach. They are the Logansport Berries. Loganberries?

The Cloverdale Clovers must be of the four-leaf kind to bring good luck to that small town also blessed with the natural wonders of Cataract Falls and Cagle's Mills Lake in western Indiana.

Rising Sun is a town on the Ohio River, somewhat to the east of Madison. The Ohio, in its twists and turns, actually runs almost north to south as it flows by the riverside town. The sun, thus, actually does rise directly across the river, over the hills behind Rabbit Hash, Kentucky, with its general store more than a hundred years old. The river is extremely wide at this point and the view can be quite spectacular. Fortunately, the people of Rising Sun knew how to name their athletic teams: they are the Shiners.

The citizens of Plymouth, in northern Indiana, faced a bit of a dilemma when it came to selecting a name for their teams. Some favored Pilgrims, others preferred Rocks. The issue was resolved by calling the football teams the Rocks and all of the other teams at Plymouth High School the Pilgrims.

Talk about whimsy: Horace Mann High School in Gary is named for a great American educator, born in 1796, champion of public education, Brown University graduate, lawyer, fierce advocate of freedom for slaves, and first President of Antioch College in Yellow Springs, Ohio. Their teams, in a bit of a slurry way of saying his name, are the Horace Mann Horsemen.

Closing out our Indiana selections is Speedway, a westside suburb of Indianapolis and home to Tony Hulman's Indianapolis Motor Speedway. The Indianapolis 500 has for years been the most highly attended sporting event in the world. What would a town so surrounded by motorcars and internal combustion engines choose to call their athletic teams? None else than the Speedway Sparkplugs.

No one who has seen Niagara Falls can ever forget the awe-inspiring majesty of this spectacle of nature. It is the place where the first hydroelectric plant was built. The Niagara Falls High School teams are appropriately known as the Powercats. Some miles to the southwest, in central Ohio, is the town of Philo. An electric power plant was once located in Philo and, although it is not still in use, the Philo High School teams are still called the Electric. Sparks would fly if the Powercats and the Electric were ever to play each other, I'm sure.

Who has ever been to the Napa Valley of northern California and not marveled at the beauty of the vineyards nestled into the rolling hills of the countryside and enjoyed the taste of the fine wines produced there? It is

Fun With Names

perhaps not at all surprising that the citizens of Napa chose to call their high school Vintage and its teams the Crushers.

Across the country is the town of Northeast, Pennsylvania. Northeast is really in the far northwestern part of the state on the shoreline of Lake Erie, but it is northeast of Pittsburgh. Grapes were introduced to this part of Pennsylvania and to nearby western New York State at an early date. Although some excellent wines have come from these vineyards, the town of Northeast is even better known for the Welch grape juice operation located there. Their high school teams are the Grape Pickers. Go Pickers, Beat Crushers! Go Crushers, Beat Pickers!

In England, the male of the red deer is usually called the hart and the female the hind, as for example Sir Francis Drake's famous ship, the *Golden Hind*. In America we are more likely to refer to these animals as stags and does. The town of Hartsburg, Illinois, however, cleverly decided to call their boys' teams the Stags. Are the girls' teams the Does? No, regrettably, they are also the Stags. So it goes on this side of the Atlantic.

Elkhorn, Nebraska, does call its teams the Antlers, very descriptively, as does Deer, Arkansas.

Elkton, North Dakota, fields the Elks.

White Deer, Texas, named their teams the Bucks.

Both Buffalo, Oklahoma, and Buffalo, Wyoming, put the Bisons on the field, as does Buffalo Grove, a suburb of Chicago.

For most fun with animal names, however, my vote for the prize goes to the town of Bray, Oklahoma. The Bray teams are the Donkeys. Close behind would be the Burros of Burroughs High School in Ridgecrest, Colorado, and the Rams of both Merino, Colorado, and Big Horn, Wyoming. I hope the girls' teams at the latter two schools are the Ewes!

The "Don't tread on me" award is shared between two schools. Snake River High School in Baggs, Wyoming, fields the Rattlers and Anaconda, Montana, the Copperheads. Copperheads is perfect for a place like Anaconda (itself named after another kind of snake) where copper was once mined in great abundance. If any school is likely to violate the "Don't tread on me" caveat, perhaps it will be Atlanta Chalcedon. Why? Because their nickname is the Treaders. No fear at Chalcedon.

Before copper-containing ore was ever discovered out west, the only U.S. source for it was entirely concentrated in a small area of the Upper Peninsula of Michigan. The shafts of old mines are still evident there, as are museums dedicated to those halcyon days when copper was king. These days are well remembered by the nickname of Calumet High School, right in the middle of these once rich ore veins: the Copper Kings.

Talking about mining, I also like Bauxite, Arkansas. Bauxite is the ore from which refineries extract aluminum. The Bauxite teams are called the Miners. Then there is the town of Ishpeming, Michigan, in the Upper Peninsula, not far from Marquette and right in the middle of one of the richest iron ore veins in American history. Iron ore extracted from mines near Ishpeming was taken by railroad car to the ports of Lake Superior and dumped into the large ore boats waiting to transport it to the steel mills of Chicago, Gary, Cleveland, and Pittsburgh. This ore is called hematite, and the Hematites is the nickname selected for the teams of Ishpeming High School.

Galena, Illinois, is another historical town, nicely restored, and named for the ore from which lead is extracted. Most of the nation's early supply came from the mines around Galena. In addition to mining, however, several of the early citizens of the town were notable for taking advantage of their location on the Mississippi River to indulge in piracy. Today, the Galena High School athletic teams recognize the latter in their choice of nickname. They are the Pirates, which segues quite nicely to Thief River Falls, Oregon, whose teams are the Prowlers.

If a special prize for most intriguing name involving an insect were to be awarded, I think the winner would be the Dunn School in the town of Los Olivos, California. Now, as most of you know, *olivos* is Spanish for olives. Also Italian for olives, and few crops are more important than olives to those two beautiful countries, and to Los Olivos, California, as well, I daresay. Well, the earwig is a nasty little insect with forceps-like appendages and many-jointed antennae that is a threat to olives. What are the Dunn School

Fun With Names

teams called? Well, the Earwigs, as you may have already guessed.

Robert Fulton was born in Lancaster County, Pennsylvania, in 1765. Although he tried his hand at a variety of things he is best remembered as the Father of the Steamboat. Fulton, Illinois, on the Mississippi River, was, in its early days, a significant steamboat port. It is named, of course, for Robert Fulton. Their high school teams are the Steamers. Then there is Steamboat Springs, Colorado. This delightful little town is located far from any sizeable body of water, in the Colorado Rockies. It is a skier's delight. Several Olympians have come from Steamboat Springs. What are the high school teams called? The Steamboat Springs Sailors!

James Watt was born in Scotland in 1736. He was an inventor of considerable skill and an engineer of such stature that his name is used as the unit of measure for electric power. Perhaps his greatest invention was an improved design for the steam engine making it efficient enough to be practical and thus the driver for the industrial revolution. The town of Watts, Oklahoma, proudly calls their high school teams the Engineers in his honor.

The Roman Legions, military scourge of most of the known world for some three hundred years, were organized in units of a hundred soldiers. Thus each soldier was known as a "centurion." There are Centurions representing the town of Centuria, Nebraska.

Winters in Escanaba, Michigan, in the famous Upper Peninsula, are cold. It is not at all surprising that their high school teams are called the Eskymoes. Similarly, in Esko, Minnesota, another cold place in the wintertime, their teams are the Eskomos. Perhaps an Eskymoes versus Eskomos hockey game would be entertaining.

Elgin, Illinois, named for a town in Scotland, was for many years the headquarters of one of America's finest watch companies, the Elgin National Watch Company, founded just after the Civil War. Top of the line models were the Lord and Lady Elgin. The teams from Elgin High School were officially called the Maroons, but newspapers often referred to them as the Watchmen or, in basketball, as the Watch City Five, I am informed by my good friend, Tom Aley, who once starred for Elgin's State Championship runner-up team and then for an excellent Dartmouth team, which was one game shy of a Final Four appearance in 1958. Elgin, Minnesota, also deriving its heritage from Scotland, had, as far as I can determine, no association with the Elgin National Watch Company, yet their high school teams are the Watchmen.

Pleasant Hill, Oregon, is a tiny community, with perhaps one hundred people living there. However, it is less than fifteen miles from Eugene with its very sophisticated University of Oregon campus. Nevertheless, the people of Pleasant Hill call their high school teams the Billies. The Pleasant Hill Billies, or, equally, I should think, the pleasant hillbillies.

Across the continent, at Verona High School in New Jersey, we find the Hillbillies. One theory is that this is due to the town's location on the high plateau above the Palisades. Another, and I like this one better, is that it was a Shakespeare reversal. Some felt the school's nickname should be the Gentlemen. Right near by, in the town clearly named for its location, Summit, we find the Hilltoppers. Also close by are the Mounties of Montclair High School.

Ozark, Arkansas, is in a beautiful section of that state. It was once fairly remote but has recently been "discovered" by vacationers, fishermen, skiers, and many others interested in the out-of-doors. Here, again, we find the Hillbillies. Not far away is Hermitage, Arkansas, whose teams are called the Hermits.

For calling it like it is, and I guess that would be the Howard Cosell award, I find no place does it better than Lower East Side High School in the Borough of Manhattan. The Lower East Side is a place that first provided homes and work for hundreds of thousands of arrivals from Europe with dreams of a brighter future in the New World. What nickname did Lower East Side High School choose to celebrate its history? Why, the Immigrants, of course.

Similarly, again crisscrossing our continent, we find the Los Angeles Manual Training High School, another contender for the Cosell prize. Their nickname? The Toilers. Lanier High In San Antonio is also a vocational, and they come in a close third with their nickname: the Voks, pronounced with

Fun With Names

a long O. I am also told that at one time the Denver Manual Arts High School teams were the Bricklayers, a name I find more appealing than the current one, the Thunderbolts. An apprentice in a printing shop was always referred to as a printer's devil. What are the teams called that represent New York City's High School of the Graphic Arts? Yes, they are Printer's Devils. At the Atlanta Commercial High School the teams are the Typists. In this category I also am very fond of the nickname picked by East New York Transit Technical High School. These teams are called the Express. No locals on that track! Another one I love is just across the river, in Brooklyn, where Automotive High School teams are the Pistons. Wouldn't it be fun if the Speedway Sparkplugs and the Automotive Pistons ever got together!

Bad Axe, Michigan, is a town of some three thousand people in the windswept area of the state known as the thumb of the mitten, northwest of Port Huron and southeast of Bay City. All of this was lumbering country and the teams of Bad Axe High School are called the Hatchets.

The city of Baton Rouge, Louisiana, lies on the Mississippi River mostly west and a bit north of New Orleans. Baton Rouge means Red Stick in French, and St. Joseph's Academy teams there are faithfully called the Red Stickers.

The beautiful Penobscot River flows from northern Maine and empties into the bay of the same name and into the Atlantic Ocean. Penobscot Valley High School is located in the town of Howland, home of the Howlers.

Hialeah, Florida, has a world-renowned horse racing track. Plenty of thoroughbreds there. It also has the Thoroughbreds at Hialeah High School. Kentucky is probably better known for its thoroughbred racehorses than any other state. Harrison high School in Cynthiana also fields the Thoroughbreds. A Harrison versus Hialeah game would be a real horse race!

Rose Bud, Arkansas, is a tiny town about thirty miles north of Little Rock. With wisdom and the hint of a smile, the people of Rose Bud selected Ramblers as the name for their high school teams.

Several schools in Pennsylvania caught my eye for this section. The first is Canon McMillan High in Canonsburg. With a bow to the Golden

Go Huskies! Beat Felix the Cat!

Arches, yet fully consistent with their namesake, their teams are called the Big Macs. Not too far away is Carmichaels Area High School. There we find the Mighty Mikes. Just south of Oil City, also in western Pennsylvania is the town of Seneca. The high school there is Cranberry High and the teams are, of course, the Berries. Wouldn't it be fun to see an intersectional game between Seneca Cranberry and Logansport, Indiana. It would be a Berry, Berry good match-up!

While we're in this part of the country we cannot overlook Oil City itself and its equally historical neighboring town of Titusville, both located on Oil Creek. For perhaps centuries the Seneca Indians had been using the slick substance on the surface of what came to be known as Oil Creek to mix their war paints. Early white settlers bottled the substance and sold it as "Seneca Oil." It was not until 1860 when Colonel Edwin Drake drilled the world's first oil well near Titusville that this discovery transformed the area overnight into one of the fastest growing boom towns in the history of man. Oil City itself sprang up almost overnight and was no place for the fainthearted. Fortunes were made and lost as men strove to capture what they could of this marvelous substitute for the world's dwindling supply of sperm whale oil, used for lighting homes and lubricating the machinery of the rapidly advancing Industrial Revolution. The Oil City High School teams are, what else, the Oilers, and the local newspaper is *The Derrick*.

One more Pennsylvania entrant is the town of Boiling Springs. This is a community of around eighteen hundred people located just south of Carlisle in the east central part of the state, not far from Harrisburg. The Boiling Springs teams are known as the Bubblers. Highland Springs is an eastern suburb of Richmond, Virginia. The teams there are the Springers. How about Springers versus Bubblers some day? Of course the Springers would have the advantage on the basketball court!

Many schools in the Great Sky State of Montana have had fun with their names, as well. Consider, for example, the Shepherders of Sweet Grass County High in Big Timber, the Rustlers of Russell High in Great Falls, and the Terriers in Terry. The Troopers represent the town of Garrison, which reminds me of the similarly inspired Stockaders of Old Fort, Ohio. For the

Fun With Names

color conscious, I submit Vermillion High School in South Dakota. Their teams are called the Tanagers. The school colors? Red and white, of course.

Hereford, Texas, is located in the Panhandle, just southwest of Amarillo. Anyone who has traveled any of the back roads of America is highly likely to be acquainted with Hereford cattle, with their distinctive white faces and black and white markings over their bodies. The Hereford High teams, sometimes known as the Thundering Herd, are more commonly and affectionately known as the Whitefaces. Somewhat similarly, New Salem High School in South Dakota's teams are the Holsteins. Holsteins versus Hereford Whitefaces? Could be a stampede.

In Wyoming, the interesting town of Gillette is a good base for seeing such interesting sites as the Devil's Tower National Monument, the Thunder Basin National Grasslands, and the Fort Kearny State Historical Site. Campbell County High School is located in Gillette and the teams are the Camels, the Campbell Camels, that is.

Addison Trail, Illinois, a western suburb of Chicago, fields the Blazers. Downstate is the small Clay County town of Louisville, located between Effingham and Flora. Out of deference, perhaps, to the University of Louisville, Cardinals was the name selected for their athletic teams.

Bell Buckle, Tennessee, is a lovely little town, not far off of Interstate 24 between Chattanooga and Nashville, but worlds apart from those bustling metropolises. It was once a railroad town and the depot has become an antique store, along with several others, in a quaint, well preserved downtown. Just on the east side of Bell Buckle is the prestigious Webb School. With a bit of whimsy they have named their teams the Feet. The Webb Feet. Perhaps the mascot is a duck.

There is another Webb School across the continent near Los Angeles and once related to its Tennessee namesake. This Webb School's nickname is the Gauls. Can it be that, like Caesar's Gaul, it is divided in three parts, Lower, Middle and Upper Schools?

Nearby, in Los Angeles, is another private school with a particularly whimsical mascot. It is the Ribet Academy. Their teams are the Fighting Frogs. Ribet, ribet.

Go Huskies! Beat Felix the Cat!

Finally, in the whimsy category, is the town of Belfry, Montana. Now what would you think the Belfry teams should be called? Bats? Well, that's exactly what they are called. Yes sir, they've got Bats in their Belfry!

Favorite Names

A count of the most popular names chosen by the twenty thousand-plus high schools of America results in a virtual dead heat between Eagles and Tigers, at around 540 each. Somewhat behind are Bulldogs and Panthers. Wildcats are pretty much alone in a third tier with just under 400 schools selecting that name. Almost 300 schools have chosen Warriors and Indians for their team names. A good number of Hawks and Bears are also out there, particularly so if the various kinds of each were to be added together.

4
FUN WITH HISTORY— AND THE PRESENT

Fun With History

THE PRIZE FOR most imaginative use of history in establishing high school nicknames is shared by several communities. The town of Delphi, with its twenty-five hundred inhabitants is the seat of Carroll County in north central Indiana. The name Delphi was selected in honor of the ancient Greek city, site of the most important of all Greek temples and the Oracle of Apollo. Ancient Delphi was considered the center of the world by the Greeks, its location having been determined where the eagle Zeus let fly from the East met the one he let fly from the West. Not a bad name for a small settlement in the relatively new state of Indiana, perhaps, for the locals anyway, the second center of the world. At any rate, the Delphi High School teams are wonderfully called the Oracles. Prize Number One: the Oracles of Delphi.

In Illinois, we have two honorees. The name of Marco Polo conjures up images of a dauntless traveler to exotic lands, the bold Venetian whose journeys to far Cathay opened up the Orient to Europe. Tashkent, Samarkand, Dushanbe, the Silk Road. The town of Polo, in the north central part of the state, was quite alert to this bit of history when it selected Marcos as their team nicknames: the Marcos of Polo. Also in Illinois is the town of Monticello, named after Thomas Jefferson's fabled home near Charlottesville, Virginia. The good citizens were also aware that Jefferson's wisdom had earned him the name of the Sage of Monticello. They decided if that was good enough for him it was certainly good enough for them as well. The Monticello High School teams are the Sages. The Sages of Monticello.

In Michigan we have another contender. John Pershing was the Missouri-born General who commanded the forces who liberated Europe in World War I, the Allied Expeditionary Force, or AEF. The American troops in the AEF were affectionately known as Doughboys, much as those of World War II were known as GIs. Pershing High School in Detroit, a school that has produced more than its share of basketball stars, has teams also called the Doughboys.

Turning our attention to those brave GIs who removed the scourge of Nazism from the face of Europe, we recall D-Day, the sixth of June, 1944, when the greatest armada ever assembled stormed the beaches of Normandy. This began the assault on the Germans that culminated in Victory in Europe, V-E Day, some ten months later. Normandy High School in Parma, Ohio, remembers those events well with the name of the Invaders. More recently, North Las Vegas High School in Nevada honored another great invasion: their teams are called the Desert Shield.

In a similar vein there is Bryan Station High School in Lexington, Kentucky. Before there was even a Lexington there was Bryan Station, a fort protecting settlers, trappers and fur traders in what would be the state of Kentucky. In honor of an Indian battle, Bryan Station High School's teams are the Defenders. Perhaps they play Iroquois High School in nearby Louisville. The Iroquois teams are the Raiders. That would be much like a reenactment of the original story: Raiders versus Defenders!

Jim Bridger spent most of his life roaming the West and was believed to have been the first white man to view the great Salt Lake. He was perhaps the most famous scout in the West, although some of you Kit Carson fans

Fun With History

might dispute that. The town of Bridger, Montana, also remembers their namesake in the mascot chosen for their high school: the Scouts.

Northfield, Minnesota, was raided by the Jessie James-Cole Younger gang on September 7, 1876. The gang was after the money in Northfield's First National Bank. The townspeople were ready for the raid, however, and it was thwarted. In the ensuing gunfight two defenders were shot dead as were two gang members. Jessie and Frank James escaped. This heroic stand by the people of Northfield is commemorated in the restored bank, now an Historical Society Museum. It is also commemorated in the name selected for the Northfield High School teams. They are the Raiders.

There is plenty of history in Arlington, Massachusetts. On April 18, 1775, Paul Revere's ride took him through the towns of Cambridge, Somerville, Arlington, Lexington, and Concord on his mission to alert "Every middlesex village and farm" that "the British are coming." The next day, as the Redcoats retreated, a bloody battle was fought in Arlington, much of it taking place around a small lake known as Spy Pond. In the 1830s, a new industry was born involving cutting up blocks of ice from Spy Pond and exporting them to tropical countries. I have some trouble imagining how well that worked—and talk about a seasonal occupation. Oh yes, the high school teams—they're called the Spy Ponders.

Spencer, Indiana, is a pleasant town of about twenty thousand people located on the White River northwest of Bloomington. The United States census of 1920 determined that the center of population of the country was eight miles south southeast of Spencer. The townspeople liked this and decided to use it for their high school nickname. The Spencer High School COPS, not of the police variety, but of the Center Of Population variety!

Go Huskies! Beat Felix the Cat!

Fun in the Sun

Several schools have considered their pleasant location when selecting nicknames for their teams. Miami Beach High School teams are the HiTides, while at nearby North Miami Beach Allison Academy they are a bit more hedonistic: the Sunseekers. Everyone knows some of the best surfing in the world, perhaps the best, takes place in Hawaii. On the island of Oahu's northwestern shore is the city of Kailua. The high school teams there are known as the Surfriders. In Honolulu is a high school called the Academy of the Pacific. Their team name is listed as the *Nai'*, native for Dolphins, or Porpoises.

Pacific Grove, California, is a gorgeous oceanside suburb of Los Angeles. Their teams are the Breakers, which not only recognizes the waves crashing in from the Pacific Ocean but also serves notice of what they intend to do to the hearts of their opponents on the athletic field. Mount Clemens, Michigan, is north of Detroit, on Lake St. Clair. In the summer this is also a good swimming area and the Mount Clemens teams are called the Battling Bathers. To the west a bit, in the state of Wisconsin, are the pretty little towns of Elkhart Lake and Glenbeulah. Their high school teams are enticingly known as the Resorters.

Farther west, and for a different kind of fun in the sun, are the wonderful ski slopes of the Colorado Rockies. Aspen High School recognizes this with their choice: the Skiers. Nearby Vail, also blessed with beautiful ski slopes, is in that part of the Rockies known as the Gore Range and Gore Creek forms the valley in which the town itself is located. The Vail High School teams are known as the Gore Rangers.

Seville, Ohio, is a small town just west of Akron. When they had their own high school I am told the teams were called the Barbers. They gave their opponents many a close shave, I'm sure.

Waukegan, Illinois, a port city between Chicago and Milwaukee, was the birthplace of Jack Benny, the ageless, violin playing, Bob Hope-baiting, comedian. The original high school teams were and are the Bulldogs, but when a second school was needed it was named after their hometown hero

Fun With History

Familiarity

Several schools around the country have adopted nicknames that might belong to the person—or celebrity—next door. Here are some of them:

Minneapolis—Thomas Alva Edison Tommies and the Theodore Roosevelt Teddies.
Indiana—Jimtown Jimmies
North Dakota—Thompson Tommies.
Maine—Auburn Edward Little Eddies and the Livermore Falls Andies. (I could find no balancing Amoses.)
New York—Williamsville South Billies and the Basher Falls St. Lawrence County Larries. In Boston are the Charlestown Townies and nearby are the Haverhill Hillies.
Massachusetts—In Andover, Lawrence Regional Technical High School, the Reggies.
Ohio—Fredericktown Freddies, the Johnstown Johnnies and the Smithville Smithies. (Perhaps the latter is "Under the spreading chestnut tree"!)
Nebraska—Fairbury is the county seat of Jefferson County and their teams are the Jeffs.

Finally, we have three interesting female familiar names: In Redford, Michigan, are the St. Agatha High School Aggies, in Wilmington Delaware, the Salesianum School Sallies, and in Kankakee, Illinois, the Kays.

Go Huskies! Beat Felix the Cat!

and the Jack Benny High School (now a middle school) teams were called the Thirty-Niners!

Some Fun Play Pens

In addition to the names chosen for the teams, some fun names have been selected for the gyms in which they play. Here is a selection from around Indiana:

> The Lion's Den in Loogootee.
> The Panther's Den at Gary Roosevelt.
> The Tiger's Den in LaCrosse.
> The Rock in—where else?—Plymouth. (Their football team plays in The Rock Pile.)
> The Berry Bowl in Logansport.

Hobart's Brick Yard is where the Brickies play, named so because the major employer in town was once a brickyard (I love Dale Lawrence's observation in his *Hoosier Hysteria Road Book* that calling your basketball team the Brickies in today's vernacular is about as appropriate as calling your football team the Fumblies!)

The Cave is where the Mishawaka Cavemen play.

The Bedford Stonecutters played in the Quarry.

Kendallville is where opponents of the East Noble Knights are confronted with the problem of playing in the Big Blue Pit.

In Berne the South Adams Starfires play their games in the Stardome.

In Poneto the Southern Wells Raiders take the court in the Raiderdome.

In Argos, the Dragons breathe fire in the Dragon's Den.

Oak Hill High School is located in Converse and their teams are the Eagles. The gym is called the Eagle's Nest.

John Glenn High School is in Walkerton. Their team name is the Falcons and the gym is the Aerie.

Fun With History

Although Washington, with its three state titles, is definitely a small town (population 10,800), it has two high schools with two gyms. The Hatchets play in the Hatchet House (capacity 7,090!) and the Washington Catholic Cardinals play in the Bird Cage.

Eminence is located on the Eel River in west central Indiana, and their teams are the Eels. They ask their opponents to join them in the Eel Tank.

If you play the New Albany Bulldogs on their court you do so in the Dog House.

The Alexandria Tigers get you to play them in the Jungle.

The Eastern Green Thunderbirds invite you to the Thunderdome.

In Vincennes, the Lincoln High School Alices play in Alice Arena. Opponents may think of it as Wonderland.

My personal penultimate favorite is in the attractive southern Indiana town of Scottsburg. The Scottsburg Warriors call their gym the Pressure Cooker. How would you like to take them on there?

Now to my favorite arena. It is in Anderson, first settled in 1823 on the site of a former Delaware Indian village. Anderson itself derives its name from that of Chief Kikthawenund, an important Delaware (or Lenni Lenape) leader, who was also referred to as Captain Anderson. In keeping with the town's heritage, the Anderson High School teams are called the Indians; they play their games in the magnificently proportioned, 8,996-seat Wigwam. The Wigwam has an 80,000 tile mosaic of an Indian head on one outside wall, another Indian head painting hanging from an inside wall, and yet a third painted on the center of the floor. Before every game they have an impressive patriotic reading followed by the National Anthem, sometimes sung by Anderson native Sandy Patti. Then comes the real show. The lights are dimmed and spotlights shine on the Indian brave and maiden, dressed in authentic costumes. They perform a native dance, the drums beat, the crowd cheers. By the time the teams are introduced and the game begins you're already drained from the excitement and the noise. There are few places in this great land where a basketball game is more fun to watch than it is when the Anderson Indians fill the Wigwam.

5
Fun Groupings

Try these groupings on for size —

The Optimists

Some towns and schools are very optimistic when it comes to their choice of nickname. Lenox, Massachusetts, for example, a charming town, nestled as it is into the Berkshire Mountains. It was discovered by the social and financial elite of New York City in the nineteenth century, many of whom, including Andrew Carnegie, established summer places there. At some point in the 1920s a New York dowager summering in Lenox was said to have offered to have a fund-raiser for the poor of the town. She was supposedly informed "There are no poor people in Lenox." Maybe. At any rate, the summer home of the Boston Symphony Orchestra is at Tanglewood in Lenox, and the area is filled with music, actors, authors and artists of every kind much of the year. With all of this in mind, it may not be too surprising to learn that the Lenox High School teams are called the Millionaires.

Other optimistic choices include:

> Jane Addams Career Center High School in Cleveland, the Executives.
> Milwaukee High School of the Arts, the Crimson Stars.
> Detroit Southwestern High School, the Prospectors.

Fun Groupings

Gwinn, Michigan, a town of just over two thousand people, twenty miles south of Marquette in the Upper Peninsula, the Modeltowners. (The mascot, however, is a student dressed in a rather fierce tiger outfit.)

Wisconsin Heights High School in Mazomanie, planning to stay ever in the lead, the Vanguards.

Falmouth, Maine, High School, home of the Portland Yacht Club, the Yachstmen.

Ceredo-Kenova High School in Huntington, Virginia, and Kannapolis Brown High School in North Carolina, the Wonders.

Cascade High School in Wartrace, Tennessee, the Champions.

Haubstadt, in southwest Indiana, the Elites.

Luther, Michigan, teams are simply the Tops, which would make Cole Porter proud, I think.

And, of course, Bloomingdale Academy in Indiana, long gone now, whose mascot was the overly optimistic Immortals!

A Girl's Best Friend

Diamonds, so the song goes, are a girl's best friend. That being the case, then I suppose one of a girl's favorite high schools would be in Sallisaw, Oklahoma, where the Black Diamonds take the field. Certainly another would be at Lower Richland High School in Hopkins, South Carolina. The teams there are the Diamonds. Or perhaps she would settle for Manistique, Michigan, located on the south shore of the Upper Peninsula, on the coast of Lake Michigan. They are represented by those wonderful, dark green stones, often more valuable than diamonds: the Emeralds. Perhaps she would favor the Blue Stars, reminiscent of another precious stone, the star sapphire. She would find the Blue Stars at Port Hope, Michigan, on the shores of Lake Huron. Two Harbors, Minnesota, on the western shores of Lake Superior, is surrounded by gorgeously colored trees in the fall, and by roaring, copper tinged waterfalls. Their teams are the Agates, perhaps not a contender for the affections of the *Two Girls From Little Rock*, but also a beautiful stone in its own right and surely indicative of what can be found by a sharp-eyed beachcomber on the shores of the lake at Two Harbors. Rye, New York, is a charming town on Long Island Sound in Westchester County, a relatively easy commute to Manhattan. The high school teams are the Garnets.

Other favorites of our girls might include:

>Villa Joseph Marie High School in Holland, Pennsylvania, the Jems.
>Manhattan's St. Jean Baptiste High School, the Jewels.
>Wilkes-Barre, Pennsylvania, Bishop Hoban High School, the Argents.
>East Rockaway High School, Long Island, the Rocks.
>Pratt High School in Kansas, the Greenbacks.

֎

Light My Fire

South Park is not just a television show of dubious distinction, it is also a high school in Buffalo. Their nickname is the Sparks. S. Park. Sparks. A good choice. A useful choice for nearby East Amherst Williamsville High School, the Flames. But what is the hottest of flames? I have always thought it was the blue part. So must Pickens, South Carolina. Their teams are the Blue Flames. In Westbrook, Maine, the teams are the Blue Blazes. Then there are the Torches of Gardendale, Alabama, Tabernacle High School. This could explain the Blazers of Bush High School in Seattle. I really like this one: the Burning Bush! I'll digress for an instant and point out Pine Bush, New York, home of the Bushmen. They haven't caught fire yet, it seems. This brings us to Word of Life High School in Wichita. They are the Fire. And let's not forget the Burnsville Blaze, from Minnesota or the Effingham, Illinois, Flaming Hearts.

In several communities around the country home schooling is being done in fairly large numbers. Large enough, anyway, for the home schoolers to get together and field their own athletic teams. Manatee, Florida, is one

Fun Groupings

such place. Their entries are called the Home Educated Athletic Teams. The H.E.A.T.

Sparks, Flames, Fire, Torches, Blaze, Burning Bushes, Flaming Hearts, and Heat. What could be next? Perhaps the hottest of fires, hot enough to melt rocks and make them flow like a river of flame, the volcano. Which leads me to my final entry in this category. Chester, California, is located on Lake Almanor, just south of Lassen Volcanic National Park. The Chester High School teams are the Volcanoes. (Another opportunity-missed award is granted to Etna in the Marble Mountains of California, near the Oregon border. The Etna teams are the Lions.)

Boxers and Contenders

Brockton, Massachusetts, founded in 1700, was primarily an agricultural center until the invention of a machine for sewing shoes. The city quickly became the leading shoe producer in the nation and remained so for many years. More recently, Brockton has produced two World Champion boxers: Marvin Hagler and Rocky Marciano. The Brockton High School teams have a nickname more indicative of their later history than their earlier history. No, they are not called the Shoes. They are the Boxers. However, their mascot, seen on the sidelines of home football games, is of the canine variety.

Budd Schulberg's powerful book *On the Waterfront* was turned into an excellent black and white motion picture starring Marlon Brando as a longshoreman who was also a promising prizefighter. Circumstances were such that he was forced to throw a fight that he probably could have won, thus ending his chances to go for the title. Brando's words were haunting: "I coulda been a contendah." Faith Baptist High School in Canoga Park has a mascot that reminds me of the movie and Brando's lament. They are the Contenders. Shouldn't the Contenders have at least one shot at the Boxers some day?

Go Huskies! Beat Felix the Cat!

Clothing

I have mentioned several schools that use Blazers as their nickname, a nice triple entendre: does it refer to their uniforms, their speed, or the fire with which they attack the opposition? At the Hathaway Brown School in Shaker Heights, Ohio, at least, it originally referred to their uniforms.

Zippers, once called hookless fasteners, also have the connotation of speed. Monmouth High School, in western Illinois calls its teams the Zippers.

Then there is Regina High School in Harper Woods, Michigan. Regina is an all-girls school and its nickname is the Saddleites. I am informed by Ms. Diane Laffey, Regina spokeswoman, that the nickname did, in fact, derive from the saddle shoes long worn by the Regina girls as a part of their school uniforms. The teams of Argyle High School in Colorado are the Socks. A nice combination.

In Princeton, New Jersey, the athletes of the Stuart Country Day School have the nickname of the Tartans. Any guess which one? Mt. Pleasant High School is in Providence, Rhode Island, and their teams are the Kilties.

Another entry in this category is in San Antonio, Texas, home of the Alamo and the storied exploits of men such as Jim Bowie, Sam Houston and Davy Crockett. At least, at first it seemed to belong here, as it did to their opposition. The school is San Antonio Central Catholic. Their nickname? The Buttons. (They never upgraded to Zippers. Perhaps they'll bypass and go straight to Velcros?) Opponents of the Buttons have been known to hold up drawings of a large man with a shirt too small for his girth, the buttons flying off and the words "We'll pop the Buttons." (I seem to remember a character like that in a comic strip popular when I was young. I think it was from *Popeye*, a hamburger lover named Wimpy.) However, the truth of the matter is a much different story. As many Texans know, buttons are baby rattlesnakes and Central Catholic is a sister school to St. Mary's College in San Antonio who are the Rattlers. So, you had better handle these Buttons with care!

Waukesha, Wisconsin, is on the southern tip of the largest inland lake

Fun Groupings

in the state, Lake Winnebago. The Waukesha South High School teams are the Blackshirts.

Remember that long coat the cowboys wore in the west? A similar item was worn by drivers of the early motorcars, before they were enclosed, heated and air-conditioned. Holdredge, Nebraska, teams are the Dusters. They probably like to dust off their opponents, I'll bet. And, of course, that most ubiquitous of all American apparel, blue jeans, once the nickname proudly adopted for the teams of Wheatland, Indiana, and the Hatters of Danbury, Connecticut, certainly deserve mention here! (More about these two later.)

Indy East?

Chicopee, Massachusetts, is a city of almost sixty thousand people, a suburb just north of Springfield, nicely situated on the Connecticut River. I was intrigued to learn the mascots of the two schools there, Chicopee High and Chicopee Comprehensive. The high school itself has selected Pacers as theirs while Comprehensive has chosen Colts. I'll bet they beat Indianapolis to those names, too.

East Meets West

San Anselmo, California, is north of San Francisco on the peninsula created by the Pacific Ocean to the west and San Pablo Bay to the east. Proviso Township in Illinois incorporates the western suburbs of Maywood and Hillside. One of the high schools in San Anselmo is named for the great English admiral and explorer who visited the west coast of North America early in the seventeenth century, Sir Francis Drake, conqueror of the vaunted Spanish Armada in 1588. Their teams are the Pirates. Their crosstown rival, San Domenico High School fields the Panthers. Back in Illinois, the original Proviso High School, now East, was one of our great rivals at Oak Park, the Pirates. When Proviso West was established their choice of team name was the Panthers. East meets west.

Go Huskies! Beat Felix the Cat!

Good Things

Good things often come in small packages. Perhaps that was the thinking of several schools in selecting their team names. For example, the town of Butternut, Wisconsin, has the Midgets representing the local high school. Not to be outdone are the Bantams of Clarkston, Washington, right across the Snake River from Lewiston, Idaho, both named for the great explorers of the nation's new Louisiana Purchase. There are also Bantams at Belfield, North Dakota, and Midgets at Dickinson in the same state. All of these schools should get together and play each other and so should Fort Worth Masonic, the Mighty Mites from Texas.

Even smaller, however, are the Atoms, representing Annandale, Virginia, and the Atomics, of Graceville High School in Poplar Springs, Florida. Both of those, however, should beware of Savannah, Georgia's Johnson High School. Old Savannah, with its wondrous layout of squares and fountains, its fine old buildings and elegant riverfront, is truly one of America's great treasures. It is also near an atomic power plant, and the Johnson High School teams are called the Atom Smashers. Atoms and Atomics, watch out!

One other school's nickname belongs in this section. Danville, Arkansas, is surrounded by national forests and must have some of the feel of England's Sherwood Forest. There may not be a Robin Hood in Danville, but the high school's teams are the Little Johns.

Sword Play

Porthos. Athos. Aramis. D'Artagnan. Alexander Dumas' *Three Musketeers* captured my imagination as a young man. Dashing swordsmen, protecting king, queen and country. "All for one, and one for all!" But why were they called Musketeers when the sword was their weapon, not the musket? Who knows? At any rate, several towns and schools have also been attracted to the

Fun Groupings

Dumas' heroes and many have selected the sword as their nickname of choice. Several are, in fact, the Musketeers, as was selected by the town of Fort Jennings in northwest Ohio. Their kinsmen are at the Temple Christian School in Perris, California, the Swordsmen, and at the very aptly named Bayonet Point, Florida, Christian School. The Christian Academy in Garland, Texas, fields the Swords and the East Bakersfield, California, teams are the Blades. Pahoa is on the Big Island of Hawaii and surrounded by lava flows from the great volcano. The Pahoa High School teams are the Daggers. Finally, there is Souhegan High School in the pretty little southern New Hampshire town named for Lord Jeffrey Amherst. They are the Sabers.

Speed

Speed is important in most team sports. Here are some schools that have chosen to emphasize that:

- Apopka, Florida, and Lockesburg, Arkansas are both called the Blue Darters.
- Calhoun Falls, South Carolina, teams are the Blue Flashes.
- Bessemer, Michigan, and West Philadelphia high schools are the Speed Boys and the Speed Girls.
- Hartford, Arkansas, and Melbourne, Florida, Central Catholic are both the Hustlers.
- Newcastle, Oklahoma, fields the Racers.
- Dietrich teams are the Movin' Maroons and Decatur fields the Runnin' Reds, both in Illinois.
- Sebring, Florida, home of some speedy racecars, has the Blue Streaks.
- Faster yet are the Bullets of Jamestown, North Carolina, and the Blue Bullets of Knoxville, Illinois
- Fastest of all are the Lasers of Atlanta Southside, in Georgia.

Go Huskies! Beat Felix the Cat!

Irresistible Pairings

Some things just go together: Rogers and Astaire; pretzels and beer; baseball and Wrigley Field; marshmallows and campfires. Try these on for size:

The Rotan, Texas, Yellow Hammers and the Chattanooga, Tennessee, Harrison High School Purple Pounders.
The Memphis, Tennessee, Southside High School Scrappers and the Westport, Connecticut, Staples High School Wreckers.
The Brooklyn, New York, St. Ann's High School Steamers and the Tower City, North Dakota, Clams.
The Laona, Wisconsin, High School Kellys, and the Red Bank, New Jersey, Catholic High School, Caseys. Caseys and Kellys. Sounds like an Irish pub. God bless all here.
The Cloverdale, Indiana, Clovers, and the Dublin, Ohio, Shamrocks.
The LeRoy, New York, O-At-Kan Kats and the Bay St. Louis, Mississippi, St. Stanislaus High School Rock-A-Chaws. (I put these together just because I would love to hear the opposing cheers if they met each other on the playing field.)
The Salts from Epsom and the Peppers from Pimento, Indiana.

Brookline, Massachusetts, is notable for several reasons. For one, it is a very wealthy suburb of Boston, home of one of the few remaining Lawn Tennis Clubs in the country. Perhaps more importantly, it is the place where John Fitzgerald Kennedy was born and his birth house is now a National Historical Site. For another, it is the location of my wife's alma mater, Wheelock College, generally recognized as the finest school for training teachers for grades K-4 in the country. It is also the location of Maimonides High School, whose teams are the M-Cats. I am pairing them with the Y-Cats of Gardner high School half way across the country in Topeka, Kansas.

Booker T. Washington High School in Norfolk, Virginia, is named for the great African-American scientist who saw the value of education and learning as a route to a better, more fulfilling and economically rewarding

Fun Groupings

life. His own first name speaks to that value in the vernacular of today and is the mascot of the school—the Bookers. Wouldn't they go well with the Academics of Hillhouse High School in New Haven, Connecticut?

※

Steelton grew up around a steel mill in western Pennsylvania. In the early days of the local high school the teams were called the Ingots. In the twenties, however, Steelton High school was enjoying considerable success on the gridiron, defeating their opponents by immense margins. Soon the newspapers were referring to Steelton's "steamrolling" over their opposition and the students decided they preferred Steamrollers to Ingots, and that's what it is today. How would it come out if the Iron Heads of Eufala, Oklahoma, were to play the Steamrollers of Steelton (now Steelton-Highspire)? You wouldn't want to get in the middle of that one.

One final, more historical, pairing involves New Orleans Alfred Lawless High School, home of the Pythians. The Pythians were related to the Oracle at Delphi in ancient Greece. Every four years, similar to the Olympiad, they engaged in games at Delphi. Thus the Pythians could be matched either with the Olympians of Columbus, Indiana, North, or perhaps most exquisitely with the Oracles themselves, from Delphi, also in Indiana.

AND THESE:

The Gents of Crowley, Louisiana and the Fredonia, New York, Hillbillies.

The Maple Leafs of Geneseo-Darnall High School in Illinois and the Canucks of North Plainfield, New Jersey.

The Black Jacks of Dawson-Boyd, Minnesota and the Hearts of Sacred Heart Academy in Waterbury, Connecticut. (Or maybe with the Bridgemen of Ambridge, Pennsylvania.)

The Rock Island, Illinois, Rocks, and the Rockville, Indiana, Rox. (Or perhaps a triangular meet including the Jug Rox from Shoals, Indiana? A rocky road, indeed.)

The Warrensburg, New York, Burgers and the Big Macs of Canon McMillan High School in Canonsburg, Pennsylvania. Or, perhaps, the Frankfort Hot Dogs from Indiana: Go Hot Dogs, Beat Big Macs! Hold the mustard!

The E-Rabs of East High School in Rockford, Illinois, and the O-Rabs of Sheldon, Iowa.

The Purple Roses of St. Rose High School in Belmar, New Jersey, and the Ramblers of the nearby Carteret School.

The Campers of Allegany High school in Cumberland, Maryland, and the Townies of East Providence, Rhode Island.

The Savannah, Missouri, Savages, and the Quakers of New Philadelphia, Ohio.

The Blugolds of LaCrosse Aquinas and the Purgolders of Madison in Wisconsin.

The Wheelers of Audubon, Iowa, and the Hubs of North Hagerstown, Maryland.

6
SOME TOUGH ONES

SOME NICKNAMES TAKE a bit of deciphering. We are a nation that enjoys mysteries, puzzles and inside jokes.

Orabs and E-Rabs

Sheldon, Iowa, is in the far northwestern corner of the state. I was mystified by their nickname, the Orabs, until I was able to get in touch with the school. The answer was simple and straightforward. Their colors are orange and black. *OR*ange *A*nd *B*lack: Orabs. A bit to the east, in northern Illinois is the city of Rockford, named because it was the point at which early travelers would ford the Rock River. When I was in school Rockford had two high schools, East and West. We had annual swimming meets with both. West has since become a middle school and East has been joined by several newer high schools. East, however, has retained its nickname, the E-Rabs. The "E" stands, as might be imagined, for East. The Rabs? Well, their colors are red and black. *R*ed *A*nd *B*lack. E-Rabs. How about the Orabs versus the E-Rabs some day?

Whip-Purs

Hampshire High School is located in a northwestern suburb of Chicago. I often wondered what a Whip-Pur was. The answer was pretty simple. Their colors are the same as Northwestern University's: *Whi*te and *Pur*ple. Hence Whip-Purs.

Bonackers

East Hampton is some 150 miles from Manhattan, on the southern shore of Long Island. In driving from New York City to East Hampton one passes by some of the best farmland in New York state, the Shinnecock Indian Reservation, Suffolk County Whaling Museum, several college campuses and golf courses too numerous to count. Originally a seafarer's settlement, East Hampton has more recently become a resorter's and beach resident's paradise. The past is honored, however. The original European settlers, fishermen, whalers, and clammers, clustered around a beautiful bay that the Indians had called Accobanac, or "place where groundnuts are gathered." These settlers were referred to as "Bonackers," originally a name of derision indicating something like "hick," or "hayseed," or more specifically "lazy clam digger." Over the years, similar perhaps to the evolution of the word "Hoosier" in Indiana, the name became more of a badge of honor. For years, the area around East Hampton was rather isolated and certain words spoken by the locals were still pronounced as they had been in Elizabethan England three hundred years earlier rather then evolving into the Americanized pronunciation that happened elsewhere. Thus the term Bonacker also implied steadfastness, resistance to change, determination. The athletic teams of East Hampton High School are proudly known as the Bonackers, teams intent on doing their best, that never give up.

Kares

The Rio Hondo Prep School in Arcadia, California, is small, the high school portion having only eighty students. There are also comparably sized lower and middle schools and I am told that something like 85 percent of their graduates not only go on to college but get their degrees. When I saw that their school nickname is the Kares I could not imagine what that meant.

Some Tough Ones

Was it Spanish? Or French? Not in any of my dictionaries. Was it some kind of bird or animal? Apparently not. So I called them and was informed that the school itself grew out of an effort called the Care Youth Leagues. These leagues were established to give every child an opportunity to play sports, regardless of level of talent. Soon this became a school with the same philosophy as well as one of close individual instruction. The result was the Rio Hondo Prep School. The nickname, the Kares, is from the Care Youth League, spelled with a K to emphasize and differentiate it.

Tologs

I had heard that the nickname of Sacred Heart Academy in LaCanada Flintridge, California, was the Tologs, a name that really had me mystified. Again, I looked in every dictionary I had, checked my Colliers and Britannica's encyclopedias, but no Tologs. I even tried my Spanish language dictionary. After all, it was California. No Tologs there, either. So, I called the school. The answer was simple. It is an all girls school; Tologs is an acronym. For what, I asked. It stands for To Our Lady of Great Success was the answer. Pretty wonderful, I thought, and she added that the mascot itself was a Teddy Bear. There is definitely a place for mascots and nicknames like this in our sometimes all too competitive world.

Naps

Holy Name Central Catholic High School occupies a beautiful setting on a hilltop with spacious grounds in Worcester, Massachusetts. Their nickname, the Naps, had me mystified—were they sleepy?—until Athletic Director and Holy Name alumnus Jim Manzello kindly clarified it for me. Holy Name was not always so grandly located. The original school was in a mostly French-speaking parish of the city where it had been founded and run by the Sisters of St. Anne. The teams were then called the Lions, but a sportswriter, cognizant of the French heritage of the athletes, wrote that they "Played with the heart of Napoleon." Soon the teams were only referred to as the Napoleons, eventually shortened to Naps. Mystery solved.

Obezags

The Key School is an independent school located in Annapolis, Maryland. Recently, I have had the opportunity to revisit the historic sites of the old town, see the stunning state capitol building, walk the grounds of the grand old campus of St. John's College, enjoy the hospitality of the Midshipmen at the Naval Academy, and enjoy lobster and crab dinners on the balcony of our room overlooking the harbor. Which brings me to the Key School. I had noticed that their athletic teams are called the Obezags, which I found puzzling. I began to understand when I saw their pretty campus with its several gazebos. Obezag, as I am sure you have already deciphered, is merely gazebo spelled backwards.

Chitwins

Taholah, Washington, is located on the Pacific Coast at the foot of the often fog-enshrouded Olympic Mountains, and in the heart of the Quinault Indian Reservation. Their teams are the Chitwins. The word *chitwin* means bear in their language, a wonderful choice.

Pam-Pack

Washington, North Carolina, was first settled in the 1690s and was originally called Tar River Fork. When it was renamed in honor of the Father of Our Country it is believed to be the first locale in the country to have been so. The Tar River, a prominent name in the Tar Heel State, is actually a feeder to the much broader Pamlico River on the shores of which Washington is located and which flows into Pamlico Sound and the Atlantic Ocean. Washington High School's athletic teams are called the Pam-Pack, because many years ago there was a pack of wolves roaming the north shore of the Pamlico River, which captured the imagination of the local populace.

Some Tough Ones

Sauras

When I first heard this one as the nickname of the South Stokes High School teams in Walnut Cove, North Carolina, I was stumped. Could it be some kind of lizard? Or a treasure, or a collection of something? A call to the school quickly cleared things up. A very pleasant young lady with a delightful Carolina accent was happy to tell me that Walnut Cove is located in the Saura Mountains, once the home to the Saura Indians. She further told me that the school mascot is a student dressed in the tradition of the Sauras . . . and, she added with considerable pride, the Sauras just won the state baseball championship!

Piasa Birds

The first white men to explore what is now the state of Illinois were the Jesuit Priest Pere Jacques Marquette (1637–1675) and his companion Louis Joliet (1645–1700). On one of their trips down the Mississippi, in 1673, near St. Louis in what is now the city of Alton, they spied, painted on the walls of a quarry, a colorful, monstrous bird, described by Marquette in his journal in the following words: "As we were descending the river we saw high rocks with hideous monsters painted on them . . . birds as large as a calf, with head and horns like a goat, eyes red, beard like a tiger's and face like a man's. Their tails are so long that they pass over their heads and between their forelegs, under their belly and ending like a fish's tail. They are . . . red, green, and black." He went on to say that no Indian would look upon them, they were such a fearsome sight. The Indians called them Piasa Birds. Now there is a high school in that area of Illinois, called Southwestern High School. It is on U.S. Highway 67 in Piasa. A large sign saying HOME OF THE PIASA BIRDS is painted on the water tower, the bird itself is on a sign at the north end of the football field, and another in the gym. Their teams are, of course, the Piasa Birds.

Go Huskies! Beat Felix the Cat!

Jug Rox

Shoals, Indiana, is a small town in the south central part of the state. It is located on U.S. 50, a national road that goes from coast to coast. The glaciers of the last great ice age pretty much flattened out the northern half of Indiana, but they pushed some interesting piles of earth and rock around in the southern part. One of the most impressive of these is just outside of Shoals, a mile or two only to the west, also on U.S. 50. It is a sixty-foot-tall monolithic rock structure that, from a certain angle, resembles a huge jug. It is thus called the Jug Rock. The Shoals High School teams are therefore called the Jug Rox. Inside the Shoals High School gym there are no less than four renderings of this rock, the more enjoyable ones being two versions of it playing basketball!

Briar Jumpers

Somerset, Kentucky, is a city of just over ten thousand people located near the many outdoor opportunities afforded by Cumberland Lake. Some years ago, I was told by Somerset High School principal and former football player there, Thomas G. "Tommy" Floyd, before the school had a mascot or nickname for their teams, the football team had enjoyed minimal success. Then, one Saturday in October of 1916 the Somerset team traveled north to play the blue clad, heavily favored Louisville High School team. When the final whistle blew, however, and the dust had settled and the last cheers faded into the twilight, the surprising score read SOMERSET, 51; LOUISVILLE, 6! The Louisville press was amazed. Now, from the Somerset High School athletic brochure:

> Louisville sportswriters were knocking themselves out trying to describe the drubbing that was perpetrated. One writer, Mr. Johnny Head, was

Some Tough Ones

frantically searching for some previous occurrence with which to compare the extraordinary speed and skill used to evade Louisville tacklers. That is when he remembered the story of Uncle Remus, the briar patch, and the elusive ways the Somerset team had of getting around, or evading obstructions. He also remembered the expression 'bawn and bred in de briar patch'. Immediately he christened the Somerset team the Briar Jumpers . . . and Briar Jumpers at home in their Briar Patch it has been ever since.

More recently the boys' teams have been joined by the girls' teams, called the Lady Jumpers.

Hoggers

While I was in graduate school at Dartmouth, I coached a swimming team at a nearby prep school, Kimball Union Academy. One of our meets was against the Mt. Hermon School in north central Massachusetts, just across from New Hampshire. They have since merged with a girls' prep school, and become Northfield-Mt. Hermon, their two fine campuses straddling both the Connecticut River and the state line. I have recently learned that their nickname is the Hoggers. Why? So, I called. Originally the Mt. Hermon campus was a farm. Apparently a swine farm, at least in part. So they are the Hoggers. And the girls' team? I inquired. The Lady Hoggers. They would give the Somerset, Kentucky, Lady Jumpers a good run for their money!

Hubs and Cogs

Hubs and Cogs. Sounds like someone is making reference to wheels. That's not the case, as I was to discover. Genoa and Rochelle are two towns not too far apart, in north central Illinois. Genoa is a town of some thirty-one hundred people, located on the Kishwaukee River, just southeast of Rockford. I had heard that the team name of Genoa-Kingston High School was the Cogs, a name that had me mystified. There must have been a factory there that produced cog wheels for industry. When I called, I got the right story. I should have guessed. Community of Genoa Schools. COGS. An acronym. However, I was pleased to learn that their mascot is a student who dresses up like a cog wheel and turns hand springs during their games.

Rochelle High School athletic teams are the Hubs. The hubs of the wheel I thought, at first, then I discovered that there is a Railway Park in Rochelle and that the times of the more than one hundred trains that pass through the town and the park daily are posted so that people can come and view them. Perhaps it is called the Hub City because it is a railway hub. So, I inquired that of the Chamber of Commerce and I loved the reply I received back from the aptly named spokesman, Greg Query. As follows:

> *You are on track (no pun intended) with your logic. We are known as the Hub City because we are at the crossing of two transcontinental railroads (Burlington Northern-Santa Fe & the Union Pacific) as well as being the intersection for two interstate highways (I-39 & I-88) and two major state routes (IL 251 & IL 38). Hope this helps.*

It did indeed.

UNIS

New York City's United Nations International School has an acronym nickname that really appeals to me. They are the UNIS. Since *unis* is French for united, the United Nations International School is also United. They would also be a good match for the Bodine School of International Affairs in Philadelphia, whose teams are the Ambassadors.

Some Tough Ones

Trevians

New Trier Township High School is located in Winnetka, Illinois. When I was in high school, New Trier was one of our fiercest rivals. It seemed as if whoever won our head-to-head competition in almost any sport was going to win the Suburban League Championship, if not the state title. At that time New Trier's teams were called the Indians, stemming in part from the Indian name of their hometown. Some time later the school became too small to hold the burgeoning student body and a new campus was built farther to the west. This resulted in the old school being renamed New Trier East and the new one becoming New Trier West. Now, what team name would you select if you are a school with west in your name and your obvious biggest rival, across town, is called the Indians? Why, Cowboys, of course. And so it was for several years. Eventually, however, two things happened: school demographics shifted so that only one campus was again needed and sentiment shifted from approving the appropriateness of an Indian mascot. The reconstituted New Trier decided to look to its heritage for the resulting nickname. The original settlers of Winnetka, which dates back to 1892, came to this country from Trier, Germany, a city on the Moselle River with Roman antecedents. People from Trier are called Trevians, and that was the nickname selected for the reconsolidated New Trier High School whose symbol is a Roman centurion's helmet.

Hyaks

Ocean Shores, Washington, is beautifully situated on a peninsula of land with Grays Harbor to the east and the rolling surf and rugged rocks of the Pacific Coast to the west. The North Beach High School teams in Ocean Shores are called the Hyaks. I had no idea what a Hyak was until I talked to some people at the school. It turns out that Hyaks is an Indian word that means "swift-moving." The symbol of Ocean Shores high School is a Winged Foot. The Hyaks.

Go Huskies! Beat Felix the Cat!

Caxys

Lake Forest Academy is located in the beautiful and exclusive far north suburban suburb of Chicago, Lake Forest. The school was founded for boys only in 1857 and a commensurate girls school named Ferry Hall was established in 1869. The two were combined in 1974. Their teams are known as the Caxys, a name that had me stumped until I had it cleared up by Ms. Ruth Novak, to whom I am indebted for the following history:

> *I am sending to you a paragraph out of a book called* Many Hearts, Many Hands, *which is a history of Ferry Hall and Lake Forest Academy written by Jay Pridmore in 1994.*
>
> *Football soon established itself as a bulwark of school solidarity, and football fever surfaced in many ways, including organized cheering. One of the academy's early chants pretended to be rooted in Greek verbs:*
>
> *"Tera-too-lix, too-lix, Kicka-bah-bah, kicka-bah-bah, 'cademy, 'cademy, rah rah rah." A few years later, "Caxy, coax, coax, coax," a refrain of the chorus from Aristophanes' comedy* The Frogs *provided the background din at games.*

The LFA mascot is, in fact, a frog.

Hoyas

Georgetown University, in Washington, D.C., has one of the most intriguing nicknames around. They are known as the Hoyas, which apparently is a combination of words in Greek and Latin that somehow mean "what rocks." Georgetown Prep, in Rockville, Maryland, is known as the Little Hoyas . . . would this be akin to "what pebbles"?

Some Tough Ones

Wamps

Massasoit was the *sachem*, that is chief, of the Wampanoag tribe of Indians who lived in what is now Rhode Island and the south eastern shore of Massachusetts. In 1621, one year after the Pilgrims had endured that first horrific winter, Massasoit visited the new arrivals in Plymouth. His own tribe had been severely depleted by famine and disease and he was accompanied by Samoset and Squanto of the Pawtucket tribe. Massasoit became a friend of the pilgrims, negotiating long-lived treaties with them. In memory of this great Sachem and his Wampanoag tribe the town of Braintree and its high school have selected Wamps as their team nickname.

Kofa

Kofa High School is in Yuma, Arizona. The question is, "What is a Kofa?" The answer: "King of Arizona." Naturally, their teams are the Kings.

Hummers

This one really had me stumped. The high school run in association with Philadelphia's Girard College has team names called the Hummers. Why? Perhaps it was a music school. Perhaps there is something about Philadelphia related to Hummers that I should know. If so, I couldn't recall it. Perhaps I had it wrong, and it was Mummers, something well associated with Philadelphia. When I called the school, of course the mystery was quickly solved. Years ago Philadelphians, or at least some of them, would pronounce the word "home" as though it were "hum." Thus, the Hummers are simply the Homers, and the high school is their home. I found that rather comforting.

7
A Boy Named Sue

SOME YEARS AGO, the late Johnny Cash, "The Man in Black," had a hit song called "A Boy Named Sue." You may remember it, the gist being that a boy named Sue had to be twice as tough as one named, say Lance, or Mike, or Joe. Well, that may be true for athletic teams as well. Otherwise, how do you explain the selection of some of the nicknames in this section?

Let me start with Benson High School in Omaha, Nebraska. Benson has a fine record of turning out scholars, athletes, and leaders in many walks of life. Two of the finest executives I ever knew came from Benson. But their team name? They are the Bunnies. Neither one of my friends knew, or at least would admit to knowing, why.

Fisher, Illinois, just fourteen miles north of Champaign, also fields the Bunnies. I do know their story, however. The vivacious young woman tending the cash register at Casey's General Store in Fisher said her grandfather, now ninety years old, played on the team that first earned the nickname Bunnies. The story as he told it was that they were having a terrible football season, couldn't seem to win a game, so one day the whole team went out hunting together and eventually every player shot a rabbit. They then took a rabbit's foot for each of them and actually wore them on their uniform for the next game. To almost everyone's surprise they won that game and they have been happily called the Bunnies ever since.

A Boy Named Sue

Next, we have Hickman High School, in Columbia, home of the beautiful campuses of the University of Missouri and of Stephens and Columbia colleges. The tough football players at Hickman, and all of their other athletes, are known as the Kewpies. This name was reportedly given by a sportswriter in the 1920s when the football team was losing big but kept their heads up and continued plugging along. The newspaperman wrote after one of their games that the team took the loss in stride "smiling like kewpies" and it stuck.

Vincennes, Indiana, was the first territorial capital of Indiana, when William Henry Harrison, destined to become President of the United States, was the Territorial Governor. The Vincennes Lincoln High School teams are the Alices. This one is a little easier to understand, although there are two theories that seem to have equal credence as to the selection of Alices for the school's nickname. The first theory refers to the 1923 State Championship Vincennes High basketball team that played, according to one sportswriter, "Like Alice in Wonderland." The other, preferred by most of the locals to whom I have spoken, is that it stems from a novel written by Maurice Thompson about the Revolutionary War called *Alice of Old Vincennes*, which was popular in the early days of the twentieth century. Either way, it is, in some respects, a nickname that requires some overcoming by the boys' athletic teams.

Fort Collins, Colorado, was originally built to protect the Overland Mail as well as travelers and settlers from Indian raids. It is located due north of Denver on the Cache La Poudre River. Today it is home to the impressive campus of Colorado State University, the Rams. It is also home to Fort Collins High School, whose teams also are ovine in origin, but, perhaps, a bit harder for the boys teams to take: their teams are called the Lambkins. Some years ago there was a move to change this to the Black Sheep, but it failed. The people of Fort Collins love their Lambkins.

Compton, California, is a suburb of Los Angeles. It is not too far from the famous LaBrea Tar Pits that claimed so many dinosaurs in their sticky, unyielding grasp. The Compton teams are the Tarbabes. Not far away is Lakewood, also a Los Angeles suburb. There the St. Joseph High School teams are the Jesters. Now, how are opponents supposed to take any team seriously that calls itself the Jesters?

Just down the Pacific Coast Highway or the Ventura Freeway from Los Angeles is the port city of Ventura. One of the famous missions of Father Junipero Serra, the Mission of San Buenaventura, founded in 1782, is in Ventura. Today Saint Bonaventure High School fields teams with the very mildest of nicknames, the Seraphs. No cherubim, just seraphim.

In Zeeland, Michigan—which is, unsurprisingly, close to Holland—the teams are called, somewhat more surprisingly, the Chix. The small town of Chickasha, Oklahoma fields the Chicks, the Fighting Chicks to be sure, but still something to be overcome to at least a certain extent. Similarly, at the Doane Stuart School in Albany, New York, are the Chickens, this time the Thunder Chickens. The mascot himself is indeed impressive. The Thunder Chicken stands six and a half feet tall, is yellow and orange, carries a lightning bolt and plays the bagpipes! That should capture any opponent's attention. The Stuart home basketball games are played in the Chicken Coop. Fighting Chicks and Thunder Chickens! Now who's kidding whom?

Our next entry in this category is Effingham, Illinois, a city of eleven thousand in the central part of the state. Founded in 1854 on the Cumberland Trail, Effingham is truly a crossroads town, bisected east-west and north-south from the time of its first settlement by trails, railroads, and major highways. The Effingham High School teams, now located in an impressive new facility just west of town, are known as the Flaming Hearts. When I asked a student where that name came from she told me it was because they consider Effingham to be the heart of America, and a hot place to live. Sam Rickeleman, a very pleasant and knowledgeable man, Editor of the local *Daily News*, added that some years ago a football coach tried to change the name to Tigers. This would not have been particularly distinctive, however, since one of Effingham's big rivals are the Paris Tigers. Anyway, the citizenry rose up against the idea and Flaming Hearts was there to stay.

Then there is Wild Rose High School in Alamo, North Dakota. Alamo is a tiny town, population sixty-nine, in the far northwestern part of the state, just twenty-five miles from Saskatchewan. Their teams are the Roses, the Wild Rose Roses.

The Salesianum School is an all-male institution in Wilmington, Delaware. Their nickname is the Sallies, which might take a bit of overcoming on occasion.

Agawam, Massachusetts, is a town just southwest of Springfield in the south central part of the state. I think their nickname belongs here as well. They are the Brownies.

Finally there are the Barbs of DeKalb, Illinois. DeKalb is a lovely town, home of the Huskies of Northern Illinois University and their impressive campus. But why the Barbs? The answer is simple. Two residents of DeKalb during the nineteenth Century combined to invent and produce barbed wire. The inventor was Joseph Glidden and the manufacturer was Isaac Elwood. Their combined contribution is sometimes called the wire that tamed the plains as it made possible large enclosures for cattle and sheep to graze without getting lost. Glidden's clever designs and Elwood's efficient manufacturing processes earned DeKalb the title "Barbed Wire Capital of the World" and it earned them each a fortune. It also earned DeKalb High School teams the name Barbs and anyone who has done so knows you must handle barbed wire with great respect and extreme care. What more can you expect of any nickname than that?

8
ANTIHEROES

SOME SCHOOLS HAVE chosen team names that appear, at first glance at least, to have negative connotations, but, on closer inspection are seen to be reflective of the history of the town in most cases.

Outlaws

Consider Rawlins, Wyoming. Today, Rawlins is a peaceful and pleasant town, a nice place to stop for a steak dinner after a glorious day exploring the wonders of the Flaming Gorge. In short, quite civilized. But it was not ever so. Rawlins was founded for the Union Pacific Railroad by General John Rawlins who found the springs in the area the best source of water in the Great Basin. Water, of course, was essential for the workers, townspeople, and the steam engines that would come. Apparently Rawlins was a particularly wild railroad town in the 1870s with "Bad characters, male and female, . . . drawn to it as by a great magnet." Fights, killings and general roistering were common occurrences. Outlaws flocked to Rawlins. So, what are today's Rawlins High School teams called? They are, in fact, the Outlaws.

Criminals

Yuma, Arizona, located on the Colorado River, was seen as an excellent crossing place, the gateway to the marvels of California. Two mission churches were built there but for a time Yuma lay dormant, to be

Antiheroes

rediscovered by the renowned Kit Carson. Today, Fort Yuma Quechan Museum, and the impressive American Historical Society house, gardens and aviary are worthy attractions for the interested tourist. So, too, is the Arizona Territorial Prison, once large enough to house 3000 inmates. At one point the prison was not fully occupied, however, and the town needed a high school. The solution was to start the school in an abandoned wing of the prison. When the football team defeated one opponent, either the players themselves or their disgruntled fans called the Yuma boys "nothing but criminals." At first this was not received lightly by the Yuma people, but eventually they began to take pride in this page of their history and for some time now the Yuma High School teams have been called the Criminals. I am told that their athletic teams actually wear uniforms of horizontal black and white stripes!

Highwaymen

The charming suburb of Teaneck, New Jersey, is located just across the Hudson River from New York City, a bit north of the George Washington Bridge. They are the Highwaymen. Now the most interesting highwayman I remember was the one in the poem by Alfred Noyes:

> *The wind was a torrent of darkness among the gusty trees*
> *The moon was a ghostly galleon tossed upon stormy seas*
> *The road was a ribbon of moonlight over the purple moor*
> *And the highwayman came riding—*
> *Riding—riding*
> *Up to the old inn door.*

Is this who the Teaneck teams are named for?

Bandits

Then there is the town of Pembina, North Dakota, just south of the

Go Huskies! Beat Felix the Cat!

Manitoba line. Pembina was founded in 1797 making it not only the oldest European settlement in the Dakotas but one of the oldest in the entire American West. Preconsolidation the Pembina High School teams were called the North Border Bandits. (Since consolidation they have become the North Border Eagles.)

Somewhat surprising to me is the choice of Bandits for the all girls' teams of Chicago Resurrection High School. I am informed that this was chosen some years ago by vote of the student body and the mascot herself roams the sidelines dressed like a bandit, complete with mask.

Maniacs

Outlaws, Criminals, Highwaymen, Bandits. But that's not the end of it. Orofino, Idaho, is located in beautiful country on the Nez Perce Indians tribal reservation. The town is on the Clearwater River and surrounded by the Clearwater National Forest. In 1805 Lewis and Clark stopped near present day Orofino on their monumental exploration of America's newest and grandest acquisition, Jefferson's Louisiana Purchase. Gold was discovered near Orofino in 1865, adding impetus to its growth and, no doubt, a wild and wooly atmosphere. In 1927 the Orofino High School basketball team went the twenty-two miles to play a game against the Kamiah Kubs by railroad, as there were no roads in those days between the two towns. Money was also scarce and the Orofino boys' uniforms were described as somewhat "ragtag." The game was pretty rough and one of the Kamiah fans said the Orofino team looked and played "like a bunch of maniacs." Well, the name took and the Orofino High School boys teams are the Maniacs to this day. When girls play began in the 1970s their teams were called the Lady Maniacs. Although there had been a state hospital for the mentally ill in Orofino even before the '20s it was not until the new State Hospital North was built . . . right across the street from the

Antiheroes

high school . . . that objections to the nickname began to arise. However, since it was selected well beforehand and in no way was meant pejoratively, it has not been changed. (Thanks to school principal Jerry Nelsen for this account, and for the Maniac pin, T-shirt, and other memorabilia.)

Vandals

Vandalia, Illinois, is one of my favorite Midwestern towns, located in the rich farmland of the south central part of the state, on the Kaskaskia River and on the Old Cumberland Trail. Vandalia was Illinois' state capital before Springfield and the original white brick, beautifully proportioned state house, dating from 1836, has been meticulously restored. Abraham Lincoln received his license to practice law in Vandalia and also served in the Illinois State Legislature there. With considerable history and culture abounding, the Vandalia High School teams are alliteratively named the Vandals. The Vandals were a marauding Germanic tribe that terrorized medieval Europe and I suppose that is in part what Vandalia's fans hope their locals will do to the opposition on the playing fields of Illinois. Perhaps they will Vandalize them!

Others

Winston-Salem, North Carolina, is another highly civilized city. It is home to the magnificent campus of Wake Forest University, the Demon Deacons of the Atlantic Coast Conference. We not only have those collegiate demons to contend with in Winston-Salem, we have the teams representing Bishop McGuiness High School. They are the Villains.

The last time I looked, rustlers were distinctly *personae non gratis* in the Wild West. Men like John Wayne and Jimmy Stewart went after them and locked them up, then defended them against angry mobs wanting to "string 'em up." No, I don't have positive images of rustlers at all. Still, the teams at both Ethan and Miller high schools in South Dakota are the Rustlers.

Eldred High School is in Duke Center among the beautiful hardwood

Go Huskies! Beat Felix the Cat!

and evergreen forests of northwestern Pennsylvania, east of Bradford and just South of Olean, New York, nearby the campus of the St. Bonaventure Bonnies. The Duke Center teams are the Terrors.

Deer Lodge, Montana, is the second oldest city in the state. It is located on the Clark Fork River, between the glories of Yellowstone and Glacier National Parks. With the Old Montana Prison, now a museum, and the Montana Law Enforcement Museum both in town it is not surprising that the Deer Lodge High School teams provide us with exactly what we need in our present circumstance for they are the Wardens. Or, equally possible, we could use the help of Jonathan Law High School in Milford, Connecticut. Their teams are the Lawmen. Other help could be provided by Marshall County High School in Benton in the western part of Kentucky. Marshall teams are the Marshals.

But, we're not quite done with the anti-heroes. For instance, Paoli, Oklahoma, fields the Pugs. As I remember it, a pug was a poor fighter, a pugilist who perhaps took one more punch than he should have, getting a pug nose. Anyway, they are the Paoli Pugs and maybe they give very bit as much as they get! Chances are Paoli never met Mifflin High School in Columbus, Ohio, but, if they did, it might just explain where the Pugs came from. After all, Mifflin's teams are the Punchers.

Some others:

Colonial Beach High School in Virginia fields the Drifters.
Medford, Wyoming High School teams are the Renegades.
Blue Spring, Mississippi, teams are the Urchins. (The Renegades and the Drifters: sounds like a 1930s movie starring James Cagney and the Little Rascals.)
Laurel Hill, Florida, teams are the Hoboes.
Mt. Tamalpais High School in California teams are the Boneheads.
Grand Rapids, Michigan, St. Joseph Seminary High School teams are the Rogues.
Portland, Maine, High School teams are the Red Riots. Nearby Orono teams are simply the Riots.

9
Our Daily Bread

MANY OF OUR towns were located where they were and grew to the size they did because of the things that were produced or extracted from the earth there. Thus it is not surprising that the way we earn our daily bread is often reflected in the choice of mascot or nickname made for our local school.

The Oil Patch

The northwestern section of Indiana is highly industrialized. With steel mills, foundries, breweries, refineries, and a major port, it much more resembles Chicago, its neighboring "City of the big shoulders, husky brawling...." than it does most of the rest of the state. It is known to residents and other Hoosiers as "The Region." The town of Whiting on the shores of Lake Michigan is in the Region. It was first settled in 1885 and four years later the Standard Oil Company built one of the world's largest refineries there. It was here that chemist William Merriam Burton discovered a process for producing more gasoline per barrel of crude oil called thermal cracking, which revolutionized the industry. Burton rose to become president of the company and the Whiting High School teams have always been proudly called the Oilers.

A similar history occurred in the Mississippi River town and St. Louis suburb in downstate Illinois, Roxanna. Roxanna could not afford to build its own high school until the Royal Dutch Shell Oil Company decided to build a refinery of its own in the town. With the tax base and employment opportunities provided by the refinery, Roxanna soon had its high school and this explains its nickname, the Shells. Next door, in Wood River, another town dependent upon the refinery, are the Oilers.

Oil was also extremely important to the economy of Oklahoma. Thus, in the town of Elk City, Merritt High School is also represented by the Oilers. The workers in the oil fields were called rough necks, and Crooked Oak High School in Oklahoma fields the Ruf-Nex. In White Oak, Texas, are the Roughnecks.

There are many oil wells to be seen in the south shore area of Los Angeles, California, and it is not surprising that Huntington Beach teams are called the Oilers. Just north of Los Angeles, at the southern end of the San Joaquin Valley, is Bakersfield. Oil and natural gas were each important discoveries there and the Bakersfield High School teams are the Drillers.

Sunburst, Montana, is located just eight miles south of the Alberta line and about thirty miles east of the many glories of Glacier National Park and its dramatic Highway to the Sun, one of the world's great scenic drives. With the discovery of natural gas and petroleum the economies of the entire area became dominated by these two prime nourishers of the insatiable hunger for energy of twentieth-century America. North Toole County High School in Sunburst recognizes this with their choice of nickname. They are the Refiners.

Drillers, Oilers, Roughnecks, and Refiners. This should just about get the job done!

The Gold Diggers – and More

Last winter we were enjoying one of those wonderful first days in Florida, having just left the northern cold and grey, the sun so warm, the breeze so balmy, the water colored in impossible shades of green and blue. We were having lunch outdoors on the dock of a charming little seafood restaurant, enjoying the moment and discussing high school team names when our waitress chimed in by announcing that her high school's was the Gold Diggers. At this point one of the waiters observed, *sotto voce*, that it must have been an all girls school. Of course it wasn't. She happened to be from

Our Daily Bread

Idaho Springs, Colorado, site of the first significant gold strike in Colorado, in 1859 and present day home to the Double Eagle Gold Mine, the Phoenix Mine and the Argo Gold Mine, Mill and Museum. No apologies necessary for calling your teams the Gold Diggers there!

She could also have been from Lead, South Dakota, pronounced like someone who is in front. The word actually refers to a kind of vein of ore that promises to lead to a particularly rich strike. That was eminently true in Lead, the particular vein being the richest gold strike ever discovered in the Western Hemisphere. The result was the Homestake Mine, begun in 1876 and only recently closed. Lead, home to the Black Hills Mining Museum, is built rather precariously on the sides of a mountain and pretty much the whole town is a National Historic District. The Lead High School teams are, of course, also the Gold Diggers.

Nearby is Sturgis, a town that evolved out of the original Camp Sturgis, a Cavalry outpost named for the youngest officer to be killed in the Battle of Little Big Horn. Sturgis has had its fair share of wild individuals over the years, male and female, including the notorious Poker Alice. Many Sturgis citizens have also been involved in the mining of gold. One of the techniques used is called scooping, and the men who do it are called scoopers. Thus, the Sturgis Brown High School teams are nicknamed the Scoopers.

Silver was discovered in Tonopah, Nevada, in 1900, a major strike, second only to the famed Comstock Lode of earlier days. When the boom died, Tonopah lived on, unlike its neighbor, Goldfields, once the territory's largest city and now almost a ghost town. Thus, Tonopah has a high school and that school's teams are called the Muckers. At first I thought that was a bit negative, thinking of the word in terms of mucking out stables or the like, but a call to the school assured me that my fears were groundless. Muckers in this case are those who clean up the dirt and debris left over

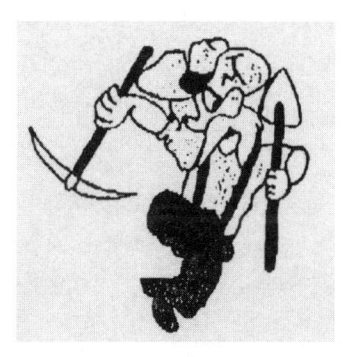

73

from the gold and silver ore during the mining process. The mascot is a student dressed as a miner, complete with pick and shovel.

Rapid City was founded by unsuccessful miners who turned their attention to providing goods and services needed by their more successful brethren. The nickname chosen for Rapid City Central High School's teams is quite representative of this reason for the city's founding. Certainly the miners and other settlers needed shoes, among a variety of other things. The nickname: The Cobblers.

North of Rapid City is the town of Newell, an agricultural area today. Rainfall is not great in the Black Hills and Badlands, so it is perhaps with excellent reason that the Newell High School teams are called the Irrigators

The Eastern entrance to the Badlands National Park is just a bit west of Kadoka. Kadoka means "hole in the wall" in the Lakota Sioux language. The Kadoka teams are the Kougars. One of the many outstanding geological formations making up the park is called the Wall. The name is an accurate description of what it is: a tall, narrow range of cliffs running north-south, which can be seen from a great distance, in a variety of shapes and colors, colors that change with the angle and intensity of the light. The town of Wall is named for this phenomenon. Wall is adjacent to the Buffalo Gap National Grasslands and is also home to a well-known tourist attraction, the block long Wall Drug Store. The Wall High School teams are the Eagles, and eagles are not an uncommon sight in the skies over the grasslands and the Badlands of South Dakota.

Mount Rushmore National Park, with its massive sculptings of the heads of Presidents Washington, Lincoln, Jefferson, and Theodore Roosevelt, is indeed a stunning site, not to be missed. Nearby is Hill City, where the Rangers take the field. Also nearby is Douglas High School, located on Ellsworth Air Force Base, and the Douglas teams are very appropriately the Patriots.

Miners

Telluride and Silverton, Colorado, are only about twenty-five miles apart as the crow flies, high up in the beautiful San Juan Mountains of southwestern Colorado. Silverton was named after an anonymous miner stated, "We may not have gold, but we have a ton of silver!" Silver there was, in abundance, and eventually gold, lead, zinc and copper as well. Saloons, also. At the peak, there were more than forty, and undoubtedly some bawdy houses as well, on notorious Blair Street. Telluride also has a rip-snorting history. Gold was discovered there in 1875. The town is named for Tellurium, a mineral often found in conjunction with gold or silver ore. The Smugglers Mine, so named because it was nestled between the claims of two other mines, produced immense quantities of rich gold and silver ore. Butch Cassidy held up his first bank in Telluride. The nicknames of the high school teams? Both Silverton and Telluride teams are called the Miners.

Salt Lake City is only about fifteen miles from the Kennecut Open Cut Copper Pit, the world's largest. Murray, a suburb of Salt Lake City, teams are the Smelterites.

Yreka, California, a name meaning "mountains" in the Shasta Indian language, is in far northern California. Yreka was begun as a gold mining camp and the Siskiyou County Museum there tells a fascinating tale of those early days when visions of gold clouded the minds of many an adventurer into the wilderness. Today the Yreka High School teams capture those memories with their nickname, also the Miners. Nearby Happy Camp fields the Indians.

Cripple Creek

In 1891 gold was discovered on a cattle ranch west of Colorado Springs. The town of Cripple Creek, named for the cattle that had been lamed when they crossed the rock strewn stream in the area, sprang up nearby. By 1900 Cripple Creek was a rip-roaring genuine Western boom town, inhabited by some twenty-five thousand hardy souls and boasting two opera houses, fourteen newspapers, an assayers office, town services, lawyers, and 139 saloons. Legend has it that a drugstore clerk threw his hat out over the ground and dug where it landed, resulting in the rich Pharmacy Mine. The

Go Huskies! Beat Felix the Cat!

Cresson Mine hit a vein of almost pure gold. The Independence Mine and the Mollie Kathleen were also highly successful operations. Some $500 million-worth of gold was extracted from the mines around Cripple Creek before they were essentially exhausted. With all of those people brought to this rich spot can it be a surprise that the Cripple Creek High School athletic teams are called the Pioneers?

Granite Diggers

Mellen, Wisconsin, is a small town of nine hundred people located almost as far north as you can get in the state. It is great country for outdoorsmen, fishing, hunting, hiking, cross-country skiing, and the like. One of the treasures of the area is the red and black granite quarried there. This stone is widely used for monuments and buildings and the Mellen High School teams are proudly called the Granite Diggers.

Sandstoners

Potsdam is in far upstate New York, close to Canada. Winters in the Potsdam area are only for the hardiest of souls and the cold comes early and stays late. One of the prime activities in Potsdam was the quarrying of sandstone found in abundance locally. Sandstone from Potsdam quarries was used extensively in the construction of buildings in Ottawa, Ontario, and Syracuse, New York, as well as in many other cities and towns in both countries. The Potsdam High School athletic teams are the Sandstoners.

The Slaters

Fair Haven, Vermont, is just over the New York state line, about nine miles east of Whitehall and three miles southwest of beautiful Lake Bomoseen. The area around Fair Haven was rich with slate deposits and became the center of the industry in the early days of our country. Many Welshmen and Irishmen migrated to Fair Haven to work in the quarries around the town.

Our Daily Bread

The Fair Haven High School teams are faithfully called the Slaters.

The Stonecrushers

Lakeside, Ohio, is on the Marblehead Peninsula jutting out into Lake Erie, west to east, creating the pleasant harbor of Sandusky Bay. Danbury High School is in Lakeside. There are significant limestone deposits in the area, many of which are very close to the surface. This has led to the development of several limestone quarries on the peninsula and, particularly in the time before the days of automation, much of the employment in the area involved working in those quarries. When the high school first fielded football teams the field was placed, almost unavoidably, in a position where the limestone deposits would continually work their way up through the topsoil and sod. The Danbury players then made it a practice of walking the field prior to home games and picking up loose rock wherever it appeared and tossing it out of the way. At that time the school colors were Columbia blue and the teams were generally referred to as the Blues. However, sometime around 1931, the opponents started referring to Danbury players as Stonecrushers. This caught on and became the official mascot of Danbury High School until it was consolidated with another school some thirty years later, changing the colors to a darker, or royal blue, and the nickname to the present one, recognizing the school's proximity to Lake Erie, the Lakers. I am most grateful to Principal Karen Abbott and Librarian Jim Rinaldo who most graciously gave of their time in providing me with this information. Jim also told me there are repeatedly efforts to reintroduce the name Stonecrushers, which he hopes will succeed, as I do, as it is indeed a most distinctive and historic school team name.

Linton

Linton, Indiana, is smack in the middle of some of the nation's richest, close to the surface veins of coal. Since the veins were so close to the surface no shafts were necessary and the coal was removed by miners using strip mining techniques. Once the topsoil was removed the coal was exposed and then it was dug and removed by some truly giant equipment. Railroad lines were built right into the mines to haul the coal to the various points where it was needed. Many of Linton's men worked in those open air pits. When the coal was exhausted the result was a pretty ugly scar on the surface of the rolling hills of the Indiana countryside. However, the topsoil was then carefully replaced, fields and trees were planted, and the result is a return to an area of beautiful ponds and woods. The teams of Linton-Stockton High School were and are proudly called the Miners.

Iron and Steel

Perhaps no industry was of greater importance to the building of America than was iron and steel. Several towns have recognized the importance of iron or steel to their development in the selection of nicknames for their high schools. Joliet, Illinois, named for one of the early explorers of the state, is a southwestern suburb of Chicago. Steel mills were an important employer in Joliet and their high school teams are the Steelmen . . . and the Steelwomen. Close by, using that steel to build the iron horses that truly tamed the west, are the Bradley-Bourbonnais Boilermakers. Few states are more closely identified with steel than is Pennsylvania. There we find the Steelers in Farrell and the Steel Valley Ironmen in Munhall. There are also Ironmen in Mancelona, Michigan, a town due east of Traverse Bay. An enormous statue, some twenty feet high, of a foundry worker pounding a giant hammer into a piece of steel stands on the grounds of Mancelona High School.

Birmingham, Alabama, was a second Pittsburgh when it came to steel. Nearby Holt High School also fields the Ironmen. Lackawanna, New York, near Buffalo, is an industrial and railroad town. Its high school teams are the Steelers. My favorite nickname in this category, however, goes to a school in Hobart in north central Indiana called River Forest. The River Forest teams are the Ingots. An ingot is defined by Webster's New Collegiate as "A mass

Our Daily Bread

of metal cast into a convenient shape for storage or transportation to be later processed." Yea, rah, metal mass. Go Ingots.

The Chemics

Midland, Michigan, is now a city of thirty-nine thousand people located due west of Bay City, at the southern tip of Saginaw Bay. Midland's location at the confluence of the Pine and Chippewa Rivers made it a natural for the fur trappers and traders who originally settled there in 1856. In 1891 Herbert H. Dow, a chemist, developed an efficient new process for extracting chemicals from the area's brine deposits. Soon Midland became the headquarters for the booming and prosperous Dow Chemical Company. Today the home and six-acre gardens of the Dow estate are a major attraction for tourists and residents alike. The overwhelmingly main employer in Midland continues to be the Dow Chemical Company, now a worldwide operation. The Midland High School athletic teams are the Chemics.

The Tractors

In 1915 Henry Ford bought two thousand acres of land in Michigan, near the farm where he was born, on which he intended to build a totally vertically integrated manufacturing plant to build and assemble his Model T cars and his tractors. The concept was to go from steel mill to finished product, utilizing Ford's principles of efficient assembly lines and interchangeable parts. The factory was called the River Rouge Plant, after the name adopted by French trappers who came to the area after the War of 1812. The town was called Fordson. In 1928 Fordson became a part of the city of Dearborn. Today Dearborn is still the headquarters of the Ford Motor Company, but it is also home to the Henry Ford Museum and the living history establishment known as Deerfield Village. The high school in Dearborn, named for the town in which Henry Ford built his enormous River Rouge

Plant, is Fordson High School, proudly represented on the fields of athletic competition by the Tractors.

Brickmakers

Hebron was a Canaanite royal city, nine miles south of Jerusalem and thirteen miles from Bethlehem, founded more than three thousand years ago in an area of abundant water from both wells and springs. There are several Hebrons in the United States, one of which is in southern Nebraska on the Little Blue River, just west of Gilead. The Hebron, Nebraska, High School teams are the Brickmakers.

Northampton, Pennsylvania

Northampton, Pennsylvania, a town of fewer than ten thousand in the eastern part of the state, north of Allentown, is in an area that produces immense quantities of cement and concrete. The Saylor Cement Museum is in Allentown. However, it is in nearby Northampton that pride in the concrete industry is at its highest level. Their teams are the Konkrete Kids. Their wrestling team, often among the best if not the best in the nation, uses a hold called the "cement mixer." I know one thing for sure: you never want to get caught in a cement mixer, particularly if it is being operated, or applied, by a Konkrete Kid!

Iron Horse

The building of the railroads was the greatest industrial enterprise our young country ever attempted, and it was accomplished only through tremendous effort, ingenuity and management skill. Cities were made and broken depending upon the choice of roadbed made by the railroads. Land grants made a checkerboard march across the nation as the railroads used the land to raise the funds necessary to meet the immense expenses they incurred. Towns were often essentially totally dependent on the work provided by the railroads for their entire economic development. It is no surprise that many of them selected nicknames related to the iron horse for their high school teams. I have covered much about the railroads in other sections of this book, from Monon to Billings, from Henry Flagler to Will Durant. (A few more are described in the sidebar on the following page.)

Tarriers were Irish railroaders, many of whom came over to the United States to help build ours. The old Irish song "Drill, Ye Tarriers, Drill" relates to these men. When Charles Wright decided on the site for the western terminus of the Northern Pacific Railroad he chose a natural harbor on Commencement Bay of Puget Sound and soon port facilities and sawmills were built. The nearby settlement of Commencement City had been established in 1868, and the name changed to Tacoma, the Indian name for Mt. Rainier, shortly thereafter. Wright's daughter, Annie, founded a school for girls in Tacoma and later a new school for boys was established and named for Charles Wright. Their teams were called the Tarriers and their mascot is a burly Irishman who carriers a large sledgehammer, reminiscent of Purdue University's Boilermaker Pete. (I am indebted to Phil Havens, former Master of School at the Charles Wright Academy, for this account.)

The real Iron Horse, of course, was the fire-breathing, steam generating monster at the front of the train, the locomotive. Laurel, Montana, is just southwest of Billings, itself a railroad town named for a railroad man from Woodstock, Vermont, whose family farm there was purchased by Laurence Rockefeller and is now open to the public, providing a fascinating look into life as it was lived on a dairy farm in the nineteenth century. The Laurel teams are the Locomotives. Montpelier, Ohio, in the northwest corner of the state, near Indiana, also selected Locomotives for their nickname. Finally there is the town of Huntington, Oregon, named for one of the prime movers of the Central Pacific Railroad that met the Union Pacific at Promontory Point, Utah, on that proud day in 1869. The Huntington High School teams are also the Locomotives.

Not all locomotive engines were run by steam. Harlowton, Montana, in the central part of the state, northwest of Billings, was the jumping off point for the Milwaukee Road's electric line that headed west over the mountains

Go Huskies! Beat Felix the Cat!

More Railroaders

Brunswick, Maryland, is located on the Potomac River. In the 1880s it was selected by the Baltimore and Ohio Railroad to be the site for one of its repair shops. In 1907 a roundhouse, still there, was constructed. The Brunswick Railroad Museum speaks to the town's history as does the selection of Brunswick High School's nickname: the Railroaders. Ellis, Kansas, just west of Hays, also a railroad town, was an important source of labor for the Union Pacific Railroad. Ellis, too, has a Railroad Museum celebrating the importance of that phase of their history to the townspeople. It was also the boyhood home of Walter Chrysler. Before he became a Detroit automotive baron he had been an Ellis Railroader. Waynoka, Oklahoma, was also built around the railroad, in this case the Santa Fe in 1893. The impressive Santa Fe Depot in town was built in 1910 and now houses the Waynoka Historical Museum. Once again, Railroaders represent Waynoka on the high school athletic fields. Durand, Michigan, is a town of forty-three hundred people southwest of Flint. In town is the Durand Union Station Railroad Museum and Library. The Durand High School teams are also the Railroaders. In Ohio, Collinwood High School in Cleveland and Bradford High School in the west central part of the state near the Indiana line, both field the Railroaders.

When the name Altoona arises, first thoughts naturally turn to the town by that name in western Pennsylvania where the famous Horse Shoe Curve is located. Although the town's minor league baseball franchise is in fact called the Curves, a very nice double entendre, the high school did not pick up on the railroading theme, preferring Mountain Lions. Altoona, Wisconsin, did, however. The town near Eau Claire does call its high school teams the Railroaders.

Our Daily Bread

to Idaho. The advantage of the electric engine was its ability to recharge its batteries to a significant extent on downward runs. A Milwaukee Road Electric engine, built in 1915 by General Electric is on display in downtown Harlowton, near the 1908 Graves Hotel that overlooks the old Milwaukee Road Complex including roundhouse and depot. The Harlowton High School team name is the Engineers, perfect for guiding our Locomotives and our Railroaders.

The Burlington Zephyr

Galesburg, Illinois, was founded in 1836 by the Reverend G. W. Gale, who went there to establish what became Knox College, an excellent small liberal arts school. Among its many historical and cultural connections, Galesburg was a major shop for the Chicago, Burlington and Quincy Railroad (now part of the Santa Fe Burlington Northern Route), which still runs through town. Poet Carl Sandburg's father, who immigrated from Sweden, was a blacksmith for the CB & Q in the Galesburg yards and his son was born in the town. The excellent Galesburg Railroad Museum attests to the importance of railroading to the economic history of the town. In 1934, the CB & Q introduced a radically redesigned passenger train, the exterior of which was made of shining, silver-colored stainless steel—a true "streamliner" with graceful, aerodynamic lines. This beautiful train was called the Burlington Zephyr. Inside it was appointed with every amenity a traveler could desire. In 1934 it demolished all railroad speed records, cutting the travel time between Denver and Chicago in half and achieving the unheard-of speed of seventy miles per hour while the passengers ate, drank and slept in perfect comfort. Many of these trains were built and serviced in Galesburg. Can it be any surprise that the Galesburg High School teams are known proudly as the Silver Streaks?

Rails

Spooner is a town of twenty-five hundred people in the logging area of the far northern part of Wisconsin. Spooner was originally a railroad junction and was named for a railroad attorney, John Coit Spooner, who was also twice elected as a United States Senator. The railroad heritage of the town is not forgotten, however. The Railroad Memories Museum is housed in the old Chicago & Northwestern depot and the Western Great Northern Railroad operates sightseeing and dinner trains with vintage cars and engines. And the Spooner High School teams are the Rails. Proctor is a suburb of Duluth, not far from Spooner. The Proctor High School teams are also the Rails. As far as I know, there is no third rail, which, we were always told, is the most dangerous one.

Valley City

Valley City, North Dakota, is about fifty miles due west of Fargo. It was on the main line of the Great Northern Railroad located in the spot where it had to cross the Sheyenne River. The original bridge over the river was frequently flooded out and impassable. Thus a second, higher bridge was built. This bridge has been described as one of the most impressive engineering feats of its era, spanning a distance of 3,838 feet at a height of 126 feet. Opened in 1908 and still in operation today, the bridge is known as the High Line Bridge to differentiate it from the original Low Line Bridge. The Valley City High School athletic teams are the Hi-Liners.

The Packers

Phillip Danforth Armour founded the giant meat processing company that bears his name and the town of Armour, Montana, has named its teams the Packers. Cudahy, Wisconsin, was settled in 1892 by Patrick Cudahy, founder of another large meat packing company. Many of the streets in Cudahy are named for meat packers, as are the high school's teams, again, the Packers. There are also Packers in Austin, Minnesota, home of George Hormel, who in 1887 founded the Hormel Meat Company, yet a third member of the largest meat processing and packing operations in the world.

Other Vocations

Several other vocations are honored by their local high schools. One that intrigues me is in Freeport, Texas. Freeport is a town of about twelve thousand on the Gulf Coast, due south of Houston. The Freeport Brazosport High School teams are called the Exporters.

Mullins, South Carolina, is a town of about six thousand near the North Carolina line and about thirty miles from Myrtle Beach. It is located in tobacco country and the Mullins High School teams are the Auctioneers. "Sold, American!"

Norwalk, Ohio, is located near Thomas Edison's birthplace, about ten miles south of Lake Erie. At one time the Ernst Hausen Trucking Company employed many locals and, although it is no longer there, the Norwalk High teams are still called the Truckers. There are also Truckers at Clinton, Wisconsin High School. Ten-four, good buddy!

Hobart, Indiana, was a center of the brick-making industry for many years. The Hobart High mascot, described as the "school spirit" by alumna Patricia Douglas Dains, is a little brickworker named Johan Petrovich, and their teams are the Brickies. (Also in Hobart are the River Forest Ingots. A game between the Ingots and the Brickies? No comment.)

Biglerville is a small town, less than a thousand people, near Gettysburg in southeastern Pennsylvania. Canning is important to the people of Biglerville and their high school teams are called the Canners.

East Liverpool, Ohio, is located on the Ohio River very near the point where it enters the state from Pennsylvania, and just across the river from the northernmost part of the West Virginia panhandle. The city was founded in 1799 in part to take advantage of the buff-burning natural clays and coal deposits of the area that were essential to the production of fine pottery. From those beginnings until the mid-1930s, firms in East Liverpool produced about half of the nation's pottery. Today it is home to the Museum of Ceramics and the Hall China Company. It is also home to the East Liverpool High School Potters. Crooksville is a town of twenty-six hundred people, southwest of East Liverpool with a similar heritage. The Ohio Ceramic Center is located in Crooksville and the high school teams are called the Ceramics. Perhaps the Ceramics do play the Potters from time to time. I wonder who cracks first?

Knippa, Texas, is a very small town, with a population of 350 people and a high school enrolling 52 students. Apparently the consolidation movement so evident in many states has not reached this part of Texas. Knippa High School's athletic teams are called the Rock Crushers. Perhaps they are the recipients of the products of Dell Rapids, South Dakota, home of the Quarriers.

These two would make quite a pair on the athletic field, along with the one-time nicknames of three other schools (also mentioned elsewhere):

Stonecrushers, Danbury High School, Lakeside, Ohio
Stone Cutters, Bedford, Indiana
Quarry Lads, Stinesville, Indiana

10

FROM THE FIELDS AND FORESTS

BRINGING FORTH THE Lord's bounty from His various storehouses on this earth has rarely been easy. Robert Frost said it best: "We were the land's before the land was ours." Many of our nation's communities were located just where they were simply because that is where the treasures could be grown from the soil or wrested from the trees.

Farmers

When the Pilgrims endured the terrible hardships of that first year in the New World they could not produce enough crops to feed themselves. But farming was our first occupation and years later the farms of America were truly the breadbasket for the world. Nothing in our history better captures the drive and initiative of the American spirit than those two facts.

Farmers are honored in many schools and towns throughout the country. Wheat Ridge, Colorado, a suburb of Denver, is represented by the Farmers, as are the teams of Farmington, Illinois, and Farmersville, Texas. Also in Texas are the Lewisville Fighting Farmers. Lewisville was farming country once, but it has been absorbed by the city as has been true of all too much of our prime farmland recently. As Will Rogers once said "Progress may have been a good thing once, but it's been going on too long." At any rate, in a bit of nostalgic reflection, the Lewisville water tower is adorned

Go Huskies! Beat Felix the Cat!

with a rendering of a football player carrying a pitchfork. The Fighting Farmers.

Monte Vista, Colorado, is located in the lush San Luis Valley. The area thrives by growing potatoes and other crops and Sargent High School, a small school in Monte Vista, aptly calls its teams the Farmers as well.

Serena, Illinois, is in prime corn growing country. The Serena High School teams are the Huskers. They would go well with another Illinois school's teams, the Hoopeston Cornjerkers (covered in detail later). Jerk it, husk it, cook it, eat it. We all love fresh sweet corn.

Ranchers

The term "farmers" is generally applied to those whose primary interest is in growing crops, though they may also have some livestock. Ranchers, however, primarily raise livestock, often having enormous amounts of grazing land for their cattle or sheep. Or maybe it's just geographical: farmers in the east, ranchers in the west. At any rate, ranchers are popular mascots for our western high schools. They are found at the White Oak School in Vinita, Oklahoma, at Power Lake in northwest North Dakota, and at Harding County High School in Buffalo, South Dakota, to name a few.

Beetdiggers and Meloneers

Whenever we visit the Eagle's Lair, the name of my sister and brother-in-law's lovely home perched atop a mountain outside of Estes Park, we seem to drive through the town of Brush, Colorado. Brush is situated on the flat, high plains, just east of the majestic Rockies and the view toward the west on a clear day is truly awe-inspiring. The town itself is one of wide, straight streets and pleasant, hardworking people. Once, when we were visiting, the Brush High School football team was scheduled to play in the final game of the State Championships in a few days and every storefront carried a sign exhorting the team to win. The teams at Brush, by the way, are named for the primary agricultural crop in the area. The signs read GO, BEETDIGGERS!

From the Fields and Forests

About 150 miles due south of Brush is the town of Rocky Ford, Colorado. It is near LaJunta, or The Junction as it would be in English, referring to the railroad junction there. Rocky Ford is prime growing area for cantaloupes and the high school teams are the Meloneers. How about a contest between the Beetdiggers and the Meloneers?

Perhaps we should include some other schools in this section as well. Certainly, Jordan High School in Sandy, Utah, just south of Salt Lake City, belongs here. They are the Beetdiggers, too. Then there's Chinook, Montana. Chinook is an Indian word meaning "warm winter wind." The Chinook High School teams are the Sugar Beeters, in acknowledgment of the many sugar beets grown in the Milk River Valley. Then there's Sugar-Salem High School in Sugar City, Idaho. The Diggers. And Wilburton, in the San Bois Mountains of Oklahoma—also the Diggers.

Cairo, Georgia

Cairo, pronounced "kay-ro," is located just over the Florida line, about twenty-five miles north of Tallahassee. It was the birthplace of the great Jackie Robinson who, in 1947, thanks to farsighted Branch Rickey of the then-Brooklyn Dodgers became the first African American to play baseball in the Major Leagues. Robinson is now honored in the Hall of Fame in Cooperstown, New York. He left Cairo before entering high school, but he is remembered there with great affection, a sort of unofficial Syrupmaker. Yes, Cairo's boys' teams are the Syrupmakers and the girls' teams are the Syrup Maids.

I asked about these names, and this is the story I got from the Cairo Chamber of Commerce: Cane syrup has for many years been an important crop in the environs of Cairo. There were, and still are, many producers, some very small. The largest was the Roddenberry Syrup Company, whose plant was located right next to the high school. It was the area's largest employer and its president was a big fan of high school football. One night, as a game was being played in a driving rain, Mr. Roddenberry went over to his factory, and returned with enough raincoats for the whole team to wear on the sidelines. These raincoats bore the inscription RODENBERRY SYRUP on the back, and from that day on the Cairo teams have been the Syrupmakers. Syrup Maids was the name adopted when girls' sports arrived on the scene, and one Syrup Maid, Teresa Edwards, has made quite a name for herself as an Olympic basketball gold medalist and a pioneering member of the WNBA.

Cheesemakers

Monroe, Wisconsin, is a town of ten thousand people in the south central part of the state. Much of the area was originally settled by immigrants from Switzerland, and the rolling country side is ideally suited for the raising of dairy cattle and the processing of various dairy products including cheese. Monroe has a charming square on which many buildings in Swiss architectural style surround the red brick county courthouse. There is also an Alpine and Dell Cheese factory, and Monroe bills itself as the "Swiss Cheese Capital of America." The Monroe High School athletic teams are known as the Cheesemakers.

Across the continent is Tillamook, Oregon, with its name coming from an Indian word meaning "land of many waters." Tillamook has long been a dairy center on the west coast with its principle products being cheeses. The Tillamook High School athletic teams are also called the Cheesemakers. Tillamook versus Monroe could make for a churning intersectional football or basketball game, I should think

Cowboys, Horses, and Cows

Kanab, Utah, is a good place to start. Kanab is in the area of spectacular scenery that is southern Utah, near Zion and Bryce Canyons, Grand Canyon and Monument Valley. In the early days of the twentieth century the great chronicler of the American West, Zane Grey, went to Kanab while writing his classic work, *Riders of the Purple Sage*. Several years later Tom Mix came to Kanab to film his movie, *Deadwood Coach*. Soon Kanab was

From the Fields and Forests

the movie capital of Utah and more than three hundred Westerns were filmed there. Just a short drive out of Kanab is a Ghost Town, created by the motion picture industry for the shooting of the television series *Gunsmoke*, starring James Arness. Today the Kanab High School mascot is the Cowboys.

There are Cowboys representing many of our high schools, of course, from coast to coast. Here are some examples:

Killdeer, North Dakota.
Custer City, Montana, near the Little Big Horn.
Chaparral High School in Las Vegas, Nevada.

Happy, Texas, is about thirty miles south of Amarillo. In this wonderfully named town we find the Happy Cowboys, which always reminds me of Gene Autry and Roy Rogers. "Happy trails to you," Happy, Texas, Cowboys!

We did not overlook the four legged animals that gave the cowboys their name, either. In fact, there are so many schools from coast to coast with cow and cow-related nicknames that I will only mention a small selection of the total. Most romantic of all of the cattle of the Old West, I think, was the longhorn. These majestic animals were driven for hundreds and hundreds of miles from grazing land to market, marshaled and kept together by the cowboys. Today the longhorn is a fairly rare sight, although I have seen them not too long ago on a ranch in the shadow of the Grand Teton Mountains of Wyoming. There are Longhorns representing Chisholm High School in Enid, Oklahoma, and many Texas high schools including Amarillo Caprock, Aqua Dulce (Sweet Water), and Bronte (no relation to the sisters from Haworth, England).

Fort Benton, Montana, is located at the head of navigable waters of the Missouri River and was an agricultural and shipping center for the entire region. In 1867 it is reported that thirty-nine steamboats arrived at Ft. Benton every day. The city became quite prosperous until the railroad bypassed the town and the economy suffered until an overland trail to

Go Huskies! Beat Felix the Cat!

Canada was opened to serve that growing nation's needs in its remotest outposts. Longhorn cattle became an important source of revenue for the area. The high school teams today are also the Longhorns. Wibaux, in the Badlands of Montana, is named for a wealthy French settler named Pierre Wibaux who came to Montana in 1883. At one time his herd numbered one hundred thousand head and the town became an important center for shipping cattle to the markets of the south and east. The Wibaux High School teams are, again, the Longhorns.

Ogden Nash once wrote some clever lines about a purple cow—he'd rather see than be one. That may be well and good, but if you should go to Brownwood, Texas, you might indeed see a purple cow and you would surely meet a lot of people who are quite proud to be one. Those would be the students, alumni and fans of Early High School. It is home to the Early Longhorns, whose colors are purple and gold. Definitely Purple Cows, and surely proud to be so.

Big Spring, Texas, is on the Santa Fe Trail, a route long used by the Comanches to take advantage of the waters there. The first white men to view these springs arrived in 1849, followed in 1882 by the Texas and Pacific Railroad. Today the Big Spring High School teams remember the days of the great cattle drives with their nickname, the Steers.

Marfa was another Texan town that took root and grew because of water. Marfa is located in the stunningly beautiful, yet sparsely populated area of the state known as the Big Bend because of the turn taken by the Rio Grande. The distinctive Highland Hereford cattle were first introduced to American ranchers in Marfa. In the early twentieth century many western movies were filmed there. The Marfa High School teams are the Shorthorns.

The Holstein is a breed of large dairy cattle originating in northern Holland and Friesland. It is believed that Holsteins have been bred for their dairy qualities for some two thousand years. First imported to this country by the Dutch in 1795, today they account for ninety percent of the milk production in the United States. In New Salem, North Dakota, the teams are the Holsteins.

From the Fields and Forests

An unbranded range animal is generally referred to as a maverick. The name comes from Samuel Maverick, an American pioneer who did not brand any of his cattle. The word may also be applied to any iconoclast, or freethinking rule breaker, one who does not go with the crowd. The Lordsburg, New Mexico, teams are the Mavericks.

"Git along little dogie . . . I'm headin' for the last roundup . . ." was part of a well-known cowboy song. Dogies are calves with no mothers. Forsythe, Montana, is on the Yellowstone River. Founded in 1875, it was named for General James Forsythe, and the high school teams are the Dogies.

Brahmas, or Brahmans, are large, humpbacked cattle from India. After their introduction to the United States they were cross bred with the zebu to produce a heat- and tick-resistant animal that was particularly well suited to husbandry in the south and retained the name of the Indian breed. Brahmas are a popular nickname at highs schools in Texas, particularly. We find them at Bellville, the seat of Austin County, and at Hallettsville, while the Brahmans take the field at Furr High School in Houston. Falfurrias High School fields the Bulls . . . and the Belles. Carlisle High School brings the entire Thundering Herd to the fray. Dewey, Oklahoma, was founded in 1898 by John Bartles (shortly after he founded nearby Bartlesville), and named for Admiral Dewey the hero of Manila Bay. Bartles also established the Dewey Hotel, now a museum. Tom Mix once lived in Dewey and a museum bearing his name pays tribute to this celebrated American cowboy entertainer. The Dewey High School teams also recognize their cowboy heritage. They are the Bulldoggers, and what they do to cattle they also expect to do to their opposition!

Closing out this section are three high schools in Wyoming with imaginative nicknames. The first is in Glenrock, where the Herders take the field. The second is Lingle-Ft. Laramie, home of the Doggers. It would be fun to see what would happen if they played Dewey High School. Finally, what could better represent what cowboys do and at the same time represent what athletic teams are trying to do to their opponents than the nickname of Big Piney High School. They are the Punchers.

Go Huskies! Beat Felix the Cat!

Riders who round up horses prefer not to be called cowboys. They are wranglers. There are Wranglers representing Pinedale High School in Wyoming, on the Platte River and the Oregon Trail. The ruts created by the Conestoga Wagons on the Oregon Trail are still visible in the area. Geyser, Montana, which is near Great Falls, and Rosebud in the eastern part of the state, also field the Wranglers. The Horsemen represent Plains High School, near beautiful Flathead Lake in western Montana

Nor are the horses themselves forgotten. America has long had a love affair with the horse, not only in the West. Here are just a few examples:

Jefferson High School in Lafayette, Indiana, the Bronchos.
Chariton, Iowa, the Chargers.
Schlagel High School in Kansas City, Kansas, and Sierra High School in Colorado Springs, the Stallions.
Pendleton Heights High School in central Indiana, the Arabians.
Owen High School in Black Mountain, North Carolina, and Barnwell, South Carolina, High School, the War Horses.
California, Missouri, the Pintos and Stillwater, Minnesota, the Ponies.

(I had hoped to find the Navajos in San Antonio so that I could reflect the words of Johnny Mercer's wonderful song: "Across the alley from the Alamo lived a pinto pony and a Navajo. . . ." But alas, it was not to be. The Apaches of Antonian College Prep was as close as I could come.)

Havre, Montana, was originally called Bull Hook Bottoms, and was renamed by railroad magnate James Hill in 1887 when he selected the site on the Milk River for a station on the Great Northern Railroad line he was building. The name Havre came from that of a French settler's home town, Le Havre. Today Havre is the site of Northern Montana College and the Havre High School teams are the Blue Ponies.

Do you remember when Bill Clinton first ran for the Democratic Party's nomination for president, how he was often described in the press? In the New Hampshire Primaries? Well, I think I do. He was not the favorite, he was the dark horse. Well, believe it or not, the town of Clinton, South

From the Fields and Forests

Carolina, has a high school and their teams are, you guessed it, the Dark Horses.

Chesterfield, Missouri, is a far Westside suburb of St. Louis. There are two high schools in Chesterfield that make an interesting pair. Marquette High School teams are the Mustangs and the Parkway Central High School teams are the Colts.

Rangers

Rangers are also important to the West. There are Rangers representing the tiny town of Regent in southwest North Dakota, and at the wonderfully named Big Pasture High School in Randlett, Oklahoma. One cannot mention Rangers without thinking of Texas, although Texas Rangers do have a slightly different connotation. There are Rangers at Patton Springs Afton High School, east of Lubbock, and at El Paso Riverside High School.

Aggies

Park River, in northeast North Dakota, is proud of its agricultural heritage, calling its teams the Aggies. There are also Aggies at Tate High School in Gonzalez, Florida, as well as several other places.

Cotton

We should never forget King Cotton. Cotton drove the economy of the South for many years. Robstown, Texas, located in the fertile "Valley" region, just west of Corpus Christi, does not forget. Their teams are the Cotton Pickers. Where do they play their games? In the Cotton Gin!

Hoopeston

Hoopeston, Illinois, a town of some sixty-five hundred, was first settled in 1871. It is located on the Great Prairie, not far west of Lafayette, Indiana, on

Go Huskies! Beat Felix the Cat!

Illinois Route 1, the former Hubbard Trace from Danville to Chicago. Hoopeston's greatest prize is corn. The soil and climate of the area are ideal for growing corn, and the crop is perennially strong throughout the area. A sign on the Fair Grounds, bordering Illinois 1, reads "Hoopeston, Sweet Corn Capital of the World." In the early days of Hoopeston High School the students were often let out of class at harvest time, also football season, of course, and went into the field to help jerk the corn off the stalks. Thus was born the nickname of Hoopeston's athletic teams, first applied to those early football teams. They are proudly known as the Cornjerkers. There it is, boldly recorded on the north wall of the Hoopeston Area High School, facing Illinois Route 9: "Home of the Cornjerkers." The athletic teams wear an ear of corn on their jerseys and the mascot is a perky creature dressed like an ear of corn!

The Huskers

When the Hickory High School Huskers won the 1952 Indiana State Basketball Championship in the movie *Hoosiers* I did not know if there were any non-fictional schools in the country who really had that nickname. I found only two. There may well be some more, but the only Huskers I discovered were those in Holdingford, Minnesota, and Serena, Illinois. Holdingford is a town of about the same size as Hickory was portrayed to be, maybe even smaller, at 561 people. Serena, with a population of 250 is smaller yet. I hope the Holdingford and Serena Huskers have seen and enjoyed *Hoosiers* as much as I have. Perhaps it has provided them with some motivation to win the Minnesota and Illinois State Championships "For all the small schools"!

From the Fields and Forests

Makin' Hay

You have to make hay while the sun shines. Everyone knows that. And making hay is important to the farm animals of this country that depend on it for their daily repasts. Several schools and towns have recognized this in their choice of nickname. Take Cozad, Nebraska. Grain fields may be seen in abundance in the area, and the Cozad High School athletic teams are the Haymakers.

Somewhat to the south of Cozad is the town of Haskell, Oklahoma, not far southeast of Tulsa. The Haskell High School teams are also the Haymakers. It could be quite a slugfest if Cozad and Haskell try to lay their Haymakers on each other!

They could both use the help of the boys from Hollister, California. Hollister is about thirty miles northwest of Monterey, and very close to the fascinating Mission of San Juan Bautista. The climactic scenes of Alfred Hitchcock's memorable movie *Vertigo* starring Kim Novak and Jimmy Stewart were filmed in San Juan Bautista, and the first time I went there I had a tremendous sense of déjà vu and it was not until days later that I realized it was because of the movie and the impact it must have had on me. Anyway, back to why Hollister's teams would be useful to Cozad's and Haskell's. Perhaps you've guessed. They are the Hollister Haybalers!

Actually, before anyone can bale the hay, someone has to cut it down. For that purpose, I think we must turn to the town of Hesston in central Kansas. Hesston High School teams are the Swathers, and I'll bet they cut quite a swath through their opposition as well!

Come to think of it, all three of the above schools could use the help of the teams from Tustin, California, Plano, Illinois, and Pampa, Texas. Tustin is a suburb of Los Angeles and their teams are the Tillers. Pampa is in the Panhandle, northeast of Amarillo, and their teams are the Harvesters. Plano is in northern Illinois, southwest of Chicago and their teams are the Reapers. Before you can grow the grain you have to till the soil and before you can dry and bale the hay you have to harvest, or reap, the crop. Add in the Noblesville, Indiana, Millers, and now we have the whole package!

The Appleknockers

Cobden, Illinois, is a town of about one thousand people in the far southern part of Illinois, about fifteen miles south of Carbondale. The town of Cobden is surrounded by orchards, both peach and apple. The growing and harvesting of both fruits has long been central to the economy of the town, as has been the manufacture of baskets for their storage and transport. One of the most efficient ways of getting the ripe fruit down from the trees was to take long sticks and hit the trunks and branches, causing the ready-to-pick fruit to come tumbling down into the waiting cushions, blankets and, eventually, air pillows that had been placed under them. The men and boys who did the hitting were known as Appleknockers, and Cobden began to describe itself as "The Appleknocker Town." Naturally enough, the Cobden High School athletic teams are called the Appleknockers as well.

Timber-r-r!

Nothing was of greater importance to the development of our country's economy than the lumber industry. Houses, furniture, ships, the wagons that headed west, the ties that held the rails for the fire breathing iron horses, barns, and eventually paper and paper products came from the extensive forests that dotted our landscape so extensively.

Perhaps no lumberman is more famous than Paul Bunyan. Paul Bunyan is said to have been so huge that he picked his teeth with pine logs and his footsteps created Minnesota's many lakes as he roamed the state. Bemidji is known for the severity of its winters, located as it is in the far northern part of this rugged state. It is a place for the hardy, indeed. No wonder the most rugged lumberjack of them all was claimed by the citizens of Bemidji. In 1937 they erected a statue of Paul Bunyan that was eighteen feet tall, accompanied by Babe, his great blue ox. This was done in recognition of Bemidji's tremendous logging heritage: in the early 1900s as many as ten thousand lumberjacks were in the immediate area using two-man saws,

From the Fields and Forests

skidders and peavey hooks to fell the mighty trees. Bemidji High School's teams are the Lumberjacks.

Butte Falls, Oregon, is a very small town—only 252 people live there. The town is located near the Rogue River National Forest and the high school teams are the Loggers. A bit farther north is Eugene, home of the University of Oregon. Eugene was once also a logging center, surrounded by spruce, Douglas fir and Sequoias. The Eugene South High School teams are the Axemen.

Wabeno, Wisconsin, is located in the Nicolet National Forest in the northern part of the state, near the Potowatami Indian Reservation. The Wabeno High School teams are the Logrollers. Not far away is the Paul Bunyan ski area. Farther west and a bit to the north is the town of Drummond in the Chequamegon National Forest. Drummond's teams are the Lumberjacks.

Boyne Falls, in the northwestern part of Michigan's Lower Peninsula, is now a popular winter and summer resort destination, near beautiful Walloon Lake and the Boyne Mountain Ski area. It is in the Mackinac State Forest: the high school teams are the Loggers. Somewhat east of Drummond is Saginaw, once a major logging center. The Saginaw Arthur Hill High School teams are the Lumberjacks.

One of the most dramatic parts of the beautiful state of New Hampshire is the area in the White Mountains around the towns of Lincoln and Woodstock, with tall waterfalls, forests, Cannon and Loon Mountains, and the intriguing series of shorter falls and rushing waters known as the Flume. The Lin-Wood High School teams are also the Lumberjacks. Greenwood, Indiana, calls its teams the Woodmen.

Lake Winnebago is the largest lake in the state of Wisconsin. It has long been a center of the paper-making industry with Marathon Paper being located in the twin towns of Neenah and Menasha and Kimberley Clark in the nearby town of Kimberley. The Kimberley High School teams are the Papermakers. Not far away, also on a substantial lake named Petenwell, is the town of Nekoosa. The Nekoosa High School teams are also the Papermakers. Kleenex versus Bond?

Go Huskies! Beat Felix the Cat!

Although the town of Hayfork, California, certainly sounds like it would be a farming community, it is, in fact, located on the Hayfork River in the Coastal Ranges of Northern California and is surrounded by the Trinity National Forest. The Hayfork High School teams have the wonderfully imaginative nickname of the Timberjacks.

Two more entrants in this category are in Oklahoma and Pennsylvania. Wright City, in the far southeast corner of the former, fields the Lumberjax and Forrest City, in the far northeast corner of the latter, is represented by the Foresters.

Now that we have all this lumber, who can we get it cut it up into boards and make it useful for the craftsmen who will build our homes and furniture? Perhaps we should turn to the Hudson River town of Saugerties, New York. There we find just what we need. They are the Sawyers. And once it is cut into boards, where can we go to get the skills to build those houses and that furniture and all of the many wood products we depend on for modern day life? One place would be in Taunton, Massachusetts, at Plymouth Regional Tech. There we find the Craftsmen.

Trees

Joyce Kilmer said it best:

> *Poems are made by fools like me,*
> *But only God can make a tree.*

Several schools have indeed selected a specific tree as their mascot. Stanford University has the Pine Tree on its Crest and Dartmouth College has its own Old Pine on its Presidential Flag. Indiana State University teams are the Sycamores. At the high school level, perhaps the oak is the most popular choice. A good example is Oakland, a small town in south central Illinois, and home of the Oaks. There are also Oaks in the town of Oak Hill, Ohio. Coventry, Rhode Island, is a town with considerable history. It was

From the Fields and Forests

the home of General Nathaniel Greene, second in command to George Washington during the Revolutionary War. The Coventry High School teams are the Knotty Oakers. Other trees:

Lakewood, New Jersey, are the Piners.
Geneseo-Darnall High School in Illinois fields the Maple Leafs.
Birmingham, Michigan, Seaholm High School are the Maples.
Northwind High School in Minong, Wisconsin, are the Evergreens.

One of the definitions of chaparral in my Webster's is "a thicket of broad evergreen oaks." There are several schools that have selected Chaparral as their nickname, including Fort Worth Wyatt.

Potatoes

Potatoes are a staple of most good diets. They are loaded with nutrients, an almost complete food. Growing this marvelous crop has long been important to many American communities. Moorhead, Minnesota, is a good place to start. Moorhead is located on the Red River. It was settled by Norwegians and one of the town's claims to fame is a seventy-seven foot long replica of a Viking ship in a local museum. Potatoes are important to the people of Moorhead, too. Their teams are the Spuds. Way out west is the town of Ridgefield, Washington. Ridgefield is on the Columbia River, not far north of Portland and their teams are the Spudders. However, when girls' teams were added they marvelously were called the Sweet Potatoes.

Russets

Salmon, Idaho, is on a difficult mountain road, just south of the Lost Trail Pass, 7,014 feet above sea level, that connects it to the road north to Missoula, Montana. Salmon was first discovered by Lewis and Clark on their expedition of discovery and later was home to mountain men such as Jim Bridger and Kit Carson. After that came the miners and well after them came my wife and I. Our trip was memorable because the road south from the top had been washed out by storms and was being rebuilt under very difficult circumstances. Every day the road was completely closed for three hours of construction beginning at noon. We just missed it and were stopped at the top of the pass, first in line, en route to Salmon and Sun Valley. There was no other option, but we hated to sit there for three hours on what was a very hot July day. The very pleasant young lady traffic controller who stopped us suggested we go back three miles and have lunch at a lodge just off the road on a rushing trout steam. This we did, enjoying not only a nice fresh pan-fried steelhead, but some engaging conversation with the owner of the lodge, his wife and son. They had bought the lodge after he, an engineer and former naval officer, had retired from the service. We enjoyed our visit so much that we barely got back by the three o'clock reopening time. Our host had suggested we take some large, cold cokes to the traffic controllers, which we were glad to do. When we got back out on the road the lineup of cars, trucks and campers was miles long, but, when we gave the coke to the young traffic controller at the rear he waved us through to the front so that we could give our refreshments to the two up at the top as well. So, back we were at the front of the line again, everyone behind us no doubt grousing a bit and wondering who we were! Anyway, when we got to Salmon I discovered that potatoes were as important as trout to the good people of that pretty little town. They hold a Potato Festival every year and their high school teams are the Russets. Later, after another wonderful stay at the Sun Valley Inn, on our way back east, we passed through the town of Shelley, just north of Pocatello, and discovered that they, too, were the Russets.

11
DOWN TO THE SEA IN SHIPS

IN A COUNTRY bounded by two great oceans and the Gulf of Mexico, tied together by a network of great rivers and blessed with five Great Lakes, it is not at all surprising that many communities would owe their reason for being and derive most of their wealth from activities associated with water.

The Sea Itself

Fair Oaks High School in Sacramento, California's teams are the Waves as are those of Ponchatoula, Louisiana. There are Blue Waves at Riverhead, New York, and Darien, Connecticut, while Mattoon, Illinois, and Dover, New Hampshire, have the Green Waves. Grundy, Virginia, teams are the Golden Wave, reminding me of some pleasant sunsets I have seen.

The tide is another significant factor in life by the sea. We find the Tides representing the teams from Ludovici, Georgia, High School and the Blue Tide at Harrison, New Jersey. The Crimson Tide is not only in evidence at the University of Alabama, but at Minden, Louisiana, and Dunbar, D.C., highs as well. Roll, Tide!

The king of the sea in Roman mythology was the God Neptune, often depicted with a three-pronged spear, known as a Triton, in his hand. Tritons

Down to the Sea in Ships

represent the aptly named Mariner High School in Cape Coral, Florida, near Ft. Myers, and at the California town made famous by President Nixon's Winter White House, San Clemente, on the beautiful coast just north of San Diego.

❧

Fish

Several different kinds of fish have also been selected by our schools. Those of perhaps the most predatory bent have chosen the shark. One such is the magical town of Malibu, California, on the Pacific Coast Highway, east of Los Angles, home of the Malibu High School Sharks. Sharks, it seems, are popular team names at some other very desirable places as well, including:

Boca Raton Spanish River, Cedar Key, and Port Orange high schools in Florida; Oceana High School in Pacifica, California; and Sheepshead Bay High School on Long Island.

Virginia Beach has two schools that have fish for their team names. One is also the Sharks, at Cape Henry Collegiate School, and their neighbors are the Marlins of Bayside High School. I understand that Marlins can hold their own very nicely, thank you, in a tussle with Sharks, certainly in Virginia Beach!

Another predator fish that I have developed a healthy respect for whenever I swim in salt water is the barracuda. Opponents of New Smyrna Beach High in Florida also have a healthy respect for the Barracudas of that school.

Among the more playful sea creatures are the dolphins, those lovable animals who leap and dive behind the boats and in the bays around Gasparilla Island. They're also popular at several other places in this country, including the following who have selected Dolphins as their team name: South Yarmouth High School, on Cape Cod; Marathon, in the Florida Keys; Queens Beach Channel High School in New York; and Whitney Young High School in Chicago.

Tarpon, I am told, is among the finest fighting fish an angler can ever experience, though not good for eating. The World's Greatest Tarpon Tournament takes place early every summer in Gasparilla Pass, when the tarpon are attracted to the area because the little fresh water crabs that they find so delectable come flowing down the Peace River into the Pass. Nearby Charlotte High School in Punta Gorda fields the Fighting Tarpons, and their big rivals across the Peace River in Port Charlotte are the Pirates.

Whidden's Marina on Gasparilla Island is now on the National Register of Historic Places. Part of it is a fascinating Marine Museum. The current proprietor, Barbara Whidden, told me that the island once had its own high school, named for the island's principal town. When Barbara graduated with seven other classmates from Boca Grande High School their teams were known as the Tarpons.

When it comes to fighting fish, if you're on the northern lakes it's hard to beat the muskellunge, or muskie, another fish primarily sought after for the fight it offers. We find Muskies representing the teams from Muscatine, Iowa, and Jamestown, Pennsylvania.

However, if it's good eating you want, there are the famous redfish of New Orleans, where the concept of blackened fish took root. There are Redfish representing high school teams in Tivoli, Texas. For more good eating we can turn to the Tunas of Our Lady Star of the Sea High School in Grosse Pointe Woods, Michigan, and the Coho Salmon, of Cascade Christian High School in Wenatchee, Washington.

The French find eels more of a treat to their taste buds than I do (there really are no eels in Indiana streams, anyway). However, the Eel River winds its way through west central Indiana and, sure enough, there are Eels representing both Eminence and Clay City high schools in that part of the state, never to be confused with central France, however!

Other Water Animals

Unique not only in appearance but because the male carries the eggs, the Sea Horse has captured the imagination of the good citizens of Burlington, Vermont, Christchurch, Virginia, and Far Rockaway on Long Island, in choosing team names for their high schools. Here are some other selections:

Beaver Falls, New York, has naturally chosen the Beavers.

Otters represent the teams from Fergus Falls, Pennsylvania, and Brandon, Vermont.

Algonac, Michigan fields the Muskrats.

Sand Crabs are the choice of Daytona Beach Seabreeze—and wouldn't you love to go to a school with a name like that—and of Calhoun High School in Port Lavaca, Texas. (Shouldn't the latter be the cows?)

Selinsgrove, Pennsylvania, teams are the Seals.

Florida is not just the Sunshine State, it is also the Gator State. It would be surprising if there weren't many high schools down there that had selected the mascot of the University of Florida as their own, and, again, Florida does not disappoint. Just to mention some, there are Gators representing Pensacola Escambia, Hialeah Golenam, Palm Beach Gardens, Everglades City, and Land o' Lakes high schools.

Elsewhere, there are Gators at Port Allegany in the beautiful hardwood and evergreen forests of northwestern Pennsylvania, and, perhaps scariest of all, the Wild Gators of Lake View, South Carolina. Excuse me. Are there tame gators anywhere?

The Fishermen

Gloucester is located north of Boston on the south shore of beautiful Cape Ann. As soon as you enter the town you know it is a fishing port. All roads lead to the Harbor, wonderfully sheltered and open to the south. You smell the fish. You see the fishing boats, the nets hung to dry, the statue of the Gloucester Fisherman, the light house. You begin to sense the history of fishing permeating the area. Gloucester has been a fishing port continuously since 1623, just three years after the Pilgrims landed some fifty miles to the south at Plymouth. You visit the Fishermen's Memorial and stop at the church of Our Lady of Perpetual Voyage. You discover that some ten thousand Gloucester men—that's ten thousand—have died at sea since 1623. One cannot help but think of the haunting "Naval Hymn" with these words:

> *Eternal Father, strong to save,*
> *Whose arm hath bound the restless wave,*
> *O hear us when we cry to thee*
> *For those in peril on the sea.*

It is a prayer you share. How could the Gloucester High School teams be anything else than what they are: the Fishermen?

The Anglers

It's hard to beat casting for a nice rainbow, brown, or steelhead trout on a summer afternoon in a swiftly flowing stream, unless of course it's pan frying the catch in butter over an open flame and dining in the open air under the shade of an old oak tree. This kind of fun happens a lot in Trout Creek, Michigan, where the high school team is called the Anglers.

The Trollers

On the lee side of the Bayfield Peninsula in the Upper Peninsula of Michigan is the wonderfully preserved Victorian town of Bayfield with its sheltered deep-water harbor. Once a contender to be a port rivaling Duluth, this never developed, although commercial fishing began as early as the 1870s. Today, Bayfield is primarily a resort community where people can enjoy whitefish and lake trout fishing, sailing, and power boating in the summer or such pursuits as cross country skiing and ice fishing during the winter. The Bayfield High teams, remembering their fishing heritage, are called the Trollers.

Down to the Sea in Ships

Clippers I

Newburyport, Massachusetts, on the north shore of Cape Ann, has a special place in American history. The craftsmen of Newburyport were skilled shipbuilders, pioneers and leaders in the design and construction of the mighty sailing ships known around the world for their speed and grace: the famous Yankee Clippers. In the early days of the Revolutionary War when a cash-strapped Continental Congress could not afford funds for a fledgling Navy, the good people of Newburyport took it upon themselves to build a frigate and give it to the country. Fittingly, the Newburyport High School athletic teams carry this heritage proudly forward with their nickname, the Clippers.

Clippers II

For most of its early years New Hampshire was merely a northern portion of the Massachusetts Bay Colony. Most of the early settlement of what would one day be New Hampshire occurred around the site of present day Portsmouth. Many of those first settlers were Scotch-Irish Presbyterians who left the area around Boston when they became disgruntled with the Puritan life style. Thus Portsmouth gained an early, perhaps deserved reputation for being somewhat wild and wooly. At any rate it was located on an excellent natural harbor and the profusion of fine shipbuilding timber led the way for Portsmouth to be a leader in the design and construction of sailing boats. Portsmouth's rich history, particularly its shipbuilding heritage is well preserved by Portsmouth High School's athletic teams—also the Clippers.

Clippers III

Door County is the peninsula that creates Green Bay out of Lake Michigan. At its southern end the city of Sturgeon Bay with its fine natural harbor, is a major harvester of Chinook salmon and one of the largest ship building ports on the Great Lakes. The Sturgeon Bay High School athletic teams are also the Clippers.

Ships

At Manitowoc, Wisconsin, a town of 32,500 people on the shore of Lake Michigan, located on an excellent harbor, shipbuilding has been an important profession since the 1830s. In the nineteenth century Manitowoc was known as the "Clipper City." The schooner *Citizen* was launched in 1848 and hundreds of ships have been built in Manitowoc since then. Manitowoc Lincoln High School athletic teams are called the Ships.

Shipbuilders

Bath, Maine, on the west bank of the Kennebec River has been an active center for shipbuilding for almost four hundred years. The townsmen once built the large wooden sailing ships that sailed the seven seas before the advent of steam and steel. Today, the Bath Iron Works builds nuclear vessels and large merchant ships not far from the Maine Maritime Museum. The Bath High School teams are the Shipbuilders.

Windjammers

Camden and Rockport were once one town. They split into two in 1891 but are pretty much of a close-knit pair again today. Each is extremely picturesque and each is devoted to seafaring pursuits. In the mid to late summer every year there is an impressive gathering of the tall sailing ships of today in the area's harbors. It is a great time to see these lovely, graceful creations and to enjoy coastal and blue water cruises in great comfort. The Camden-Rockport High School teams are wonderfully known as the Windjammers.

Down to the Sea in Ships

Whalers

Whaling was an important industry in the early days of our country. Before the discovery of petroleum whale oil was widely used for lighting, lubrication and a variety of other purposes. The center of the whaling industry was located on that picturesque island off of Cape Cod, Nantucket. Initially the settlers harpooned right whales, a species that swam close to the shore, but eventually they learned how to range farther afield and harvest the much larger sperm whale with its more valuable oil. Now a tourist and vacationer's delight, whaling has not been forgotten as a visit to the Nantucket Whaling Museum will readily demonstrate. And, to this day, Nantucket High School teams are the Whalers.

Four thousand miles from Nantucket Island, closer to Russia than to Massachusetts, is the northernmost Alaskan town and therefore the northernmost American town of Barrow, located at the edge of the permanent ice pack, fully 340 miles north of the Arctic Circle. For eighty-two days in the summer the sun never sinks below the horizon and for fifty-one days of winter it never appears above the horizon. Barrow is home to one of the world's largest, if not the largest, population of Eskimos. Whaling has long been a source of food, oil, and other necessities for the Eskimos. It is comforting to me that two such different places, with different climates, cultures, and ethnicity as Nantucket and Barrow can find, under the umbrella of the American nation, much in common. One of those things: they both call their high school teams the Whalers.

Harpooners

Point Hope, Alaska, is about three hundred miles southwest of Barrow (and farther west than anyplace in Hawaii), also on the Arctic Ocean. It is a small town, only six hundred or so people live there, and most of us can only imagine the tough, isolated winters endured there by the residents. Point Hope, however, supports a high school, called Tikigag. The Tikigag High School athletic teams are the Harpooners.

Go Huskies! Beat Felix the Cat!

Whalers II

New London, Connecticut, was founded in 1646 by John Winthrop at the point at which the Thames River forms an elegant natural harbor as it enters Long Island Sound. Whaling began in New London in 1784 and after the War of 1812 there were eighty whaling vessels registered in the port. Whale Oil Row is a series of mansions built in the 1830s, testimony to the prosperity that whaling brought to the city. At nearby Mystic, a wonderfully realistic nineteenth-century whaling village has been faithfully reconstructed and an impressive whaler, the *Charles W. Morgan*, may be boarded.

New Bedford, Massachusetts, is in the southern part of the state, near the Rhode Island border. In the nineteenth century, New Bedford was also one of America's largest whaling ports. In the 1840s some ten thousand seamen worked on New Bedford ships. One of those was Herman Melville, author of *Moby Dick*, who also described New Bedford as having "Patrician-like houses," many of which still exist. The nickname of the New London and New Bedford High School athletic teams? They are both, of course, the Whalers.

Anchors Aweigh

Lakeland, Florida, surrounded by and encompassing seventeen different lakes, is home to the Lakeland High School Dreadnaughts. A dreadnaught is a warship with many large caliber guns, a battleship, the scourge of the Seven Seas. Dexter, Michigan, a small town near Ann Arbor also fields (or is it "floats"?) the Dreadnaughts.

Somewhat smaller and generally faster than a battleship is the cruiser, still a devastating naval fighting ship. We find Cruisers representing the athletic teams of Powers, near the coast of Oregon, at Eatonville, Washington, a stone's throw from Mt. Rainier National Park, and at equally landlocked Groveport, south of Columbus, Ohio.

Down to the Sea in Ships

Faster yet, though smaller than cruisers, are destroyers. Dunellen, New Jersey, near Plainfield, sends the Destroyers on to the field against their opposition. Dreadnaughts, Cruisers, Destroyers. A pretty good start to a fleet. Elsewhere, we have identified several Admirals and Commodores who could command this fleet of ours. So, too, could the mascot of North Kingstown, Rhode Island, High School, the Skippers, as befits their location near the Quonset Point Naval Station on Narragansett Bay. Nearby Narragansett High School itself fields the Mariners.

Cohasset, Massachusetts, on the coast south of Boston, was discovered in 1614 by Captain John Smith (six years before the Pilgrims landed at nearby Plymouth) and its beautiful natural harbor led to its success as a fishing, whaling and shipbuilding port in the early days of our nation. The high school's nickname is also the Skippers.

Scituate is another seafaring town on Boston's south shore. Locals like to recount the Revolutionary War story of the lighthouse keeper's two teenage daughters who fooled the British into thinking the lighthouse was well defended by playing the fife and drum and thus sending the marauders scurrying off. Scituate High School teams are most appropriately called the Sailors. Sarasota High School in Florida is close to beautiful Sarasota Bay, the Gulf Keys and the gorgeous Selby and Ringling Gardens and Estates. Their teams are also the Sailors. Even in that perhaps most unexpected of all places, Nebraska, we find Sailors representing the town of Sutherland. Sutherland is located just west of the point at which the Platte River splits into practically parallel North and South branches and is on the somewhat narrow stretch of land between them, so it is not far from water. Still, the Nebraska Navy? Sailors near the sea of grass? Yes, at Sutherland High School!

Now we have ships, captains, and crew, and our little armada is ready to see action, guided by the Navigators of Chicago Payton Preparatory School. When they're done, they'll need the skilled services of St. Clements High School in Somerville, Massachusetts. They are the Anchormen.

The Jolly Roger

Sailors beware in northern Illinois! In addition to the many pirates representing schools from Galena to Palatine, there are also the Buccaneers from Belvedere and the Corsairs from Carmel High School in Mundelein. The Corsairs were the pirates from the Barbary Coast of North Africa.

Hampton, Virginia

Hampton Roads is the name given to the area of Virginia where the James River empties into Chesapeake Bay. Four cities overlook Hampton Roads: Norfolk, Portsmouth, Newport News and Hampton. These cities and the entire area of Hampton Roads have a long and fascinating history of maritime and naval activity, one of the most famous pieces of which was the Civil War battle between the *Monitor* and the *Merrimac*, the first involving ironclad vessels. It is also an area where shell fishing has long been a central activity and the Hampton High School athletic teams are named for those hardy souls who extract a particular treasure from the waters of Chesapeake Bay: They are the Crabbers.

Clinton, Iowa

Clinton, Iowa, is located on the Mississippi River about forty-five miles south of Dubuque. Before the bridge on the Lincoln Highway (U.S. 30) was built, Clinton was a ferry crossing, from Iowa to Illinois, and vice versa. It was also a town made wealthy by lumber, cut down in the north and shipped to the south on the Great River. With a location and history involved so closely with the mighty Mississippi River what nickname was selected for the Clinton High School teams? The River Kings. The girls' teams are, happily, the River Queens.

Down to the Sea in Ships

Key West

There are so many beautiful drives throughout this great country of ours that it is dangerous to single any out, but one of the most spectacular is surely the 126 sun-kissed miles from Florida City to Key West on Florida's Route 1 on a fair day. This causeway, a series of bridges from island to island, surrounded by the colorful waters of the Gulf of Mexico, was basically built from roadbed of the Florida East Coast Railway that Henry Flagler had constructed in 1912, destroyed in 1935 by a strong hurricane.

Upon arriving in Key West you find that the conch is very important to the local residents. You can eat conch stew, conch fritters, conch chowder, conch salad, and probably any other conch concoction you can think of, and you can do it at Sloppy Joe's where Ernest Hemingway once held forth. You can go conch shelling and enjoy the sunset on the grandstands set up for the purpose at the westernmost point of the Keys while being serenaded by conch shell blowers. You can even buy Conch Republic flags, for that is the special name the citizens of Key West have given to their little slice of paradise. And, if you go to any of the games played by Key West High School, you will have the chance to join the other fans rooting for their beloved Fighting Conch teams.

The Spongers

Near Tampa is Tarpon Springs, founded by Greeks who brought their sponge-diving expertise to America very early in the twentieth century and specifically to this town near abundant sponging grounds. Although synthetic sponges have diminished the demand for the natural variety, sponge diving is still a significant activity here. A drive down Dodecanese Boulevard parallels the wharfs and sponge boats can be seen at the docks or cruising the river. There is a Sponge Museum and diving exhibitions are available as are cruises to the sponge beds. The Tarpon Springs High School nickname? The Spongers.

Manta Rays

While swimming in Florida, I have frequently seen small delta wing skate-type fish that the locals refer to as stingrays, but the most I had seen at one time was six or seven, lazily gliding around. However, one day while swimming in the Gulf, not far from shore, I was suddenly surrounded by a school of many hundreds of them each about two feet across, so many that the water was actually churning with them. Rather cautiously, I worked my way to shore, and marveled with the others there at the size, perhaps fifty feet wide by one hundred feet long, of the school of manta rays that had been my surprising, but docile, companions. Our local high school, Lemon Bay, has the nickname Manta Rays (they play their basketball games in the Tank) and, across the state, Miami Senior High School teams are the Stingarees.

12

LIONS AND TIGERS AND BEARS — OH, MY!

WHEN DOROTHY AND her new friends, the Tin Man and the Scarecrow, entered the dark forest they had no way of knowing that they had more to fear from angry apple trees and beautiful poppy fields than they did from fierce beasts, but that has not stopped many of our schools from selecting those beasts for their team names.

Perhaps a good place to start is in Alamogordo, New Mexico, that lovely city near the White Sands National Monument. Three of the schools in Alamogordo fill Dorothy's bill completely. There is Alamogordo High, the Tigers; and there is Alamogordo Community Christian School, the Lions; and there is the New Mexico School for the Visually Impaired, the Golden Bears.

Similarly, in Dallas we find Lions at Lutheran and, of course, at St. Mark's, and Tigers at Lincoln; and, appropriately, since *ursa* means "bear" in Latin, the Bears at Ursuline Academy. The menagerie in Dallas also includes the following animals: The Molinas Jaguars, the Woodrow Wilson Wildcats, the Adams Cougars, the North Dallas Bulldogs, the Sunset Bisons and the South Oak Cliff Golden Bears.

El Paso, also offers Lions at Faith Christian Academy, Tigers at El Paso High, and Bears at Bowie High School. And these others: The Franklin Cougars, the Mountain View Lobos, the Socorro Bulldogs and the Jefferson Foxes.

LIONS

Lions abound all over the country, but not of the cowardly sort. Here are some of them:

> South Lyons, Michigan.
> Lyons, New York.
> Lyons, Kansas.
> Lyons, Colorado.
> Lyons Township High School in LaGrange, Illinois.
> Lyons County High School in Kentucky.
> Leo, Indiana.
> Red Lion, Pennsylvania.

Central Daniel High School in North Carolina also fields the Lions where it is the opponents who are in Daniel's Den, not the other way around, I should think.

Tallahassee, Florida, has Lions fittingly at Leon High School.

Mountain Point East High School in Phoenix, Arizona, teams are the Pride.

Mesa, Arizona, Red Mountain High School, and Green Mountain Falls, Colorado, are the Mountain Lions.

St. Mark's School in Southborough, Massachusetts, are the aptly named Lions . . . they would be the Lions of St. Mark's, of course.

Curiously, in Lawrence, Kansas, are the Chesty Lions. That almost sounds like a commercial I may have heard once.

Martin Luther King High School in Tampa is also known as the Lions. I turn this one around in my mind, realizing that they are the King Lions, not the Lion Kings!

Lions and Tigers and Bears — Oh, my!

Bears are equally ubiquitous. All kinds of bears. Grizzlies are truly huge and fearsome. They may be found at Griswold High in Helix, Oregon, in Fowler, Colorado, at Rocky Mountain High in Byron, Wyoming, and in Hoquiam, Sunnyside and Newport, Oregon, among others. The equally fearsome Kodiak bears represent Widney High School in Los Angeles. One of their crosstown rivals is Loyola, the Cubs. Hardly seems fair that those two should play—the Kodiaks versus the Cubs. There are also the Cubs in Madison, Indiana, so I am well aware that cubs can handle any opposition they are asked to deal with!

Where might you expect to find bears? In caves, much of the time. Thus it is hardly surprising to find the Bears representing La Cueva High School in Albuquerque, New Mexico. There are Polar Bears in Ohio, in the town of Dola, at Hardin Northern High School. Must be the Northern that attracted the Polar bears to roam that far from Canada. Even more to the point, and even farther south, are the Polar Bears of Frost, Texas. Larimore, North Dakota, just west of Grand Forks, probably seems cold enough for Polar Bears in the winter, but the only ones to be found there are at the local high school.

Nome, Alaska, is located on the Seward Peninsula in the Bering Sea. It is the financial and commercial center for the northwestern portion of the state. Gold was discovered on the beaches at what was to become Nome in 1898. At the peak of the gold rush the population of Nome, which seems to be a contraction of "No name," reached twenty thousand eager souls. Today it is less than 40 percent of that, but serves the needs of a larger population spread out over the area. In 1925 a diphtheria epidemic resulted in rushing serum by dogsled the eleven hundred miles from Juneau to Nome. Today the famous Iditarod Race commemorates that event. The Nome High School teams are called the Nanooks (or Nanuqs), the Eskimo word for Polar Bears.

Haines, Alaska, was settled in 1881 by a Presbyterian missionary on a site earlier selected by the naturalist John Muir. Haines is located in the beautiful Chilkat Mountain Range and became a major jumping off point for the Alaskan Gold Rush. The Haines High School teams are the Glacier Bears. Juneau, the capital city of Alaska, is located in the southern panhandle of the state, a narrow strip of America between British Columbia and the Pacific Ocean. It is a city of about twenty-six thousand, and Douglas High School fields the Red Bears.

Finally, there is the town of Kodiak, located on an island of the same name, most of which is a National Wildlife Refuge. Kodiak was the first capital of Russian America, from 1792–1804, when the capital was moved to Sitka. Kodiak High School teams are, what else, the Bears.

Back in the contiguous forty-eight, there are Black Bears at Glidden, Wisconsin, and, perhaps my favorite, in the Smoky Mountains, at Sevierville, Tennessee, located on Dolly Parton Parkway, representing Sevier County are the Smoky Bears. Stamp out those cigarettes and quench those campfires. There are many Bruins around the country, including those at Bear Creek High School and Bear River High School in Stockton and Grass Valley, California, respectively.

There is some question about whether or not pandas should be classified as part of the bear family but I have decided to do so pending some other resolution of the issue. Here are some:

Lee High School in Maine.
St. Pius V in the Bronx.
St. Xavier across the East River in Brooklyn.
Notre Dame High School in Park Hills, Kentucky.

Koalas are those cuddly little creatures generally associated with

Lions and Tigers and Bears — Oh, my!

Australia and popularized by QANTAS Airlines. They seem very sleepy most of the time and subsist on eucalyptus leaves. Perhaps that is why they are so drowsy. At any rate, they do not seem fierce, but are, I guess fierce enough for the following schools:

Bishop Keogh High in Pawtucket, Rhode Island.
Ursuline High in New Rochelle, New York.
Anaheim, California, High.

The word for bear in Spanish is *oso*. Thus it is very reasonable to find the Bears representing West Oso High School in Corpus Christi, Texas. Equally appropriate are the Bears of Bear Creek High School in Denver, Colorado, and at Bear River High School in Garland, Utah. The only Green Bears I could find were at Ottawa Hills High School, a very pleasant south side of Toledo suburb. One of my favorite bear mascots is in Upper Arlington, a suburb of Columbus, Ohio. Their teams are the Golden Bears and one of their most famous alums is golfer Jack Nicklaus. There are also Golden Bears at Evansville Central High School, I am reminded by Clarence Doninger, former Indiana University athletic director and proud Central alumnus.

Peru, Indiana, is named for the South American country. No one I spoke with there seemed to know why. It is also frequently referred to as the Circus City. Everyone knew why that was so. In the nineteenth century, Peru was a favorite winter resting place for several major touring circus troupes. The present day Circus Festival Museum on Broadway bears excellent testimony to this and is worth a visit. What is the mascot of Peru High School? Why, in this circus town, the Tigers, of course!

There are two towns in Alabama that have also chosen the Tiger for their mascot and are deserving of special mention. They are Meek and Minor. Now, I suppose with town names like that you might be particularly interested in choosing a mascot that would engender considerable respect, hence the Tiger, which certainly achieves that goal. However Minor went one step further. Minor is located just outside of Birmingham, to the north and east. Their teams are not just the Tigers, they are the Tenacious Tigers. 'Nuff said.

Meek is another case altogether. They are the Tigers, plain and simple, and, yet, when you put it all together they have a bit of a predicament in trying to be fierce because they are, after all, the Meek Tigers. The Meek Tigers. An oxymoron? Or something from the back of a cereal box? A kin to Tony the Tiger, perhaps? Certainly a kindred spirit to Dorothy's Cowardly Lion. I say more power to them. May the Meek Tigers inherit, if not the earth, at least their conference championship!

13
Man's Best Friend

WHO AMONG US has not had at least one dog who was loved as a family member? Certainly no one in our family, where several have had the run of the house and been treated like royalty!

Malamutes and Huskies

Fairbanks, named for Senator Charles W. Fairbanks, later to be vice president of the United State under Theodore Roosevelt is located near the geographic center of Alaska. Fairbanks became the northern terminus of the Alaska Railroad and, when gold was discovered nearby in 1902, prospectors flocked there in search of their fortunes. From the area's history, still a present day favorite, comes a sled dog with great stamina, a beautiful coat and penetrating eyes, a very regal animal, named for an Alaskan people, the Malamutes. Fairbanks Lathrop High School has selected the Malamute as the name for its teams.

At Newhalen, on the shores of Lake Iliamna, between Katmai and Lake Clark National Parks, southwest of Anchorage, the Iliamna Newhalen High School team names are also the Malamutes.

The Huskie, in addition to my own at Oak Park, is also the choice of many other schools, one of which is in Alaska where the selection is particularly appropriate. The town of Akiachak, on the Kuskokwim River, just south of the Yukon River and the town of Russian Mission, has a population of four hundred extremely rugged souls, for the winters there cannot be for the faint of heart. Oak Park has sixty thousand inhabitants, it is adjacent to Chicago, and the climate is Midwestern. One school is small, one large, one urban, one rural, one on a river surrounded by mountains and National Parks in an extremely cold place, the other on a railroad line in flatlands, surrounded by other suburbs and a big city, with a comparatively mild climate. We both have the Huskies to cheer for. We both are American. That's enough to make us kindred souls, I think.

How 'Bout Them Dawgs?

Winston Churchill, who rallied the English people during World War II and is considered one of the twentieth century's great leaders, was often said to have the strength and tenacity of a bulldog. This is recognized in several places, no more so than at Winston Churchill High School in Potomac Maryland, whose teams are the Bulldogs.

Haddonfield, New Jersey, a suburb of Camden, has Americanized its nickname just a bit. They are the Bull Dawgs. Copperas Cove is in Central Texas, a long way from the streets of Jersey, but they have something in common with their countrymen up north: they, too, are the Bull Dawgs. Further west is Las Cruces, New Mexico, home of the Lobos of New Mexico State University. It is also the home of the Las Cruces High School Bull Dawgs. So now we have three, the makers of a good old fashioned dawg fight.

Ft. Madison, Iowa, on the Mississippi River, was founded in 1808 and named for President James Madison. Ft. Madison High School teams are the Bloodhounds. You can't hide anything from them.

Aurora, in the far southwestern part of Missouri, is good hunting country and their high school teams are the Houn' Dogs. Corbin, Kentucky, sports the Red Hounds. The Huntington School in Ferriday, Louisiana, is represented by the Hounds

Man's Best Friend

The Swiss use the St. Bernard to find lost skiers, putting a small cask of brandy around the dog's neck so that the downed skier might have the warming comforts of VSOP while awaiting the ski patrol and the welcoming fireside of the lodge. At the All Saints Academy in Winter Haven, Florida, they have selected the St. Bernard from the other saints for their team name. After all, it was a winter haven the Swiss St. Bernards were bringing their rescued skiers to, wasn't it?

Sister Elizabeth Seton, a Daughter of Charity of St. Vincent DePaul, was the first American saint. Mother Seton High School's all-girls teams in Clark, New Jersey, are known as the Seton Setters. My guess is that they have a very good volleyball team.

In California, Redlands High School fields the Terriers while the Bluedogs represent Santa Monica Wilshire West High School.

No one who has ever seen those sad-eyed, low-slung dogs known as basset hounds can help falling in love with them. They are hardly, however, what most of us would refer to as a "big" dog. Lovable, yes, big, no. Not true in Kingsfield, Maine. There we find the Carabasset Academy, home of the Big Dogs. That's the CaraBASSET Big Dogs, of course.

And who would dispute that the Great Dane is a big dog, considerably larger, in fact, than the miniature horses my cousin and his wife raise. Maranatha Christian School in Boise, Idaho, is represented by the Great Danes.

We once owned an Airedale, a lovable old female called Inga. She wasn't good for very much other than giving love, but that was enough for us. They love their Airedales in Arkansas, too, the team name chosen by Alma High School.

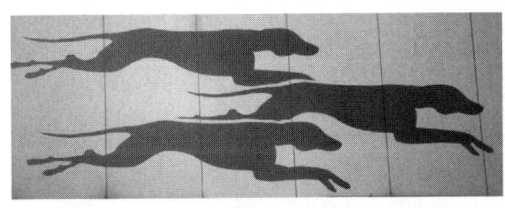

Gray, Georgia, is near Macon. They field the Grayhounds there, while at Carmel, Indiana, they cheer for the Greyhounds.

The Miami Indians were relocated from Ohio and Indiana and ended up in Oklahoma. The city of Miami, Oklahoma, is on the Neosho River in the far northeastern corner of the state. It was founded in 1891 by two men, one of whom was a chief of the Miami tribe. Today the Miami High School teams are the Wardogs.

If you want your home to be properly protected, perhaps you should contact the good folk of Beresford, South Dakota. Beresford is a town of 1849 people in the far southeastern part of the state. The Beresford High School teams are the Watchdogs. Tippecanoe, Indiana, once was also a good source of canine protection. Their teams, preconsolidation, were the Police Dogs.

Camas County High School is in Fairfield, Idaho. Fairfield is near Ketchum and Sun Valley in the great ski and outdoor sports country of that part of the state. Just south of Fairfield are the Shoshone Ice Caves and the City of Rocks. Just north is 10,095 feet high Smoky Dome and the Sawtooth National Forest. Sleds drawn by dogs might indeed be the best way to get around during the winter days in these mountains and it is perhaps not at all surprising that the Camas County High School teams are the Mushers.

Salukis

The saluki is a tall slender, swift, keen-eyed hunting dog with a silky coat, found originally in North Africa and considered the royal dog of the Egyptian pharaohs. It is the mascot chosen by Southern Illinois University, located in Carbondale, which is in that part of the state known as Little Egypt. Bridgeport is north and east of Carbondale near the Wabash River, the dividing line between Illinois and Indiana in that part of those states, and is a member of the North Egypt Conference. The teams of Red Hill High School in Bridgeport are also the Salukis.

Whippets

A small, slender, swift dog of greyhound type is the whippet, a cross between a greyhound and a terrier. Several schools all over the country have selected Whippets as their team name. One of the most interesting is the town of Minden, Nebraska, which has a fascinating Pioneer Village. It is also home to the Minden Whippets, which also run in Kosciusko, Mississippi, Frisco City, Alabama, Downingtown, Pennsylvania, and Shelby, Ohio.

Oak Park Huskies

And now for the story that began this book. Dr. Sue Bridge is currently the superintendent of Oak Park River Forest High School, carrying on the tradition of excellence in this position since the school's inception in 1873. I cannot improve on her words describing the adoption of the Siberian Huskie as our mascot:

"Up into the 1920s, there were lightweight and heavyweight football teams, with 145 pounds being the dividing line. At one point in the '20s, one of our most outstanding heavyweight player's last names was Huskie or Husky. A *Trapeze* writer wrote an article and referred to the heavyweight team as the Huskies, a pun of sorts. It stuck. At the same time, the Siberian Huskie became a very popular dog in America. So, here we are in 2001, still the happy home of the Huskies. Go, Huskies!"

Research from an old friend, Herb Knight, Oak Park Huskie '47, Dartmouth Indian/Big Green '51, Tuck Tycoon '52, has determined that the player was named William Huskie and that the nickname was adopted in 1913. The Oak Park football stadium was opened on September 27, 1924—my mother's sixteenth birthday!—with a 13–7 victory over the Chicago Austin Tigers. With a capacity of ten thousand, it was then believed to be the largest high school stadium in America. It is still in operation and my wife and I enjoyed seeing a game there last fall and being given a tour of the recent renovations by Athletic Director Sandy Abbinanti. My father graduated from Oak Park in 1924, and would have been a freshman at Oberlin by the time the new Stadium was opened. He played lightweight football and was a member of the Huskie State Championship track team that spring.

14
OUR FEATHERED FRIENDS

WE ARE CERTAINLY a nation of bird lovers. We are captivated by their grace and beauty, strength and color, and, I am sure, their freedom.

There are enough bird nicknames right here in central Indiana to start an aviary. On the south side of Indianapolis, lined up in a row, are three schools with excellent credentials, all great rivals, all birds. They are the Southport Cardinals, the Perry Meridian Falcons and the Decatur Central Hawks. On the west side of town are the Orioles of Avon and just north of the city, the Zionsville Eagles. Not far away are the Owls, at Seymour to the south and the Golden Owls at Muncie Burris to the northeast. Birds, in fact, are very popular team names all over the country.

In Iowa, the skies are filled with hawks, as you might expect in the Hawkeye State. Here is a sampling:

Cedar Rapids Prairie High School Fighting Hawks.
Cedar Rapids Jefferson High School J Hawks.
Waterloo West High School Wahawks.
Emmetsburg E Hawks.
Colfax-Mingo Tiger Hawks.
Waverly Go Hawks.
Moorhead Thunder Hawks.
Lansing Kee Hawks.
Natoma County (in Traer) Red Hawks.

Go Huskies! Beat Felix the Cat!

Mid Prairie Community High School (in Wellman) Golden Hawks. Hastings Black Hawks.

Not all of the hawks are in Iowa, of course. Fairborn, Ohio, near Dayton, is the home of Wright Patterson Air Force Base and its impressive Museum of American Airpower. The Fairborn High School teams are the SkyHawks. Boothbay Harbor, Maine, was discovered by Captain John Smith in 1614, six years before the Pilgrims arrived in the New World, on his way back to England from the Jamestown Settlement in Virginia, which was first begun in 1607. This marvelous natural harbor has been a center of seafarers, fishermen, shipbuilders, and, more recently tourists who come for the picturesque town, marvelous vistas and mouth watering fresh lobster, as we happily did. The Boothbay Harbor teams are known as the Seahawks.

Here are some other interesting hawks: Grand Rapids, Minnesota, Thunderhawks; Winona, Minnesota, Winhawks; Oyster Bay, New York, St. Dominic Bayhawks; Winter Park, Florida, Silver Hawks; Mill Valley, California, Tamalpais Red Tail Hawks

Way up north, and way out west, is the town of Nightmute, Alaska. At Nightmute High School are found the Nighthawks. Their neighbors at Seward, named for Secretary of State William Seward, perhaps the one man whose vision was most responsible for our acquisition of Alaska in 1867—hardly "Seward's Folly" at all—are located on Resurrection Bay. The bay was so named by the Russians who first sailed into port there on an Easter Sunday (a Russian Easter Sunday, of course, not ours). Seward High School teams are also the Seahawks. Again, we have the unity of team names that crosses the continent, from Boothbay Harbor, Maine, with stops at Cape Cod Academy in Osterville, Massachusets; Hilton Head and Myrtle Beach in South Carolina; Redondo Beach, California; and Anacortes, Washington, to Seward, Alaska, Americans all—and Seahawks all as well.

Hawks are certainly not the only predator birds that have been selected for our team names. These birds fall under the general heading of raptors and the teams of Eaglecrest High School in Centennial, Colorado, are just that, the Raptors.

Our Feathered Friends

One of the largest birds ever to fly in our skies is the endangered species California condor with a wingspan of up to ten feet, a body up to fifty inches long and weighing as much as twenty-two pounds. These birds are making a comeback in California and are honored by Whittier High School in California, who call their teams the Condors as does O'Brien Technical High School across the continent in Ansonia, Connecticut.

Olathe, Kansas, is on the Santa Fe Trail. There are now three public high schools in Olathe: East, North, and South. East fields the Hawks, North the Eagles, and South the Falcons. Eagles and Falcons are so popular that I can only name a few of the schools that have selected them. Lindbergh High School, in Renton, Washington, is a good example of Eagles, named as it is for the Lone Eagle himself, Charles Lindbergh. There are also Eagles at the small town of Lohn, Texas, the Lohn Eagles, of course. Here are some other examples of Eagles:

- Mid Lakes High School, Clifton Springs, New York, Screaming Eagles.
- Mt. Assisi High School, Lemont, Illinois, Screeching Eagles.
- Bald Eagle Area High School in Wingate, Pennsylvania, and Eagle Grove, Iowa, High School, also field the Eagles as does the wonderfully named town of Freedom, Oklahoma.
- Owings Mills, Maryland, Golden Eagles.
- Duchesne, Vermont, Bald Eagles.

Canyon, Texas, is near Amarillo in the beautiful Palo Duro Canyon. Every year the citizens of Canyon perform an unabashedly patriotic musical called "Texas" around the Fourth of July. As *USA Today* stated, the performance "brings everyone to their feet in a peak of national pride." Thus, not surprisingly, we note that the Canyon High School teams are the Eagles.

The Peregrine Falcon is making a dramatic comeback in central Indiana, thanks in large measure to this magnificent bird's symbiotic relationship with some of the tall buildings in Indianapolis whose perches are proxies for mountain aeries. Well, these birds never left the town of

Falconer, New York, at least not on the athletic fields where the Falcons have long held sway.

Then there are pelicans. Klamath Falls, Oregon, is on the Pacific Flyway, and there are six National Wildlife Refuges nearby. Upper Klamath Lake is the largest freshwater lake in the state. The Klamath Union High School teams there are the Pelicans.

Louisiana, the Pelican State, is a logical place to find these big-beaked birds and there are Pelicans representing the high schools in Spearsville, Homer and Port Allen there. Finally, in the northeast, Pelham High School in Westchester County just northeast of New York City has alliteratively chosen the Pelican as their mascot.

Back in Oregon is the interesting town of Lakeview. Lakeview, at an elevation of forty-eight hundred feet, is at the foot of the Warner Mountains. The Lakeview High School teams are the Honkers. And the lake the town views is Goose Lake.

To keep them company, there are the Flying Geese of Weathersfield High School in Kewanee, Illinois, the Goslings of Watertown, Wisconsin, and the Ganders at Rondout Valley High School in Accord, New York.

Having played at Geese and Ganders, now we can play a bit of Ducks and Drakes. Havana, Illinois, is about forty miles southwest of Peoria, at the confluence of the Illinois and the Spoon Rivers, close to the Chautauqua National Wildlife Reserve, a forty-five hundred-acre wetland that attracts some 350,000 waterfowl on their semiannual migrations north or south. In appreciation of this, the Havana High School teams are called the Ducks.

The Drakes are at Black Duck, Minnesota, High School. Keeping them company are the Mallards of Worcester High School in Berlin, Maryland, and of Henry, Illinois, High School. Then, of course, there are the Mighty Ducks, in this case those of Douglass High School in Baltimore.

Remaining with our fowl theme, there are the Roosters of the Rhode Island School for the Deaf in Providence and of Milligan, Nebraska, as well as the latter's more literary influenced neighbors, the Ord Chanticleers. It was Chanticleer, you will recall, who convinced himself that it was his own clarion call that roused the Sun from a night's rest only to discover, to his

Our Feathered Friends

dismay, that one morning when he did not crow Old Sol came up nonetheless, and right on time. A painful lesson, that.

More menacing are the Gamecocks of New Brockton, Alabama, Sumter, South Carolina, and elsewhere, and the Fighting Cocks of Cocke County High School in Newport, Tennessee. Then there are my particular favorites, the Gobblers of Aitken High School in Minnesota and of Broadway High School in Virginia.

Pheasants are a choice meal, as well, and there are Pheasants representing the high schools in the towns of Parker and Redfield, South Dakota, as well as the South Dakota School for the Deaf in Sioux Falls. Do they feast on their opponents or is it the other way around?

Several other seabirds have found favor as team names. Seaside, Oregon, High School has selected the Sea Gulls as has Old Orchard Beach, Maine, High School, again drawing us together across the country. There are also Sea Gulls representing Mariner High School in Everett, Washington, while it is just the Gulls that fly for Raymond High School in the same state. A bit more colorful are the Garnet Gulls of Point Pleasant Beach, New Jersey.

There are Cranes at the Cranbrook-Kingswood School in Michigan and at Crane, Texas, we find the Golden Cranes. Their relatives, the Herons, are found at the Gunston Day School in Centreville, Maryland, and at Brantley County High School in Nahunta, Georgia. I could find only one school with auks as mascot: the Auks of Archmere Academy in Claymont, Delaware.

Victoria, Texas, east of San Antonio, near the Gulf Coast, is a nice town with a distinctly Mexican flavor. The high school teams are the Roadrunners. Several other schools have chosen the same team name, including Santa Monica, California, Crossroads High School. Again, meep, meep, and keep an eye peeled for Wily Coyote!

Then, there are the Ridgerunners of Grove, Oklahoma, and the Ringnecks of Hill City, Kansas. Can you imagine what the Ringnecks do to the opposition? Or what a coach might say to his players before a game? "If you don't play hard, I'll wring your necks!" Sorry. I'm even sorrier before I get started on this next one. It's the town of Perry, also in Kansas. This is the home of the Kaws. Why the Kaws, you ask? Someone must have once told them, "Just be Kaws." Why? "Just because."

Raytown, Missouri, a suburb of Kansas City, boasts two high schools that make an interesting pair. Raytown High fields the Blue Jays and Raytown South the Cardinals.

Harvard, Nebraska, is a long way from Cambridge, Massachusetts, both geographically and philosophically. Harvard High School, however, does share one thing in common with Harvard University: the color red. Harvard high teams are the Cardinals, though, not the Crimson. There has been a flag with a white cross on a cardinal field in what is now Switzerland for close to a millennium. Geneva, Indiana, High School teams are also the Cardinals.

Sharing the color red is the town of Red Wing, Minnesota. Red Wing is named for many Dakota Indian chiefs who took their names from the headdresses they traditionally wore, the wings of a swan dyed red. The Red Wing High School teams are the Wingers.

Up near the Canadian border is the town of St. Albans, Vermont. Because of its proximity to Canada, St. Albans has seen many an instance of smuggling across that border, in both directions. The town was also the target of the farthest north incursion of the Civil War when a group of Confederates attacked it from the north, the famous "Raid on St. Albans." Things are much more peaceful today. Even the St. Alban's Free Academy teams are not very provocatively named. They are the Bob Whites.

Here are several other birds of the nonvicious, nonpredatory type:

Highlands High School in Ft. Thomas, Kentucky, Baltimore Lake
    Clifton High School and Goessel, Kansas, are all the Bluebirds.
Sublette, Kansas, the Larks.
A martlet is a small wren, the relative of a marten. Martlets are the
    unique nickname of the Westminster School in Simsbury,
    Connecticut.
St. Francis High School, San Antonio, Texas, fields the Skylarks.
Stanley, North Dakota, and Athens, Wisconsin, field the Blue Jays.

Our Feathered Friends

And these others:

Patoka, Indiana, Wrens.
Nazareth, Texas, Swifts.
Antigo, Wisconsin, Red Robins.
Swanville, Minnesota, Swans.

I have dealt with the Ravens at some length in another section, but I would like to mention one here as well. Ravenna, Ohio, is just east of Kent and the attractive campus of Kent State University with its solemn Memorial to those killed by the National Guardsmen in May of 1970. There we find the Ravenna Ravens.

Keene, New Hampshire, is of significance to all Dartmouth graduates because it was there, in the Wyman Tavern in 1770 that Dartmouth's trustees held their first ever meeting. The Tavern, still there, was already eight years old, so seven years older than the College, also still there! In 1775 a platoon of Minutemen were dispatched from that same Wyman Tavern to assist the "embattled farmers" at Lexington. Keene High School teams had no nickname at all until 1948. Up until then they had always been referred to as the Elm City Nine, Eleven, or Quintet. Basketball Coach Jim Hatch, however, felt that something else was needed to alert fans to the excellent season he expected that winter. At the time the Long Island University Blackbirds, coached by Claire Bee, were the class of college basketball and LIU's orange and black colors were the same as Keene High School's, so the coach settled on that. The release of hundreds of blackbirds before a big game was envisioned and new words were written for the song "Bye, Bye, Blackbird," which the student body was quick to learn and loved to sing whenever their team was winning. One backfire, however, was that the opposing fans often took great glee in singing the original words whenever their team was in front, vigorously waving handkerchiefs at the crestfallen Blackbird fans. Undaunted, Keene High School has changed neither their team name nor their song! (With thanks to the Keene Historical Society and *A Keene Sense of History* by David R. Proper.)

Go Huskies! Beat Felix the Cat!

I am unaware of any mina birds or cockatoos, but I could find two parrots. Both were at Polytechnic schools, so it is clearly the Poly Parrots in each case. One is in Sun Valley, California, the other in Fort Worth, Texas. Polly want a cracker?

One of my favorite birds doesn't fly, likes to swim, loves cold water, and always looks spiffy in a tuxedo like outfit. The penguin. There are Penguins representing the Cushing Academy in Ashburnham, Massachusetts, and at Tri County High School in Plainfield, Wisconsin. Perhaps their relative is to be found at St. Mary's High School in Gaylord, Michigan, where the Snowbirds take the field.

I also like the nickname of Las Plumas High School in Oroville, California. Las Plumas means "the feathers" in Spanish and their teams are the Thunderbirds.

A visit to the prime duck hunting country of Stuttgart, Arkansas, discloses the Stuttgart High School Ricebirds. Ricebirds? Yes. I don't know why. They also have Ricebirds at El Campo High School in Texas, so there must be something to it.

Our final entry in the category is in the city of Allentown, Pennsylvania, sister city to Bethlehem. The area, of course, is known for its steel mills and coal mines. Who has not heard of the value of a canary in a coal mine? The Allentown Allen High School teams are the Canaries. But I'm told there is more to it than that. The canary is apparently a more tenacious bird than I had realized, the only bird that is able to fly through a hurricane. At least that is what some Allen High School students thought. I don't know if a canary can really fly through a hurricane or not. Maybe it depends on the hurricane. At any rate, Allen High School's great rival was Liberty High School in Bethlehem. They are the Hurricanes. Some years ago the Allen students, confident that their team would fly through the opposition, chose the name Canaries. The teams wear canary yellow and blue uniforms and the basketball teams play their home games in—where else?—the Cage.

15
MORE FROM THE ANIMAL KINGDOM

WE HAVE OFTEN gone far afield in our choice of animal mascots. Some are, in fact, quite surprising.

Where the Deer and the Antelope Play

Several schools have selected team names of deer, antelope or their relatives. Adrian, Oregon, is a tiny place, rather isolated, near the Idaho line. There are only 131 people in Adrian, but they have a high school and its teams are the Antelopes. There are also Antelopes representing Antelope Valley High School in Lancaster, California.

Palmer, Alaska, was founded during the Great Depression as a place where farmers from the Dust Bowl could be resettled and try their hand at agriculture under somewhat different conditions than they were used to in Oklahoma. The town now has twenty-nine hundred inhabitants and is located just north of Fairbanks near the majestic beauty of the tallest mountain in North America, Mt. McKinley. The name chosen for Palmer High School's teams suits the area: the Moose.

Sacred Heart High School in Bloomfield Hills, Michigan, fields one of the fastest and most graceful of the animals in the antelope family. They are the Gazelles.

At the northern entrance to Penobscot Bay in Maine is the town of Bucksport whose high school teams are the Golden Bucks. Down the coast a bit, in Portland, is Cheverus High School, which fields the Stags. In New York City the Stags also represent St. Agnes Academy. That would be the ST. AGnes Stags, of course. Here are some more from this branch of the animal kingdom:

Elk Rapids, Michigan, Elks.
Bonanza, Oregon, Antlers.
Seligman, Arizona, Antelopes.
Deerfield Beach, Florida, Bucks.
Ft. Collins, Colorado, Poudre High School Impalas.
Yankton, South Dakota, Bucks for the boys' teams and Gazelles for the girls'.

Clarkton, Missouri, is tucked in between Tennessee and Arkansas, in that bit of southeast Missouri that spills down the west side of the Mississippi River. Clarkton is a smallish town, but perhaps Santa Claus visits there with unusual frequency. At any rate, the Reindeer are there all year long, whenever Clarkton High teams take the field. In Milwaukee, at Divine Saviour-Holy Angel High School may be another reindeer. At least their nickname is the Dashers. I could not find any reference anywhere, however, to Donner, or Blitzen.

Farson and Eden are two very small towns in a spectacular part of the state of Wyoming. They are located north of the Flaming Gorge and south of the equally glorious Grand Teton National Park, the Bridger-Teton National Forest, and on the Big Sandy River. The Farson-Eden High School teams are known as the Pronghorns, after an antelope-like animal found in the western United States.

Whiteface is located in the Texas Panhandle, west of Lubbock, near the New Mexico line. The nature of the landscape is indicated by the name of a nearby town: Levelland. The Whiteface High School teams are the Antelopes, sometimes referred to as the Angry Antelopes. It would be fun to see the Whiteface High Antelopes play the Hereford High Whitefaces some day!

More From the Animal Kingdom

My Favorite Cat and Dog Fight
(After Huskies vs. Felix, of course)

My (second) favorite cat and dog fight takes place on the gridiron at least once every year in North Central Ohio. One year it is held in Massillon and the next in Canton. It involves the Massillon Washington High School Bulldogs and the Canton McKinley High School Tigers. These two schools have been going at each other with gusto for a long, long time and had played 110 times at last count. Both schools are listed among the top five in the country for all time most football victories by the National High School Federation. It is a rare year when the winner of this rivalry does not play a significant role in determining the eventual Ohio State Champion. The original team nicknames were selected because they were those of the two most famous college teams of the time, Yale and Princeton. The foundations of the NFL can be traced to these two towns, which is why the Hall of Fame itself is located in Canton.

Ground Hog Day

Every year the nation sits spellbound on February 2, Ground Hog Day, awaiting the news as to how long winter will last, with the answer coming from the town of Punxsutawney in the hills of west central Pennsylvania. There, several tuxedo-clad dignitaries lead a special ground hog, Punxsutawney Phil, out of his den in Gobblers Knob into the sunlight . . . or the shade. If he sees his shadow: six more weeks of winter. This ritual, introduced by German immigrants celebrating Candlemas day has been observed since 1887. Another name for a ground hog is a woodchuck. So I guess it's not too surprising that the Punxsutawney High School athletic teams are called the 'Chucks.

Three Stingers

Woodstock, Vermont, is one of the prettiest, most charming villages I have ever seen. Any season of the year is a good time to visit. In October the yellows and reds of the trees are at their peak, in the winter a blanket of snow adds to the quiet serenity of town and countryside, in the spring the white and pink dogwoods, red flowering crabs, yellow forsythia and many hued azaleas and rhododendrons are a feast for the eyes. Flowers bloom all summer long in the area, bees buzzing in them, of course, and the Woodstock Union High School teams are known as the Wasps.

Nearby is Windsor, a town on the Connecticut River that lays claim to being the birthplace of Vermont because it was there that the leaders of the Colony met to establish a constitution in 1777, precursor to Vermont's becoming the fourteenth state in 1781. The Windsor High School teams are the Yellowjackets.

Farther north, and on the western edge of the state is the city of Burlington. Burlington is home to the beautiful campus of the University of Vermont Catamounts and is nestled on the shores of Lake Champlain, itself a wonder of nature. A suburb of Burlington is the town of Essex. Essex High School teams are the Hornets.

So, there you have it: The Three Stingers, Wasps, Yellowjackets, and Hornets.

More Stingers

Three other schools in different parts of the country have bees in their nicknames for somewhat different reasons. Two towns northwest of Chicago combined long ago to support one high school. They were the towns of Zion and Benton and they called their school, as one might predict, Zion-Benton. Their teams are the ZeeBees.

New York City's Martin Van Buren High School is named for the eighth President of the United States. Van Buren was known as "The Little Magician" by his supporters and "The Sly Fox" by his opponents. The Van Buren High School teams are the VeeBees.

More From the Animal Kingdom

Stubborn As . . .

Malverne, New York, is located on Long Island, not far from Queens. It is perhaps not the first place one would go to in search of that very stubborn animal, the mule. However, if you were to go to Malverne High School you would, indeed, find the Mules. No doubt the Malverne athletic teams show considerable stubbornness themselves on the fields of honor. Perhaps you would feel more inclined to expect to find mules in a town named Muleshoe. Muleshoe is located in the Texas Panhandle, close to the New Mexico border and their teams are, in fact, also the Mules. Certainly you would expect to find plenty of mules in Missouri, and the Show-Me State does not disappoint. There are Mules representing high schools in Poplar Bluff, Lathrop, Wheatland, and the marvelously named Lone Jack in Missouri.

In Fairfield, Illinois, we find the Fighting Mules. I am told their fans send out a cheer something like this: "Hee-haw, hee-haw—fight, Mules, fight. Hee-haw, hee-haw—bite, Mules, bite." I don't know.

Temperance, Michigan, is just north of the Ohio line in the very far southeastern part of the state, a suburb of Toledo. It doesn't require a great deal of insight to guess which side of the Wet-Dry dispute the good citizens of temperance were on! Today, perhaps reminiscent of those earlier days when those for or against Prohibition went at each other pretty aggressively on occasion, the Temperance High School athletic teams are fondly known as the Kicking Mules.

Go Huskies! Beat Felix the Cat!

There are also Mules at Newmarket High School in New Hampshire, but these are not the four-legged kind. It seems that many of the high school students used to work in the town's textile mills after school and summers. These students were given the most menial tasks, things the mill hands preferred not to do, and they were referred to as "mules." The name stuck, and, although the mills are long gone, the Mules are here to stay.

All of these teams had better be alert, however, when they play the teams from the St. John's Military School in Salina, Kansas. The St. John's teams are, after all, the Muleskinners. Perhaps the teams from Lauderdale, Pennsylvania, Muhlenburg High School would be safe, but I'm not sure. They are the Muhls.

More From the Animal Kingdom

Blacksville, West Virginia, is a tiny town northwest of Morgantown, right on the Pennsylvania line. The high school there is called Clay Battelle, and the teams are the CeeBees.

So there we have it: ZeeBees, VeeBees, and CeeBees. I think they all attacked me the other day, nasty little ground yellowjackets. When the sting near my right eye started swelling to the point that I could no longer see out of it, we hustled off to the immediate care facility near us. As I often do with new acquaintances, I asked Dr. Toney, who had treated me, where he had gone to high school. He informed me that his school, now closed, which had graduated seven others in his class in 1964, was in Williamsburg, Indiana, near Richmond in the east central part of the state. When I asked him what their mascot was he was stumped for a second or two. Then, with a smile, he informed me "Now I remember. We were the Yellowjackets."

But I can't stop there. There are Yellowjackets and Hornets all over Texas, at several schools. There are also Bumblebees at Lincoln High School in Port Arthur and at Little River Academy. I think I need to give all of those places a wide berth.

More Cats

Anchorage is the largest city in Alaska, as far north as Helsinki and as far west as the Hawaiian Islands. Diamond High School in Anchorage has chosen Lynx, a bobcat-like, feline carnivore, as their team name. The lynx is fast, strong and ferocious, as, it is hoped by Diamond fans, their teams will be.

The ocelot is related to the lynx. It is a medium-sized American wildcat that ranges from Texas to Patagonia. It, too, is known for speed, and the Ocelots represent Baptist Academy in Hutchinson, Texas.

Just outside of the town of Lakeville, Connecticut, in the far northwestern corner of the state, is the stunning campus of the Hotchkiss School, founded in 1781. The Hotchkiss School teams are the Bobcats.

In Jordan, Minnesota, we find the Jaguars and Smithsburg, Maryland, counters with the Leopards. Greenfield, Indiana, teams were the Tigers

Go Huskies! Beat Felix the Cat!

when famed Hoosier poet James Whitcomb Riley grew up there and enjoyed a splash in the ol' swimming hole, but they're a different kind of cat now. Consolidated Greenfield Central teams are the Cougars.

Muncie Central High School, perennial contender for the state basketball championship in Indiana, calls its teams the Bearcats. Bear or cat? A little bit of both.

The only Cheetahs I could find are those representing Challenger Middle School in Colorado Springs.

Dalton, Georgia, teams are the Catamounts, and the Mountain Lions are fielded by Red Mountain High School in Mesa, Arizona.

There are Panthers at my sons' school, Park-Tudor in Indianapolis, just as there are at my daughter's, North Central, just about two miles away. Talk about a neighborhood cat fight!

Manning Academy, in South Carolina, calls its teams the Swamp Cats. (I wonder if they ever play the Swamp Foxes, of Marion? See The Patriot) Or the Tomcats of East High School in Aurora, Illinois? The Coleman, Texas, Bluecats? The Fowler, California, Redcats? The Cats of Catskill, New York? The Wildcats of Los Gatos (The Cats), California? Or the Wildecats of Wilde Lake High School in Columbia, Maryland? The fearful sounding Saber Cats of Scottsdale Saguaro High School? Or, most modern of all, in high-tech Massachusetts, the Cybercats of Springfield Science High School.

Surprising Choices

As we have seen, many schools select a team name that connotes speed, power, ferocity, or all of these attributes. Now, let's consider some at the other end of the spectrum. The Madeira School in McLean, Virginia, is a good place to start. They are the Snails. Also in Virginia is the Chatham Hall

Names given to school athletic teams and the mascots they've selected run a wide range from dashing to whimsical to down-to-earth. No matter how they originated, however, they're all imaginative representations of school spirit.

THINGS THAT FLY: (clockwise from top left) The Piasa Birds, Southwestern High School, Piasa, Illinois; the Clippers, Columbiana High School, Columbiana, Ohio; the Hunter Dragons, Ste. Genevieve High School, Ste. Genevieve, Missouri; and the Orioles, Avon High School, Avon, Indiana.

LABORERS: (clockwise from top left) The Hubbers, Smethport Area High School, Smethport, Pennsylvania; the Syrupmakers, Cairo High School, Cairo, Georgia; the Spongers, Tarpon Springs High School, Tarpon Springs, Florida; and the Oilers, Oil City High School, Oil City, Pennsylvania.

ADVENTURERS: (clockwise from top left) The Pirates, Garaway High School, Sugar Creek, Ohio; the Vikings, Blue River Valley High School, Mount Summit, Indiana; the Black Hawks, Cowan High School, Muncie, Indiana; and the Rebels, Randolph Southern High School, Lynn, Indiana.

CHIVALRY AND ROMANCE: (clockwise from top left) The Golden Knights, Arlington High School, Indianapolis, Indiana; the Barons, DeKalb High School, Waterloo, Indiana; the Flaming Hearts (*illustrated here on the wagon of their marching band, the Marching Hearts*), Effingham High School, Effingham, Illinois; and the Arabians, Pendleton High School, Pendleton, Indiana.

More From the Animal Kingdom

School. Their teams are the Turtles.[1] Can you imagine a game between the Madeira Snails and the Chatham Hall Turtles? It could take all week, worse than some of the five-day cricket test matches I saw when we lived in Australia, stopped for tea every afternoon. Very civilized, but not too stirring.

Salome, Arizona—a place no doubt studiously avoided by John the Baptist High School—is located in the Harcuvar Mountains, southwest of Wickenburg. Their teams are the Frogs. Bret Harte High School in Altaville, California, is named for the great writer of the American West whose *Outcasts of Poker Flat* so wonderfully portrayed the tenor of the times in the mining camps of the nineteenth century, goes them one better: they are the Bullfrogs. Also in California is the town of Angels Camp where Mark Twain once rented a cabin and wrote "The Celebrated Jumping Frog of Calaveras County." The town holds a frog jumping contest every May and the high school also gallantly fields the Bullfrogs.

At Tampa Preparatory School we find the same mascot as that of the University of Maryland: the Terrapins. Similarly, there is the Thacher School in Ojai, California, an artist's colony beautifully situated above the Pacific Coast, nestled in the mountains. Their teams are the Toads. Up the coast and inland a bit is Coalinga, on the western edge of the San Joaquin Valley. The Coalinga teams are a touch more frightening: they are the Horned Toads.

Could Be in My Backyard

Winslow, Arizona is east of Flagstaff and close to the gigantic Meteor Crater, a most impressive sight that I have seen several times from the air and once from ground level. I don't think it is a squirrelly town at all, but their team's nickname sure is the Squirrels. Their cousins are in Metairie, Louisiana, near New Orleans, where the Archbishop Chapelle High School Chipmunks

---

[1] They also use Cougars, so I have chosen to emphasize the more uncommon of their two choices to make this point.

hold sway, and were once in Prairie Creek, Indiana, home of the Gophers.

Oconomowoc, Wisconsin, is a resort town, surrounded by lakes, north of Milwaukee. They are apparently also surrounded by those lovable little masked bandits with the striped tails that I see so much of in my own back yard, the raccoon, because their mascot is the Coons. Frisco, Texas, is just north of Dallas. They must have raccoons there, too—but, then, where don't they have them, I guess—because the Frisco teams are also the Coons.

Unique Choices

Many schools and towns have moved in more exotic directions when taking their inspiration from the animal kingdom for their team name. Some of these are easier for me to grasp than others. Nashua, Montana, is a small town, 375 people, in the northeastern part of the state. It is near the many recreational opportunities afforded by Ft. Peck Lake. Because Nashua is situated on the Porcupine River it is understandable that they selected those rather prickly little creatures as their team name. How do you approach the Porcupines of Nashua, Montana? The same way the animals mate: very carefully.

Avon Old Farms is a fine prep school near Hartford, Connecticut. The Avon Old Farms teams are the Winged Beavers. Another fine Connecticut prep school is Choate-Rosemary Hall, a merger of two venerable institutions, now both in Wallingford. Their teams are the Wild Boars. Wild boars bring us to the Razorback state of Arkansas. The impressive campus of the University in Fayetteville often rings to the cheers of the faithful shouting "Sooo-ey! Go pigs!" Perhaps the same can be heard at Arkansas High School in Texarkana, where their teams are also the Razorbacks.

Although it is not a high school, I believe the approach taken by the Greeley School in Winnetka, Illinois, as described to me by my granddaughter, Janie Warnock, who attends there along with her brother Marshall, is deserving of mention. Every Presidential Election year the school chooses a new animal mascot, by student vote, from a list of endangered species they have studied. The 2000 winner and current mascot

More From the Animal Kingdom

is the Black Leopard, which won out over the Emperor Tamarind! I think the high schools and colleges of America would have a hard time outdoing those choices.

Kirkland is on the shore of beautiful Lake Washington, an easy boat trip to the University of Washington campus and football stadium. Kirkland High School athletic teams also remind me of my days in Australia. They are the Kangaroos. Rochester, in northern Indiana, fields the Zebras. The Zebras of Wayne, Michigan received their name in the twenties when they started wearing striped uniforms.

Another surprising choice is that of the Oregon Episcopal School in Portland. They are the Aardvarks, which places them first in most alphabetical listings of team names and also means they are particularly well advantaged should they ever play the Progreso, Texas, Red Ants. Several versions of the Aardvark are used depending upon the circumstances, but it is the fire-breathing Fighting Aardvark that is used by the athletic teams.

San Saba, Texas, is southwest of Waco. The San Saba High School teams are named for those well-armored, low-to-the-ground creatures, that we see scurrying around the roadsides occasionally while driving through the South: They are the Armadillos, often shortened to the 'Dillos and sometimes to the Fighting 'Dillos. The girls' teams are the Lady 'Dillos.

Wildebeest is another name for a gnu, those somewhat ungainly animals that race around part of Africa, usually in significant numbers. We don't have many of them over here, but you will find them when the Friends School of Sandy Springs, Maryland, a suburb of Washington, D.C., sends its teams into action. What if they played Portland Episcopal? "Go Wildebeests! Beat the Aardvarks!" on one side of

Go Huskies! Beat Felix the Cat!

the stadium and "Go Aardvarks! Beat the Wildebeests!" on the other. Or throw the Armadillos into that mix for a real good time.

Big and Strong and Tough

Lincolndale, New York, is beautifully situated in the lakes country north of the City. Lincolndale Somers High School teams are the Tuskers. Poachers beware.

Which brings us to Fontbonne Hall in Brooklyn. The Fontbonne teams also fulfill at least one dimension that seems to be important to some in selecting a mascot: they are large. The "Don't Step on Me, Please" award is shared by the Fontbonne Elephants and the Red Elephants of Gainesville, Georgia, a charming college town on the shore of beautiful Lake Lanier. How about a game between the pachyderms of Fontbonne Hall and Gainesville High? The earth would shake.

Perhaps they could get some good competition from the high school in Hutto, a small Texas town east of Austin. The Hutto teams are the Hippos. Legend has it that a hippopotamus once escaped from a traveling circus in Austin and was found in a creek near Hutto, hence the nickname. It must have been a sizable creek. However they got it, they do receive the "Don't Roll Over on Me, Please, Award" for sure!

For size, ferocity, and speed there may be no equal in today's animal kingdom to the rhinoceros. The Taft School, in Watertown, Connecticut, was founded in 1890 by Horace Taft, a member of the rather famous and accomplished Taft family of Ohio. The Taft School enjoys a beautiful campus in the hills of the western part of the state and their athletic teams are called both the Big Red and the Rhinos. Their mascot, a two-legged creature with a prominent nose and a wicked looking horn, the Rhino himself, may be seen prancing the sidelines during Taft games!

Jumpers

Elmer Fudd's nemesis, that "wascally wabbit," may equally be that of the

More From the Animal Kingdom

opponents of Wabasso High School in southwest Minnesota where the Rabbits take the field. Forney, Texas, High School, just east of Dallas is home of the Jackrabbits as is Mesa High School in the Phoenix suburb.

Somewhere between here and the Jackrabbits or Kangaroos is where I should place the Georgetown Day School, Washington, D.C. Their teams are called the Mighty Hoppers. A game between the Mighty Hoppers and the Somerset, Kentucky, Briar Jumpers could be something to see.

Foxes and Vixens

Hartsville, South Carolina is a town of eighty-four hundred near Darlington, where the good ol' boys go racin'. The Hartsville teams are the Red Foxes. In the same state are the Silver Foxes of Dutch Fork High School in Erma, a suburb of Columbia. Across the country are the Foxes and Vixens of Ft. Sumner, New Mexico. Fox Lane High School in Bedford, New Mexico, teams are the Foxes as are those from Fox, Oklahoma.

And These . . .

For meanness and nasty looks, it is hard to beat the Tasmanian Devil. These marsupial creatures once roamed all over Australia but are now confined to the island state of Tasmania. However, the Tasmanian Devil does represent the teams of the Flint, Michigan, Open School. Is there any school out there whose team name is the Dingo, I wonder?

There are coyotes all over the country. We saw one recently in our rather urban Indianapolis neighborhood, somewhat surprisingly. Related to the dog, they are a good mascot for many schools, such as the La Joya, Texas, and the Calabasas, California, Coyotes. Some schools have had fun with the spelling, too. In Kahlutus, Washington, it's the Kayotes, and in Kimball, South Dakota, the Kiotes.

The American buffalo, or bison, once nearly eradicated from the Great Plains, is happily making a comeback. They are also to be found at several high schools, including the Buffalo Grove, Illinois, and Benton Central,

Indiana, Bisons; and the Smoky Hill High School Buffaloes in Aurora, Colorado.

Wisconsin is the Badger State and Badger High School on the shores of beautiful Lake Geneva, does not disappoint. Their teams are the Badgers, the Badger Badgers. Badgered enough?

You know where five-hundred-pound gorillas sit, but do you know where they play? Well, for one, it's for North Hollywood, California, High School, home of the Gorillas.

The Wolf Pack prowls the fields around Ridgefield High School in Bakersfield, California, and the Wolves represent Wolfe City, Texas. The Timberwolves are found at Millick, Washington. There are Wolverines in Michigan, as expected, an example being those at Mid Peninsula High School in the town of Rock.

The Angora is an Asian goat with particularly fine, silken-like hair, often called Mohair. Clarkston High School in suburban Atlanta fields the Angoras. Perhaps even more desirable is the soft wool known as cashmere. No wonder Kashmere High School in Houston teams are the Fighting Rams! Lamphere High School in Madison Heights, Michigan, also feels that their Rams represent fine wool.

16
HEAVENS ABOVE

Many schools have taken their inspiration from the Heavens.

◉

The Weather Report

Let's start with the wind. The town of Kamuela on the Big Island of Hawaii has a fascinating history. There is a museum in Kamuela established by the great-great-granddaughter of the founder of the massive Parker Ranch, which is nearby, as well as a church built in 1857. The nickname of the Hawaii Preparatory Academy athletic teams in Kamuela is the Ka Makani. In English this means The Wind.

And there is the soft breeze represented by the Zephyrs who play for Mahtomedi High School, a town located on the shores of White Bear Lake in suburban St. Paul, Minnesota.

Santa Ana, California, named for the Mexican general and later President of his country, Antonio Lopez Santa Ana, often experiences certain hot, dry winds that blow off the slopes of mountain ranges, called Santa Anas. Santa Ana High School, though officially known as the Saints, is often referred to in the press as the Winds.

A Chinook is a warm winter wind that must blow in Klama, Washington. Klama is on the Columbia River, near Mt. St. Helen's, and their high school teams are the Chinooks.

Go Huskies! Beat Felix the Cat!

Floydada, Texas, near Lubbock, has the Whirlwinds, as does the high school in Timmonsville, South Carolina. Lancaster, in central Ohio, was the birthplace of General William Tecumseh Sherman of Civil War renown and their teams are called the Golden Gales. Moving further up the scale of ferocity of winds, we come to the cyclone.

There are several Cyclones throughout the country, but my favorite comes from an agricultural school in a most unexpected place—within the city limits of Chicago. It is called the Chicago High School of Agricultural Science, more popularly "Chicago Ag," and it comes complete with a seventy-two acre farm thanks to the farsighted leaders of the city who kept the farm from the very early days of what was once Fort Dearborn, resisting all appeals to develop it, pave it over, build houses, stores, whatever. Today more than 90 percent of the mostly African-American students at the school go on to college, an excellent record in itself. And they have chosen to be called the Cyclones.

Then, of course, there are tornadoes to be concerned with. Again, there are quite a few in the high schools of this country, particularly in "Tornado Alley," who have selected that often destructive, whirling windstorm for their team names. Griggsville, for example, a small town in west central Illinois, between the Mississippi River and Jacksonville, fields the Tornados. Farther south in Illinois two other small towns, Zeigler and Royalton, have combined to form one high school and their teams are also the Tornados. Their website is, cleverly, the Vortex. And we mustn't forget the Twisters of Oldenburg, Indiana, Academy.

Next, there are the hurricanes, most closely associated, of course, with the state of Florida. Many high schools cheer for their Hurricanes in Florida, as do the fans of Miami University. In the hometown of the University of Florida Gators, are the Purple Hurricanes of Gainesville High, and in the horse country town nearby, Mt. Dora, on its lovely lake, are the Hurricanes. In Miami there are three high schools that really create a blow: there are the Tornadoes of Booker T. Washington, the Cyclones of Carrollton, and the Hurricanes of Hillel Jewish High. Now there's a storm!

I think the good people of Westhampton, New York and New Britain,

HEAVENS ABOVE

Connecticut, know a bit about storms as well. Their high schools are each known as the Hurricanes. Then, perhaps nowhere is the name more appropriate than at Cape Hatteras, North Carolina where Buxton High School also fields the Hurricanes.

Charleston, South Carolina, is certainly one of the most historic and charming cities I have ever visited anywhere in the world. It is populated by friendly folk eager to please and the Low Country cuisine—you have to love that she crab soup—is a true delight. Charleston has the Hurricanes of First Baptist High and the Cyclones of the Porter-Gaud School. Think of the winds that blow when these two take each other on!

Anyone who has ever spent any time in the Northeast is familiar with the words "Small craft warnings are up from Eastport to Block Island." Eastport is on the south shore of Long Island and Block Island is part of Rhode Island. The Block Island School covers grades K–12 with forty-five students in the high school portion. Their nickname? The Hurricanes.

Now let's get exotic! Mayfair High School in Lakewood, a suburb of Los Angeles, calls their teams the Monsoons. They blow away their opposition, no doubt!

Moving up the coast to Vancouver, Washington, there is another pairing that I find most intriguing. Vancouver today is a bustling city of forty-seven thousand people just across the Columbia River from Portland, Oregon. It was begun as Fort Vancouver in 1824 and was the center of the British fur trade for the region now comprising the states of Washington and Oregon as well as the Canadian province of British Columbia until 1846. The two high schools in Vancouver have the evocative names of Mountain View and Sky View. The former's athletic teams are the Thunder; the latter's are the Storm. It must be quite a spectacle when these two schools clash!

But there's more. Lehigh, Florida, near Fort Meyers, and Wright High School in Stamford, Connecticut field the Lightning while Tampa Bay Out of Doors Academy and Seymour, Wisconsin, both field the Thunder. To go with this witch's brew are the Franklin Central Flashes from suburban Indianapolis, the Calhoun, South Carolina, Blue Flashes, and the

Thunderbolts of Littlestown, Pennsylvania, and of Tinley Park Andrew, a suburb south of Chicago.

How about Paducah, Kentucky, the Ohio River city in the western part of the state? Tilghman High there fields the Blue Tornado while cross-town rival Lone Oak offers the Purple Flashes. Sparks must fly when those two meet! There are also the Salt Fork Storm, from Catlin, Illinois, the Red Storm from St. John's Prep in Astoria, Long Island, and the Magic Storm from Munich, North Dakota. Finally, the impressive campus of Mercersburg Academy is in southeastern Pennsylvania where their athletic teams are called the Blue Storm.

Of course it doesn't always storm. Some days, most days, thankfully, are clear and fair. That, I suppose, is why the Southwestern Academy teams in San Marino, California, are called the Sun.

Come Fly with Me.

Aurora, Colorado, is a suburb of Denver. There are several high schools in Aurora, but two of them are of particular interest to me now. As a preface, let me say that the most impressive pilots I have ever seen are those of the United States Air Force Thunderbirds and the United States Navy Blue Angels with their impressive high speed precision flying. Aurora Christian and Aurora Hinckley high schools must feel much as I do. Their mascots? The Christian Blue Angels and the Hinckley Thunderbirds. What a show these two must put on when they play!

Two smaller towns in south central Illinois, Brownstown and Mulberry Grove, are great rivals. Each is a pleasant community, surrounded by lush farmland. The Brownstown teams are known as the Bombers. The Bombers, however, must face the Mulberry Grove Aces whenever the two compete, reminding me of movies such as *Twelve O'Clock High*. I'll bet it's World War II all over again every time the Bombers and the Aces meet in south central Illinois.

Those planes in *Twelve O'Clock High* were B-17s, known as the "Flying Fortresses." The present town of Fort Edward, in upstate New York,

Heavens Above

originally was a military installation, placed strategically on the portage pathway between Lake Champlain and the Hudson River. This fort was an important one throughout the French and Indian Wars and the Revolutionary War. Today the Fort Edward High School athletic teams are called the Flying Forts.

Those Flying Fortresses and other bombers are only as effective as their bombardiers, those responsible for getting the bombs to the target. The teams of Attleboro, Massachusetts, High School, a city of thirty-eight thousand people, located between Boston and Providence are the Bombardiers.

What did those planes drop on the Nazi military and industrial targets? The big bombs were called "Blockbusters." The athletic teams of Yeshiva Academy in St. Louis are called the Blockbusters. And, across town, at the John Burroughs School in Webster Groves, the teams are the Bombers. Who could we get to fly those Fortresses and other bombers so that those bombardiers could drop their Blockbusters where they could do the most good? Probably Charles Lindbergh, who was the first to fly solo from New York to Paris in his tiny plane, *The Spirit of St. Louis*, would be a pretty good choice. Lindbergh High School in St. Louis calls its athletic teams the Flyers after one of the best who ever lived.

Some other team names in like vein follow:

Alliance, Ohio, High School teams are the Aviators.
Long Island City, New York, (near LaGuardia Airport) Aviation High School teams are the Flyers.
Norview High School in Norfolk fields the Pilots.
Alameda, California, St. Joseph-Notre Dame High School also fields the Pilots, while across town Encinal High School teams are the Jets. The Jets versus the Pilots. Interesting matchup.
There are also Jets at East Boston High School (near Boston's Logan Airport) and at Carleton Airport High School in Michigan.
In Springfield, Illinois, at Ursuline Academy are the Sonics and the Supersonics fly in Sequoia, Arizona.

Go Huskies! Beat Felix the Cat!

Indiana's aviation heritage is not always fully known or appreciated. Many people are unaware of the fact that Wilbur and Orville Wright were born in Indiana, on a farm near Millville, a small town just west of Hagerstown, in the east central part of the state. Their pioneering flight at Kitty Hawk, North Carolina, in 1904 was in a craft based on the designs of Octave Chanute, a French born civil engineer who came to America at an early age. These designs were developed by Chanute in 1896 and '97 on the sand dunes of northern Indiana in what has since become the city and steel mills of Gary. Chanute built the gliders that were the precursors to the Wright brothers successful powered flight. In the early days of aviation the city of Muncie set at least one world-wide time-in-the-air record, thrilling many on the ground. Many Indiana schools have turned to this heritage as inspiration for their nicknames including Hauser Jets, Adams Central Flying Jets, Akron Flyers, Freedom Aces, Bristow Purple Aces, Brookston Bombers, and New Market Purple Flyers.

Richland, Washington, was a sleepy town of less than five hundred residents when it was selected, along with Los Alamos, New Mexico, the Argonne Laboratories in Illinois, and Oak Ridge, Tennessee, as one of four sites for the United States Atomic Bomb Development program. The Hanford Nuclear Works are in Richland and the Boeing Airplane Company has a major installation there as well. Perhaps no company is more closely associated with the modern production of bombers than is Boeing. Today Richland is a thriving city of over thirty-two thousand people and the high school teams are, not too surprisingly, the Bombers. Their symbol is a mushroom cloud with an "R" in the center. Opposition, beware!

John Glenn was the first American to orbit the planet, a United States Senator, and also the oldest person ever to go into outer space. A high school in Westland, Michigan, bears his name. There we find the John Glenn Rockets taking the field. Alan Shepard was also one of the first seven Astronauts and had the honor of being the first American to go into outer space. In Palos Heights, Illinois, a south suburb of Chicago, is the high school that bears his name. Their teams are the Astros. How about a game between the Shepard Astros and the Glenn Rockets?

Heavens Above

Talking about the Astronauts reminds me of the innovative nickname selected by the students of Northwest High School in Indianapolis, opened in the 1960s. They are the Space Pioneers. One of their rivals is Broad Ripple, once a stop on the Monon Railroad Line from the north on its way to downtown Indianapolis, so named because of its location on a large bend in the White River. The Broad Ripple High School teams are the Rockets. Rockets versus Space Pioneers makes for an interesting space-age intracity matchup.

According to Broad Ripple alumna Paula Gable, whose source was *Centennial Celebration*, a book about the school compiled by Ralph Bedwell in 1986, this team name was selected via a contest run by the student newspaper/yearbook, *The Riparian*, in 1929. No one seems to be quite certain why Rockets was the winning entry at that early date in the science of rocketry, but the best educated guess is that it captured the sense of lofty aspirations and, of course, it was alliterative as the school is almost always referred to as "Ripple."

Milledgeville is a small town of a thousand people in northwestern Illinois. The Milledgeville High School teams are the Missiles. Guided, one hopes.

Baron Manfred Freiherr von Richtofen was Germany's leading ace during World War I. He was the Commander of the Luftwaffe's Fighter Group One and was credited with personally shooting down an incredible eighty enemy airplanes. Fighter Group One flew gaudily decorated red airplanes and were known to the Allies as the "Flying Circus." Von Richtofen himself flew a scarlet Fokker and was called the Red Baron. Today we find the Red Baron memorialized in the nickname of the athletic teams in Gatesville, North Carolina. Or is it Snoopy?

Home High School is in Highland, Alabama, and their teams are the Flying Squadron.

Remembering the famous lighter-than-air flying machines known as zeppelins, which had a bright future until the horrifying crash and fire of the

Hindenburg near Lakehurst, New Jersey, in 1937, are the Zeps of Sarahsville, Ohio.

Closing out this section are the Flying Flucos. Where do the Flying Flucos hold forth? Why in Palmyra, Virginia, on the playing fields of FLUvanna COunty High School.

Heavenly Bodies

Sorry, gentlemen. This section does not refer to the Marilyns of Monroe, Michigan, the Susans of Hayward, California, the Avas of Gardner, Montana, or the Elles of McPherson, Kansas. This deals with more astronomical bodies. Two of my favorites come from schools with intense rivalries. Take Florissant, a northwestern suburb of St. Louis. There is a McCluer North and a McCluer South in Florissant. McCluer South teams are the Comets; McCluer North teams are the Stars. Then there is Muhlenberg County, south of Owensboro, Kentucky. The county supports two high schools, again North and South, each more or less equidistant from Greenville, the county seat. Here again, North High School teams are the Stars; this time the South High School teams are the Suns.

South Central High School in Union Mills, Indiana, teams are the Satellites.

The North Stars (could be the Polarises) represent the North Syracuse High School teams in Cicero, New York, and the teams from Hella, South Dakota High School. The Komets represent Kasson, Minnesota, High School.

San Pedro, California, long an important West Coast port and now a part of the Port of Los Angeles, has been a commercial fishing village for almost two centuries. One of the high schools in San Pedro is Mary Star of the Sea. Their teams are called the Stars.

The small town of Mars, Pennsylvania, just north of Pittsburgh, fields the wonderfully named Fighting Planets. Little green men? Well, no, thank goodness. The Mars Area High School colors are Navy and gold.

Heavens Above

Meteors, or shooting stars, can be a spectacular nighttime sight. Meteors may also be found representing DeLaSalle High School in Chicago, and, at the other end of the state in Marissa, a small town of less than twenty-five hundred.

In northern Illinois there is another small town that belongs here. It is Orion, just south of Moline. Orion is a constellation known also as The Hunter and the Orion High School teams are called, you guessed it, the Orions. They hunt down their opposition, no doubt.

A quasar, or quasi star, is a location in space with a concentration of radio emissions that resemble those given off by the hot gaseous bodies that we call suns, or stars. Lakefield, Minnesota, is in the far southern portion of the state, near the Iowa line. The high school there is called Star Concept and their athletic teams are the Quasars.

Finally, there is Springfield, Vermont, where the high school's athletic teams use a nickname that incorporates everything our wonderful, expanding universe has to offer. They are the Cosmos.

More Space Travel

The Lunas

One of the most gorgeous beaches I have ever been to is on the west coast of the Hawaiian Island of Maui. It is called Kaanapali Beach. The fascinating town of Lahaina is just south of Kaanapali Beach. It is as if a New England coastal village had been picked up and moved to a Pacific isle. And, I guess that is pretty much what happened. The whalers and the Congregational missionaries were the first white men to come in any number to the islands, which were discovered by British Captain James Cook (who also discovered Australia) in 1778. These settlers created structures similar to those they had left behind in Maine, New Hampshire or Massachusetts. In 1790 King Kamehameha had a residence in Lahaina and by 1820 it had become the favorite whaling port of Americans in the Pacific. Herman Melville paid a visit to Lahaina in 1843 and referred to the town in his novel *Typee*. There is an interesting whaling museum in Lahaina as well as a whaling ship and the bones of a fully grown sperm whale. By 1860 the whaling industry had pretty much subsided and sugar cane and pineapples, and eventually tourism took over. The 1859 Courthouse is still standing and even more remarkable is the missionary school established in 1831 called Lahainaluna. On the campus of this school was the first newspaper in Hawaii, established in 1834 and called the *Hawaii Luminary*. That school still exists, it has a high school, and the athletic teams are called the Lunas.

E.T.

It might be enough for a town to be the hometown of someone like Demi Moore, but that is not the case for Roswell in southern New Mexico. Oh, no. Many UFO sightings have occurred in and around Roswell over the years and, in 1947, a Flying Saucer from outer space was believed by some to have crashed there. Not only that, but some Extra Terrestrials were thought to have survived and been spirited off to a United States Air Force Top Secret facility in the desert. Be that as it may, every year hundreds of the faithful, maybe thousands, descend on Roswell to see what they can see and to learn what they can learn. On a more serious note, Dr. Robert Goddard, generally considered to be the father of America's rocket program (Werner Von Braun notwithstanding) lived in Roswell and performed his pioneering work in rocketry from 1930–1941. Goddard High School in Roswell recognizes the significance of this work not only in the naming of their school but also in their appropriate choice of a nickname: the Rockets.

17
LOCATION, LOCATION, LOCATION

THAT FAMOUS DICTUM regarding real estate also applies to the towns themselves. This fact is often reflected in the subsequent choice of team names for the high schools in these towns.

Lakes, Coastline, Islands, and More

Long Island stretches for some 125 miles from its western, or New York City, end to the dual peninsulas, North Fork and South Fork, at the eastern end, which jut out, almost in parallel, into the Atlantic Ocean. Greenport is located on the southern side of North Fork, with a fine harbor on the outer reaches of the great Peconic Bay, across from the confidently named Shelter Island. Greenport was, in 1894, the eastern terminus of the Long Island Railroad. From Greenport travelers could ferry across to Connecticut to continue their journey by rail as far as Boston. Recognizing its heritage as a port, and as ferriers or porters of people, the Greenport High School teams are proud to be the Porters.

Oyster Bay, New York, on the northern shore of Long Island, is the site of an interesting bit of history. When the island was in dispute between the Dutch and the English, the issue was resolved by Treaty in 1650, drawing a line straight south from Oyster Bay, everything to the east being English,

LOCATION, LOCATION, LOCATION

everything west Dutch. More recently, Oyster Bay, may well have provided the inspiration for the setting of F. Scott Fitzgerald's compelling novel of wealth and envy, love and lust in the Roaring Twenties, *The Great Gatsby*. Jay Gatsby's home in West Egg, his library with real books, his closet with uncountable new shirts never opened, the yellow cocktail music wafting across the swimming pool and the vast lawn running down to the edge of the bay, the flappers, jazz bands, and, of course, the beautiful, fickle, selfish, reckless, willful, irresistible, careless Daisy, could all have been in Oyster Bay. The Oyster Bay High School teams are the Baymen and Baywomen. Glen Cove is a neighbor of Oyster Bay and their teams are the Covers. Nearby Farmingdale High School fields the Dalers.

Cape Elizabeth, Maine, extends out into the cold waters of the Atlantic Ocean, just south of Portland. George Washington himself ordered that a lighthouse be constructed there in 1790, the much-photographed Portland Head Light. The Cape Elizabeth High School teams are the Capers.

There is also an impressive lighthouse at Point Loma, California, near San Diego. Point Loma juts out into the Pacific, west of Coronado, and is a spot for magnificent views of the San Diego skyline, frequently filled with graceful sailboats in the foreground, or of the long swells and breakers rolling in from the west. The Point Loma High School teams are the Fighting Pointers. The rocky bluffs that form the striking coastline north of downtown San Diego are dotted with caves and the San Diego High School teams are the Cavers.

Onekema, Michigan, is located on the shores of Lake Michigan, north of Manistee, with lakes and rivers to the east. Canoeing, once for trapping, now for pleasure, is common in the area, and as every canoer knows, portaging is often unavoidable. The Onekema High School teams are the Portagers.

Fond du Lac, Wisconsin, French for "end of the lake," is located at the southern end of Lake Winnebago, where the river rushes through ledges, formed over many years. The St. Mary's Springs High School teams there are the Ledgers.

Hingham, Massachusetts, was settled in 1635. It is just south of Boston and enjoys a well-sheltered harbor, protected on three sides from the Atlantic storms. The Hingham High School teams are the Harbormen.

Mineral Point is in southern Wisconsin, not far from Frank Lloyd Wright's fascinating Taliesin in Spring Green. Mineral Point, however, has its own place in the history books. Lead had been mined there as long ago as when it was Indian land and in 1832 a number of Cornish miners came to Mineral Point to seek their fortune in the New World after the tin mines in their native corner of England had worn out. Many of these Cornish workers lived in hillside dugouts known as "badger holes" and it was from this description, not the feisty little animals themselves, that Wisconsin became known as the Badger State. The Mineral Point High School teams are the Pointers.

Beaver Island, in Lake Michigan, is almost due west of the Straits of Mackinaw and about equidistant from the shores of both the Upper and Lower Peninsulas of the state. The island has served as an Indian campground, as a base for French and American fur traders, as a home for Mormons who chose not to go West with Brigham Young from Nauvoo, Illinois, and, still later, for many Irishmen escaping the potato famine. Today, Beaver Island and its sole town, St. James, are mainly tourist attractions. The Beaver Island High School teams are the Islanders.

Another attractive island is Mercer Island in Lake Washington, near Seattle. There is a floating bridge across the lake for those who wish to drive there, but many islanders simply boat there, and, on football Saturdays boat right over to the University of Washington, do their tailgating on the water or on the shore, enjoy the action, and return afterwards the same way. It is an island of many lovely homes and enchanting views. The Mercer Island High School teams are also the Islanders.

There are few islands more well known than Coronado Island across the bay from San Diego. The fascinating Del Coronado Hotel there has seen many a movie star stay in its rooms and many a movie filmed on its grounds. One of my own favorites was the somewhat strange movie starring Peter O'Toole called *The Stuntman*. The Coronado High School teams are the Islanders, also.

Location, Location, Location

Skaneateles, New York, on the northern tip of Lake Cayuga, one of the most beautiful and largest of the Finger Lakes, is a very pretty little town. The block after block of white frame and white painted brick eighteenth- and nineteenth-century homes, some quite modest, others more majestic, add their charm to the allure of Skaneateles. The Skaneateles High school teams are the Lakers.

Hammondsport, birthplace of aviation pioneer Glenn Hammond Curtiss, the first man to fly an airplane a distance of one full kilometer (in 1908) and the first to build a seaplane, is on the southern end of another one of the lovely Finger Lakes, Keuka. The Hammondsport teams are also the Lakers.

Des Lacs means "of the lakes," and the tiny hamlet of Des Lacs in central North Dakota fields the Lakers, of course. There are few lakes anywhere prettier than Lake Sunapee, New Hampshire. The Sunapee High School teams in New London are well aware of this and their teams are, again, the Lakers.

In a markedly different kind of location is Lake Preston, South Dakota. Lake Preston is near DeSmet, named for the missionary father who spread the Gospel over so much of the west. It was in DeSmet that the Little House on the Prairie was built and still stands. The Lake Preston High School teams, interested, apparently, in what lies below the surface, are the Divers.

Here are a few other examples of teams that show pride in their physical location:

> Lake Shore High School in St. Clair Shores, Michigan, the Shorians; Dollar Bay, (on the Keweenaw Peninsula that juts out into Lake Superior), the Bays; Anchor Bay, Michigan, the Tars.
> Iron Mountain, Michigan, the Mountaineers; Elks Mound, Wisconsin, the Mounders; Glenridge, New Jersey, the Ridgers.
> Alma, Michigan (on the Pine River), the Rivermen.
> Tununiak, Alaska (on an island off the western coast of the state), the Coasters.
> Glenrock, New Jersey, the Rockers.

Haverhill, Massachusetts, the Hillers; Tower Hill High School in Wilmington, Delaware, the Hillies; Auburn, California, the Hillmen and Hillwomen; Glenbard West High School in Glen Ellyn, Illinois, the Hilltoppers.

Bailey, Kansas, Laramie, Wyoming, and Monterey High School in Lubbock, Texas, the Plainsmen.

Kuna, Idaho (near Kuna Cave), the Kavemen.

La Mesa, California, is an eastern suburb of San Diego. Grossmont High School is in LaMesa. Of course, La Mesa means a flat-topped, table mountain, and grossmont means a large mountain. Interestingly, the LaMesa Grossmont High School athletic teams are the Foothillers.

Glenns Ferry, Idaho, is located where the Oregon Trail crosses the Snake River; there was a cable ferry there for the travelers initially operated by the Glenn family. The high school teams are the Pilots and their symbol is the wheel of a ship.

Some towns are proud of their location on the political, not geological, map: Here are some examples:

Belvedere, New Jersey, the County Seaters.

Phillipsburg, New Jersey, (on the Delaware River, across from Easton, Pennsylvania), the Stateliners.

Houlton, Maine, the Shiretowners.

Diomede, Alaska (an island located right next to the International Date Line), the Dateliners.

Newfield, New Jersey, Our Lady of Mercy High School, the Villagers.

West Haven, Connecticut, the Westies.

In the tiny town of Calvin, North Dakota, is Border Central High School, with an enrollment of twenty-four students. Very near to the Manitoba line, their teams are the Border Aces. So, too, are the teams from Rock Lake—I almost said tiny again, but they are, after all, almost twice as

Location, Location, Location

large with an enrollment of forty-five—just ten miles or so from Calvin. Two Border Aces? Ten miles apart? That's border warfare!

Blain, Washington, is also right on the Canadian border. This time it is British Columbia that is their neighbor, and the Blaine teams are the Borderites.

The Capitals

Fifty states, fifty state capitals, ranging from big cities with several high schools, such as Boston or Atlanta, to fairly small ones, such as Montpelier or Fairbanks. I checked all fifty to see how many had high schools that recognized the governments that call their cities home. Interestingly, to me, only nine did. There are four Senators in state capitals, three Governors, one Caps and, my favorite, the Solons. Let's start with the Senators:

Carson City, Nevada, was a small, sleepy place, originally settled in 1851 by Mormons who abandoned it when called back to Salt Lake City by Brigham Young six years later. Then the Comstock Lode was discovered near there in 1859 and the boom began. By 1861 Carson City was the Nevada territorial capital and it was the state capital three years later. The state capitol building, governor's mansion, and Nevada State Museum are among the many interesting sites to see in Carson City, home of the Carson City High School Senators.

The Illinois state capital was moved from Vandalia to Springfield in 1837. Abraham Lincoln's home there is a national shrine as are his law office and the railroad depot from which he left Illinois to assume the office of sixteenth president of the United States. The Springfield High School teams are the Senators.

Dover was founded in 1683 and has been the capital of Delaware since 1777. Dover High School teams are also the Senators.

Finally, there is Little Rock, the capital of Arkansas since 1814 and known as the City of Roses. Robinson High School there fields the Senators.

How about Governors?

Go Huskies! Beat Felix the Cat!

Hawaii is the only state of the Union ever to have a royal family and a royal palace. Today, however, Honolulu is the capital of the same kind of democracy enjoyed by the other forty-nine states. Honolulu Farrington High School fields the Governers (that's their preferred spelling).

Minneapolis and St. Paul were not always as close as they are now. The former was built as a logging town at the site of some waterfalls on the Mississippi River used to power the sawmills, and the latter was situated at the river's northernmost navigable point and was primarily a transportation center. Over the years they have grown together and become the Twin Cities, but St. Paul is the state capital. St. Paul Johnson High School teams are the Governors.

Although the locals pronounce the name of Pierre, South Dakota, as though it were "peer," it is actually a French name. The location at the confluence of the Missouri and the Bad Rivers has long been an attractive one. The first European settlement was on the west bank of the Missouri and was called Fort Pierre when an influential trader from St. Louis named Pierre Chouteau arrived in town in 1832 and named it after himself. It was not, however, until the arrival of the Chicago and Northwestern Railway in 1880, stimulating growth on the east bank, that the present day city of Pierre grew up. The Riggs High School athletic teams in Pierre are also the Governors.

Raleigh, North Carolina, is another attractive town, known as the City of Oaks. It is the home of North Carolina State University (the Wolf Pack). It is also the home of the Needham Broughton High School Caps.

The capital city of Vermont, Montpelier, is named for a city in southern France. Montpelier has served as Vermont's capital since 1805, and the impressive public buildings there are made from the marble quarries in the area. Solons were wise lawmakers in ancient Greece, and is also the name chosen for the Montpelier High School athletic teams.

The Toppers

Mount Pulaski, Illinois, is located between Springfield, Lincoln and

Location, Location, Location

Salt of the Earth

Hutchinson is a city of around forty thousand people on the central plains of Kansas. The first thing that caught my eye as I entered Hutchinson for the first time was a seemingly endless grain elevator, some two miles long, purported to be the longest in the world. What you cannot see as you come into the city is the reason Hutchinson was founded. In 1887 salt mines were discovered on the site of the present day city and the mining and processing of salt began in earnest one year later. The vein of salt turned out to be 300–350 feet thick and some 600 feet below the wheat fields and city buildings on the surface. Now that much of the salt has been extracted there is a surprising and unexpected treasure stored in there: movie film. The cave remaining from the salt mines is dry, at a constant temperature, just right for protecting perishable valuables such as motion picture film. So, much of what has made Hollywood great is preserved for posterity in the salt mine caves under Hutchinson, along with other perishables, such as valuable documents from banks, securities trading companies, governments, and corporations. The Hutchinson High School athletic teams recognize the particular nature of their history in their choice of nickname. They are the Salt Hawks.

Decatur. It is really not so high up as to be called a "mount" in many places other than Illinois, with its elevation of around six hundred feet, but it does have an historic building at its highest point, a courthouse built in 1847. It is an elegant Greek Revival structure, one of only two courthouses that were on Abraham Lincoln's Eighth Judicial Circuit that are still standing. The nickname of the Mt. Pulaski High School athletic teams is the Toppers.

The Climbers

Urbana, the seat of Champagne County in west central Ohio, is also the home of Urbana College. Urbana College was founded by devotees of the Swedish theologian Emanuel Swedenborg and owes its location to the efforts of John Chapman, better known to most of us as "Johnny Appleseed." Chapman obtained the land on which the college was built. The local high school has a unique nickname. There are many Hilltoppers in the country, but Urbana is the only school to field the Hillclimbers that I have discovered.

Further west, Shelton, Washington, on an inlet of Puget Sound, is known for two of my favorite things: oysters and Christmas trees. There is also a working foundry in town that produces fine art pieces in bronze. The Shelton High School teams go Urbana one better: they are the Highclimbers.

Rainer(s)

Anyone who has ever visited Seattle has undoubtedly been struck by the majestic, symmetrical, snow capped mountain that can be seen from almost any site in the city, Mt. Rainier. Mt. Rainier was named by George Vancouver, the first white man to view it, for his friend Peter Rainier. At 14,410 feet, it is the highest mountain in the contiguous forty-eight states. There is a town of less than one thousand citizens called Rainier that is located about forty miles due west of Mt. Rainier with an equally

Location, Location, Location

inspirational view of it. The athletic teams of Rainier High School are the Mountaineers.

There is also a Rainier in Oregon. This Rainier is located on the Columbia River, just south of the state of Washington and twenty miles from Mt. St. Helens. It is also a small town, about seventeen hundred people. The nickname of the Rainier, Oregon, High School teams is the Columbians.

On the Street Where You Live

Merrillville, Indiana, was an historical stopping point for wagons headed west. Fully sixteen different trails crossed the spot now occupied by the town in the far northwestern part of the state. There are two high schools in town, essentially right around the corner from each other. They are the Merrillville High School Pirates, and the Andrean High School Fighting 59ers. Now, Pirates I understand, but 59ers seemed off by ten years until I noticed Andrean's address: 5959 Broadway.

Then there is St. Paul Central High School in the capital city of Minnesota. Their teams are the Minutemen. Why? Because they are located on Lexington Avenue.

Similarly there is Chaminade High School in St. Louis, Missouri. The Chaminade teams are the Flyers. Why? Because they are located on Lindbergh Avenue.

Marshmen and Swampers

The largest freshwater cattail marsh in the United States is found in central Wisconsin near the town of Horicon, a marsh covering some thirty-two thousand acres. It was formed by the action of the great glaciers that swept down over what is now the Midwest. This treasure for birds and plant growth was threatened twice, once by the construction of a dam to create a lake and again when the entire area was drained. Fortunately, wiser heads

Points of the Compass

There are several high schools in Denver, but I'll concentrate here on those with the somewhat unimaginative names of the four points of the compass. Though the school names are not very inventive I thought their selection of nicknames was. Let's start with Denver North. They are the Vikings. (There is also a North Glenn High School with the complementary nickname of Norsemen.) So the north side of town made good sense to me. What about Denver South? I guess that makes sense, too. They are the Rebels. So what about Denver West? I guess I should have known: they are, naturally enough, the Cowboys. That leaves Denver East. Now what would they be? The Magi? The Stars? The Shepherds? No, none of those. Denver East teams are the Angels. A good choice.

Location, Location, Location

prevailed and the Horicon Marsh is now completely restored. The local high school has recognized the importance of these marshes to the ecology of Wisconsin and, in fact, the whole world. They have proudly named their athletic teams the Marshmen.

Perhaps they could arrange a game with the team from Nashville, Georgia, High School. Located not too far from the Okefenokee Swamp, their nickname is the Swampers.

Fort Lee

For an absolutely glorious view of Manhattan, a traveler should journey to Fort Lee, New Jersey. Fort Lee Historic Park is atop the Palisades of the Hudson River and contains the reconstructed cannon batteries and a rifle parapet on the site originally built by George Washington's troops in an effort to defend New York, along with Fort Washington, its twin on the New York side, from British warships on the Hudson. Today Fort Lee is connected to the city by a graceful engineering marvel, the George Washington Bridge. Fort Lee High School teams are called the Bridgemen.

Carlsbad

The Carlsbad Caverns were formed by the action of an underground sea that existed some 250 million years ago in what is now southern New Mexico. They were discovered in 1901 by a cowboy named Jim White, but were not designated a national park until 1930. They are in the foothills of the Guadalupe Mountains and are truly enormous, extending for over twenty-one miles and attaining a depth of 1,037 feet, and they are home to millions of bats that emerge in great spiral clouds every night. The town of Carlsbad, to the north of the park, calls its high school teams most appropriately the Cavemen.

Go Huskies! Beat Felix the Cat!

The Artesians

Artesian wells bring water to the surface under pressure. When drilling for gas in the early days of the twentieth century such wells were found in abundance in and around the town of Martinsville in central Indiana. These waters contained certain minerals that were believed to have medicinal properties and much of the town's early growth stemmed directly from its attractiveness as a spa. Not only did Martinsville become known as "The Artesian City," Martinsville High School's athletes, including the incomparable John Wooden, have also long been called the Artesians.

18
The Old Country

Many towns and schools have taken the inspiration for their school names and team names from our ancestors, from the old country and, in many cases, the very old country indeed!

Faraway Places

What names conjure up wanderlust more than Venice, the Alhambra, the Volga River, or Sultans? Well, we have them all in the United States as well.

Venice, Italy. City of canals, cathedrals, arched bridges, medieval palaces, and gondolas. Venice, California, near Los Angeles, another city of canals calls their high school teams the Gondoliers.

The entire city of Granada, Spain, is a delight of Andalusian food, bright sun, warm smiles and the finest in Moorish architecture. The Alhambra Palace is an outstanding example of the latter, a wonder of archways, balustrades, gardens and fountains, pleasing to the eye, the ear and the nose. Alhambra, California, another suburb of Los Angeles, appropriately calls its high school teams the Moors.

Sioux Valley High School is located in the town of Volga, North Dakota. The Volga River in the European portion of Russia is the longest river on the continent at almost twenty-two hundred miles from its rising near Moscow to its Delta into the Caspian Sea. Far away, on the Russian-like tundra of North Dakota, in the town of Volga, the high school teams are known as the Cossacks.

Sultan, Washington, is northeast of Seattle. The word Sultan brings to mind luxurious palaces, softly flowing fountains, silk curtains, harems, and exotic foods. Nothing could be further from the truth in this small, mountainous, onetime mining town. However, the teams representing Sultan are proudly called the Turks.

Scandinavia

In El Cajon, California, Valhalla High School is named for the paradise where brave Viking soldiers who died in battle were flown by the Valkyries. I think it is quite appropriate that the Valhalla High School teams are called the Norsemen. Across the continent is Valhalla, New York, just a short drive north of New York City. These Valhalla teams are called the Vikings.

Decorah, Iowa, has a strong Norwegian heritage. It was founded in 1850 in the Iowa River Valley and named for a Winnebago Indian chief. Decorah was considered the center of Norwegian culture in the New World west of the Mississippi River. We found the Westerheim Norwegian Museum to be a fascinating experience, particularly so, I suppose, because both my wife and I had grandmothers who were born in Norway. The entire town is clean, and flowers were in evidence everywhere on the sunny summer day when we were there. The Decorah High School teams are the Vikings, too.

Many Swedes settled in the north central part of our country, including the marvelous farming land in the state of Nebraska. Gothenburg, Nebraska, is named for its counterpart in Sweden, a magnificent old university and cathedral city. The Gothenburg, Nebraska, High School teams are called the Swedes.

The Netherlands

One of my great-grandfathers was born in Holland, in the town of Arnheim. Thus I have a particular interest in towns like Holland, Michigan, on the shores of Lake Michigan about ten miles north of Saugatuck, known

The Old Country

to many sailors for its famous scarlet lighthouse. Holland was settled in 1847 by Dutch men and women who came to America to escape religious persecution and the ravages of a potato famine. Today, Holland has retained much of its Dutch heritage with the Netherlands Museum, a Dutch village, the Veldheer Tulip Gardens, Windmill Island, and the DeKlomp Wooden Shoe and Delftware factory. The Holland High School teams? The Dutchmen, of course.

Pella, Iowa, was also founded in 1847 for the same reasons Holland was. Known as "The City of Refuge" by its original settlers, today the whole town resembles a Netherlands village. There is a tulip festival every spring, the world's tallest windmill, and a Klokenspiel. The high school teams there are the Dutchmen also.

Utrecht is the capital city of the Dutch Province of the same name. New York City, once New Amsterdam, has a significant Dutch heritage and New Utrecht High School there calls its teams the Utes. Also in New York City is Brooklyn's Erasmus Hall High School, named for the great Dutch scholar, Desiderious Erasmus (1459–1536), described by *Encyclopedia Britannica* as the "greatest scholar of the Renaissance, [the] first editor of the New Testament . . . and an important figure in classical literature." Erasmus Hall High School teams are, again, the Dutchmen.

France

The Huguenots were French Protestants who left their homeland to escape persecution from the predominantly Catholic population of their country. The center of Huguenot activity in France was in the port city of La Rochelle on the Atlantic Coast. In the seventeenth century, many Huguenots arrived in Colonial America with its promise of religious freedom. Those who settled in what is now Westchester County, New York, named their town New Rochelle.

Also, in 1677, somewhat to the north of New Rochelle and on the west side of the Hudson River, twelve French Huguenots purchased over thirty-nine thousand acres of land from the local Indians and established the town of New Paltz on the Wallkill River. These settlers built solid homes out of local stone, several of which still exist on what is called Huguenot Street. This street is described by the Smithsonian Institution as the oldest street with its original houses still in existence in America. Both New Rochelle and New Paltz high schools have appropriately selected Huguenots as their nickname.

Bishop Ludden High School in Syracuse, New York, fields the Gallic Knights and Versailles, Indiana, named for Louis XIV's opulent palace just outside of Paris, once somewhat irreverently referred to their teams on occasion as the Frenchies. Wouldn't it be delicious if their biggest rivals turned out to be the Scarlet Pimpernels? Unfortunately, I could find no evidence of that being the case.

Italy and Rome

Gladiators are properly associated with ancient Rome and in particular with the great Coliseum. Now we have Gladiators representing the teams from the towns of Roma and Italy, both in Texas. Roma is a small town on the banks of the Rio Grande River in the extreme southern portion of the state and Italy is even smaller and located between Dallas and Waco in north central Texas. I have no evidence that these two sets of Gladiators ever met in the arena, but they may have. Carpe diem! While we're in ancient Rome we should mention the Chicago Latin School whose teams are the Romans. Universal City High School in California remembers the roman Legions when it fields the Centurions.

The Pied Pipers

Also in Texas, near Amarillo, is the small town of Hamlin. Most of us are familiar with the legend of the Pied Piper of Hamelin, Germany, the rat-catcher who not only rid the town of rats but also spirited off all of the children when he was not paid for his efforts. Hamelin is a city in Lower Saxony, and the legend of the Pied Piper began to be widespread in the mid-

The Old Country

seventeenth century and it does refer to an actual exodus of children some four hundred years earlier. Whether this had anything to do with the Pied Piper story is problematical. At any rate, a tourist to Hamelin can visit the half-timbered house claimed to have been owned by the famed rat catcher himself. Hamlin, Texas, is well aware of all of this and their teams are, you guessed it, the Pied Pipers.

The Irish

While we're in the great state of Texas there is one other nickname selected by the townspeople that I think is fun. That is in the town of Shamrock, east of Amarillo, near the Oklahoma line. Shamrock, Texas, is far from the Emerald Isle and the surrounding, generally dry and dusty, Texas Panhandle landscape probably very rarely if at all would show the forty shades of green so important to the people of Ireland. Still, the teams representing Shamrock are proudly called the Irish.

Dublin, Georgia, is about fifty miles southeast of Macon on the Oconee River, a location that gave it more economic significance than Macon until the advent of railroads changed the equation. It was founded in 1812 on land donated by an Irishman. The Dublin High School teams are the Fighting Irish. All Hallows High School in New York City also remembers its Irish heritage. Their teams are the Gaels.

Scotland the Brave

The towns of Glasgow, Kentucky, and Glasgow, Montana, are each many miles from Bonnie Scotland. Yet both towns field teams called the Scotties, as does Galloway High School in Atlanta, Georgia. The Royal Scots represent the high school in the town of McKay, Oregon. There is a town in North Dakota called Scotland and their high school teams are the Highlanders. Dundee, New York, nicely situated between Lakes Seneca and Keuka, calls its teams the Scotsmen and the Scotswomen. Caledonia, Michigan, is just south of Grand Rapids and is home to the Fighting Scots.

Go Huskies! Beat Felix the Cat!

Anderson Highland High School in Indiana fields the Scots, and their games are begun by a bagpipe player fully dressed in kilts and tartans.

Latin America

Cuba is really not too far away, only ninety miles from southern Florida. I was fortunate enough to be able to go to Cuba for two weeks many years ago, pre Castro. I found Havana to be a fascinating city, full of new sights and smells, a bustling harbor, great hotels, and the Moro Castle. The people were quite friendly, particularly when I tried my high school Spanish with them. Many smiles. Varadero Beach was as nice as a beach can get. My memories of Cuba are fond ones. We have several Cubas right here in the United States, as well, not to mention Miami's well-known "Little Havana":

> Cuba, Kentucky, the Cubs.
> Cuba City, Wisconsin, the Cubans.
> Cuba, New York, the Rebels.
> Cuba, Kansas, the Mustangs.
> Cuba, Missouri, the Wildcats.
> Cuba, New Mexico, the Rams.
> Cuba, Illinois (named by settlers who moved there from Havana, Illinois), the Cardinals.

Quite a broad selection of nickname for our various Cubas!

Simon Bolivar, 1783–1830, is known by the name The Liberator, or, in Spanish El Liberador. Born in the northern part of South America in what was then known as New Granada (in the part now called Venezuela) he vowed to free his country from Spain and his revolution swept much of South America. The town of Bolivar, Missouri, in the central part of the state is well aware of the hero for whom their town is named. The nickname of their teams: the Liberators!

Keeping with our South American theme is the town of Andes, in New

The Old Country

York. Andes is in ski country, the Catskills, which may be no match in size for the mighty Andes Range, the largest in South America and among the tallest in the world, but they are as beautiful as any mountains anywhere, particularly in October. The Andes high School teams are the Mountaineers.

Lebanon

The cedar trees of Lebanon have played an important role throughout history. Their wood was the best for early Mediterranean ships and other construction and the cedar enjoys a prominent place on the flag of the modern day country of Lebanon. Several cities and towns in the United States are called Lebanon, but only one, in Pennsylvania, thought to call their teams the Cedars.

Teutopolis

The town of Teutopolis in south central Illinois, population fourteen hundred, was settled by Germans, hence the name, but the name used by the Teutopolis High School teams has a somewhat Dutch sound to it. They are called, uniquely in all the land, I believe, the Wooden Shoes. According to Chris Boone's article "Mascots: Animal, Vegetable, or Mineral" for the National High School Federation, this came about in 1935 when two local businessmen presented basketball coach J. H. Griffin with a pair of wooden shoes. The coach, in turn, had them painted in the school's blue and gold colors and used them as a trophy for the annual game with the Neoga High School Indians. To this day, these two teams still play for these wooden shoes. Another rival of Teutopolis is Effingham, the Flaming Hearts (see

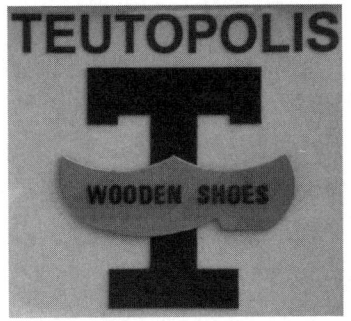

181

Go Huskies! Beat Felix the Cat!

Chapter 6), five miles to the west, in all sports the two schools both play. (Teutopolis is too small to field a football team, I was told, but they are very competitive in both boys' and girls' basketball!) When Effingham and Teutopolis play, students of both try to outdo the other side in rural dress, often wearing bib overalls and straw hats, some with long grass stems in their mouths, all in good fun.

Oriental Powers

Alexander the Great and Julius Caesar capture our imagination whenever great conquerors come to mind. But, perhaps no one has ever covered as much real estate as the amazing Genghis Khan, who lived from 1162–1227. The Tartars (or Tatars) were his tribe and the very word has come to mean a person or group unexpectedly formidable. After conquering most of modern China, Khan's armies swept westward, reaching as far as Eastern Europe. The name, Genghis Khan, is believed to have meant Universal Ruler. His descendants included the fabled Kublai Khan and Tamerlane. In the late thirteenth century the Khalanate of the Golden Horde encompassed most of eastern Russia.

Tamerlane lived from 1336–1405, and his warriors overran the territory from the Mediterranean through Persia, Asia Minor, and India, among others. Upon his death two great empires emerged, the Persian and the Mogul of India. The Moguls also dominated Russia until 1486.

Granville is a small town of twenty-six hundred in New York State, barely across the Vermont line. It has very much the aspect of a New England village and is close to pretty Lake Catherine, which is entirely in Vermont. One day we were having a late lunch in Granville when the high school baseball team came in for an after ballgame meal. They swept through the room like the Golden Horde they were, but I must confess they did not look like the fiercest warriors I had ever seen. They did, however, assure me that they had won their game that morning, and it was a playoff game, too!

The Old Country

Escalante, Utah, is a town of some eight hundred people, beautifully situated in the southwest part of the state between the glories of Bryce Canyon, Escalante Canyon, the Dixie Forest, and ninety-two hundred foot-high Canaan Peak. The Escalante High School teams are called the Moguls. (It should be noted that in ski country, a mogul is also a bump in a ski course.)

Torrance is a good-sized city between Los Angeles and Long Beach. Torrance High School athletic teams are the Tartars. There are two other high schools in town that also feature impressive warriors from the olden days as their mascots: North High School fields the Saxons and South High School the Spartans. What a battle royal when these three, Tartars, Saxons and Spartans mix it up in Torrance!

Great Battles

There are two high schools in Chula Vista, California, that recreate the Trojan Wars whenever they play. There we have the Chula Vista High School Spartans going up against the Castle Park High School Trojans.

In Beverly Hills the high school teams are the Normans and across Los Angeles in Anaheim, is Lohra High School, the Saxons. This one would be another edition of the Battle of Hastings whenever they play.

Bavaria in America

Two towns in this country are absolute musts for anyone who enjoys the many pleasures of Bavaria in the south of Germany. No, they cannot offer the fascinating castles of Mad King Ludwig, or those along the Rhine, or the Black Forest, or the Alps. There are however, many half-timbered homes, flowered window boxes, and *trompe l'oeil* facades. And there are friendly people, plenty of red beets, potato salad, sauerbraten, and beef roulade for those appetites that enjoy the German style of food. And there is no shortage of good beer and Rhine wine. One town is located in Georgia, near the highest mountain in the state, to the far north, just south of Tennessee. It is called Helen, and the town is built like so many Bavarian towns, on the sides of a rushing mountain stream, no doubt filled with *forelle*, my favorite fresh water fish. That's trout, as I'm sure you know. The other is in the northeastern part of the Lower Peninsula of Michigan. It, too, is built on both sides of a river and comes complete with a castle-like hotel. It is called Frankenmuth. The word *Franken* refers to the province in Bavaria from which the original settlers came, and *Muth* means courage, thus Frankenmuth—"courage of the Franks." Both towns are well worth visiting. Helen sends its students to White County High School in nearby Cleveland, the Warriors. Frankenmuth High School, proud of being American as well as of its German heritage, fields the Eagles.

It's All Greek to Me

The town of Greece, New York, is a northwestern suburb of the city of Rochester, founded by Greek immigrants to the New World. There are three schools in Greece that certainly attest to that kind of heritage: Arcadia, Athena, and Olympia high schools. Arcadia has selected Titans from Greek mythology as their team name, while Athena, named for the Greek goddess of Wisdom and Beauty who sprang fully mature from the head of Zeus, calls their teams the Trojans and Olympia has opted for Spartans. During athletic contests these schools relive the Trojan and Peloponnesian wars!

Athens Academy shares its home town with the impressive main campus of the University of Georgia. Their teams are the Spartans. The Athens Spartans. Both intellect and physical strength are represented in that combination.

Crawfordsville, Indiana, is a charming Midwestern town with many attractive homes, and the campus of Wabash College, nicely laid out on a small hill, well planted with trees and shrubs with buildings that are a pleasing blend of Georgian and Federal styles. Due in part to the influence of Wabash College and in part to the fact that Lew Wallace, author of *Ben-Hur*, was a Crawfordsville native, the town has long considered itself the

The Old Country

Athens of the Plains. This title is also claimed by Columbus, Indiana, more recently, due to the innovative architecture that Mr. J. Irwin Miller of the Cummins Engine Company has sponsored in that city. Clearly Crawfordsville was there first with that name and applied it to their high school teams, the Athenians. Columbus for years had just the Bulldogs—is it coincidence that Miller was a Yale man?—but, more recently, the Olympians of the newly added East High School did pick up on the Athens of the Plains theme, and their girls' teams are, marvelously, the Olympi-Annes.

Marathon, New York, due east of Ithaca, itself a Greek name, is also a long way from Marathon, Greece. The Battle of Marathon was fought in 490 B.C. and represented a significant victory for Athens as their armies, under the command of General Miltiades, repelled the Persians in their attempt to invade Greece. To bring the news to the citizens of Athens, the runner Phidippides was dispatched, ran the entire way, gave the message, collapsed and died. The distance he covered was measured as 26 miles, 385 yards and that has been the distance used for all modern marathons, Olympic and otherwise. The teams from the town of Marathon, New York, are the Olympians.

Thanks to the genius of Homer we know a good deal about the Trojan War that occurred in the twelfth century B.C. Homer's Iliad tells the story of Helen, the most beautiful woman in the world. Helen was married to Menelaus, but Paris, the son of the king of Troy abducted her and carried her off to his homeland, known also as Ilium. The Greeks were determined to recover Helen and thus began a war that would last ten years. The war was essentially a standoff until the Greeks devised a scheme whereby they would hide some soldiers in a large wooden horse, leave it outside the gates of Troy and pretend to sail away. When the Trojans succumbed to this ruse, bringing the horse inside their gates, the hidden soldiers climbed out of the horse after dark and set the city on fire. Bloom Township High School in

Go Huskies! Beat Felix the Cat!

Chicago Heights would suit the Greeks fine. They are the Blazing Trojans. The BT on their basketball uniforms fits both the school name and the nickname just fine.

Many towns and cities across the country have Troy as their name and some others are called Homer. Most of the Troys have chosen Trojans as their nickname, such as Troy, Kansas, and Troy, Texas. Other selections are: Troy, Illinois, the Knights; Troy, Tennessee, the Rebels; Troy, New York, the Flying Horses; and Troy, Michigan, the Colts. Homer, Michigan and Homer, New York, both field the Trojans.

The sea and sailing are important to Homer, Alaska, a former coal-mining and gold-rush camp, located on the southwestern tip of the Kenai Peninsula, on Kachemak Bay. The Mariners take the field for them. Perhaps they chose this only from their own experience, but it is an equally valid remembrance of Homer's other great epic poem, *The Odyssey*, chronicling the perils encountered by its hero, Odysseus, as he struggled to return home to his beloved Penelope at the conclusion of the Trojan War.

My great regret is that, to date, in all of the Homers and Troys I have discovered, I have found none whose girls teams are called what I think they should be: the Helens. If anyone does know of any, please tell me!

Spain

Ponce de Leon landed in the area now occupied by the beautiful and historic city of St. Augustine in the year 1513. Juan Cabrillo discovered California in 1542, and other Spanish explorers were all over the Prairie States and the rest of the South and Southwest as well. Our Spanish heritage is of longstanding and deep historical significance.

The Spanish soldiers under the command of men such as DeSoto, Cortez, deLeon, and others were often known as conquistadors, or conquerors. Several schools have selected Conquistadors as their mascots. My favorite is found in what is, to me, an unexpected place. That is in the

The Old Country

town of Olive Branch, Mississippi. Who would expect to find conquerors so close to the universal symbol for peace?

Following is a sampling of some other Spanish names selected by schools around the country for their teams:

Taft High School, Woodland Hills, California, are the Toreadors, and their crosstown rival, El Camino Real High School, the Conquistadors. Quite a battle when the Carmen-inspired bullfighters face the conquerors!

Monterey, California, High School teams are the Toreadores.

Bull fighting, of course, is a significant part of Spanish culture. The *matador* is the man who kills the bull, the *toro*. We find Matadors as the team name of many high schools including Shadow Mountain High School in Phoenix. Nor is his opponent forgotten. There are Toros also at many schools, including Mountain View High in Mesa, Arizona, a Phoenix suburb. One wonders what happens when Mesa Mountain View plays Phoenix Shadow Mountain. As the waiter once said, "Senor, the bull does not always lose."

A *Don* in Spain is akin to a Lord in England, a man of substance, worthy of respect. It is not surprising that there are also many Dons around the country including those at Spanish Fork, Utah, High School.

Lobo is Spanish for wolf and there are many Lobos prowling the high schools of our country, such as those at Escalante High School in Tierra Amarillo (Yellow Land), New Mexico.

Wrangling horses and herding cows was as important in Spain as it was in the West. *Vaqueros* is Spanish for cowboys and *gauchos* are skilled horsemen. Vaqueros are fielded by several California high schools, including Garden Grove Rancho Alamitos, (their cross town rivals are the Bolsa Grande Matadors, so when the two meet it is the cowboys against the bull fighters).

Gauchos may be found in the California high schools of El Cerrito, Casa Grande High in Petaluma, and Narbonne High, in Harbor City.

Father Junipero Serra constructed at least nine missions throughout California beginning with his first in San Diego in 1769, seven years before our new nation-to-be enunciated its Declaration of Independence from

Great Britain. His headquarters mission was the exquisite San Carlos Borromeo del Rio Carmelito, often called Carmel Mission, which he founded in 1770. Father Serra is buried under the altar in Carmel Mission. The Carmel High School athletic teams, with great respect, are called the Padres in honor of this amazing man. San Mateo Junipero Serra High School teams are also called the Padres.

Here are four final examples of high schools proud of their Spanish heritage with unique team names:

One is from the gorgeous San Diego suburb of LaJolla, truly a jewel by the Pacific. Not far away is LaJolla Country Day, the Torres, or Towers.

In Tucson, at the high school with the lovely, evocative name of Flowing Wells, are the Caballeros, gentlemen in Spanish. I hope the girls' teams are the Damas, not the Lady Caballeros, but I don't know for sure.

Also in Tucson, and also at a high school with an intriguing name, Canyon del Oro, or Canyon of Gold, are the Dorados. Dorados means gilded ones, and one of the quests of the early Spanish conquistadors was to find El Dorado, or the City of Gold.

Finally, in the town with the charming name of Crystal City, in the far southwestern part of Texas, are the Javelinas. Javelinas are wild boars. Sooey, as they say in Arkansas!

19
SOME STATES

I SUPPOSE I could have organized this whole book by state instead of topic. Several states did seem to make good stories in and of themselves, however, and here they are.

❂

Alaska

Two towns in Alaska deserve special mention beyond those covered elsewhere. The first is Shismaref, a settlement of only 456 very hardy souls located on an island in the Bering Sea, just south of the Arctic Circle where the Northern Lights often glow with particular brilliance. I viewed the spectacular sight known as the Aurora Borealis one night while riding on a train between Chicago and Denver. Blues, greens, reds, yellows, shimmering, rising and falling in the night sky as the train sped westward. It must be an even more amazing experience to see it from an island in the Bering Sea just south of the Arctic Circle. No wonder the Shismaref High School teams are called the Northern Lights!

Then there is the even smaller town of Seldovia, with a population of 316, on a peninsula in the Gulf of Alaska southwest of Anchorage, accessible only by boat. The town was originally a Russian settlement and the name Seldovia is derived from the Russian word for herring. Red herring? Perhaps. At any rate the St. Nicholas Russian Orthodox Church, built in 1891, is still an impressive structure. The Seldovia High School teams are called the Sea Otters.

Delaware

Newcastle, Dutch-settled original capital of Delaware, is located about six miles south of the state's major city, Wilmington, on the Delaware River. The town reflects the history of many traditions, with significant English and Swedish presence following the Dutch. Present day Newcastle is a treasure of eighteenth- and early nineteenth-century buildings around the green, many of which are among the finest examples of their kind in the country. The New Castle High School athletic teams are the Colonials. Those of Newark Christina High School are the Vikings. Nearby Bear is home to the Caravel Academy's aptly named Buccaneers. The Wilmington Friends School teams are the Quakers.

Maine

The entire "stern and rockbound coast" of Maine is a tourist's delight, a photographer's delight and a lobster lover's delight. Since I happen to qualify on all three counts, it is no mystery that I love to go there. From Portland to Eastport, through Kittery, Saco, York Harbor, Kennebunkport, Camden, Rockport, Booth Bay and Bar Harbor's Acacia National Park, the Maine coast is truly a succession of wonders. Several of the high schools reflect this in their choice of mascots and nicknames.

Old Orchard Beach, one of the oldest resort areas in America, is a magnificent strand of wide, hard packed sand. The high school's teams are the Seagulls. Yarmouth is a scenic coastal town, first settled in 1636, the year Harvard University was founded and just sixteen years after the Pilgrims landed. The Yarmouth high teams, also in recognition of the great sailing ships of America's past, are the Clippers. Freeport is considered the birthplace of Maine, as it was the town in which the colony's separation from Massachusetts was made official, paving the way for what would one

Some States

day be called the Pine Tree State. The Desert of Maine is located here, an impressive area of sand dunes up to seventy feet high. The Pine Tree Academy in Freeport fields teams known as the Breakers. This is partly due to the nearby ocean and partly due to what they hope to do to the hearts of the players and fans of their opponents. Deer Isle is located in Penobscot Bay, surrounded, of course, by water. Two of the towns on Deer Isle have the wonderful names of Sunshine and Oceanville. The Deer Isle athletic teams are appropriately the Mariners.

Kansas

Kansas is known variously as the Jayhawk State, the Wheat State and the Sunflower State. It was also Dorothy's home before the cyclone so rudely picked her up and deposited her and Toto in Oz. I must say, after hearing the song that says "I was born in Kansas, I was bred in Kansas . . . I'm a Sunflower from the Sunflower state" I had expected to find several Kansas high schools with Sunflower as their nickname. Regrettably, I found none. If there are some out there, perhaps someone will so inform me. I would be pleased to be proven wrong on this one.

There are also not a lot of Jayhawks, though they are certainly on display all over the beautiful, hilltop crested University of Kansas campus in Lawrence. Lawrence was settled by enlightened people who realized the abomination of slavery for what it was and were fervent abolitionists. All of Kansas did not share this sentiment, the state being sharply divided between those favoring slavery and those opposed to it. Those opposed were called Jayhawks. There is a town of about eight hundred people in Kansas called Mound City just south of the spot where an event called the Marais des Cygnes Massacre occurred in 1858. This massacre had nothing to do with swans. It had everything to do with slavery. A band of slavery advocates came into Kansas and executed a number of abolitionists in a ravine. Mound City is located in Linn County. The high school there is called Jayhawk Linn, and their teams are the Jayhawks.

The name Kansas comes from an Indian word meaning "people of the south wind." I don't think they had cyclones in mind as L. Frank Baum did when he wrote *The Wizard of Oz*. Ottawa was founded by Baptist missionaries who came to Kansas in 1864. Today's Ottawa High School teams are the Cyclones.

Nothing, however, is more closely associated with Kansas than is the growing of wheat. Russian and Ukrainian immigrants to the country found the perfect climate and soil conditions for growing the hard, red grain variety of wheat they had been used to in their homelands, better suited for bread than for pasta. Today, Kansas still leads the nation in the production of wheat, although the margin is small over North Dakota, and the long-stemmed varieties that gave rise to the "amber waves of grain" have been replaced by the hardier, easier to harvest shorter stemmed varieties. In the western part of the state there is a town called Grainfield. The high school there is called Wheatland. The Grainfield Wheatland High School athletic teams are quite properly called the Shockers.

Several famous Americans were raised in Kansas, including Dwight David Eisenhower, commander of the Allied forces in the European Theater of Operations in World War II, president of Columbia University and thirty-fourth president of the United States, who came from Abilene. Abilene was once a wild place, located on the Chisholm Trail, with hundreds of cowboys carousing in the streets. Before Ike was a Cadet at West Point he was a Cowboy at Abilene High School.

Bob Dole was born in Russell, Kansas, a small town in the north central part of the state, originally called Fossil. The name was changed in 1871. Before Bob Dole became a hero in World War II, vice president of the United States and Senate Majority Leader, he was a superb athlete as a Bronco at Russell High School and a Jayhawk at the University of Kansas.

North Dakota

My call to Oriska High School was answered by a very pleasant man named Roger Mulvaney who informed me that the high school was no longer in existence, having been consolidated with others in the area, and the building was now used for the elementary school. However, he said, the old nickname of the Flickers was not for a bird, as I had expected, but was for a gopher. The namesake gopher, he explained, flicks its tail. So, the Oriska Flickers, no more, but once, flicker-tail gophers. He went on to tell me that Tower City High School, also now consolidated, had been the Clams. Clams, I said, in North Dakota? What kind off clams do you have out there? He didn't know that one. However, getting into this quest of mine, Mr. Mulvaney gave me one more that I find most worthy of mention. That would be the town of Ayr, named, no doubt, by its Scottish settlers after the city of the same name back home. But how about the nickname? They were the Rifles. The Ayr Rifles. What if they played Remington, Indiana? Rifles on both sides of the field, Remingtons would seem to have the advantage over Ayrs, I guess.

Vermont

Vermont, the Green Mountain State, is beautiful from top to bottom, from the Northern Kingdom to the Massachusetts line, and from east to west, from the Connecticut River to Lake Champlain. It is beautiful in every season, particularly so when the glories of fall's colors light up the countryside and later when the deep white of snow with the blue shadows of farm buildings and church steeples cover the ground as caught so perfectly in the art of Sabra Field.

One of the nicest drives in this pretty state is Route 100, which runs north-south down the center of the state. One of the more interesting stops along the route is at the town of Plymouth Notch, boyhood home of President Calvin Coolidge. The whole town has been nicely restored and the surrounding Green Mountains provide a beautiful backdrop at all times, but particularly so in October. Plymouth Notch does not have a high school, but just a bit to the south, in Ludlow, is Black River High School, home of the Presidents.

GO HUSKIES! BEAT FELIX THE CAT!

Brattleboro was founded by William Brattle and William Dummer who purchased the land on the west side of the Connectticut River for about a farthing an acre. It was named for Colonel William Brattle, Jr. Rudyard Kipling married a Brattleboro woman in 1892, and lived there for several years where he wrote *Captains Courageous, The Just So Stories,* and *The Jungle Book*. The Brattleboro High School teams are the Colonels.

20

Happy Halloween

GHOSTS AND GOBLINS and various things that go bump in the night have long been popular selections for nicknames throughout the country.

Devils, Imps and Demons

Devils of several colors and descriptions exist. Let me begin with the Blue Devils from Quincy, Illinois, a charming town on the Mississippi River. Quincy, however, is not always considered charming by opponents who come to town to challenge the home team in basketball. After the visiting team is on the floor, the lights go out, and a cauldron appears, spotlighted at center court. Out of the mist or steam rising from the cauldron there also emerges, to the great glee and thunderous applause of the hometown fans, a Blue Devil, complete with cloven hoofs, tail, and pitchfork. Would you want to play them on October 31?

Blue Devils have also appeared at Tipton High School, a small town between Indianapolis and Kokomo, for some time. A few years ago some citizens raised an objection to the use of the Devil in any color as an appropriate representation for their school. They preferred Twisters. Eventually the issue was resolved. Tipton kept the Blue Devil, but now he has a smiling, benign expression. He is a friendlier, kinder, gentler Blue Devil. Nearby, at Indianapolis Pike Township High are the Red Devils. There are also Red Devils in California at Mt. Diablo (Devil Mountain) High School. Devils, Blue and Red, abound in every section of the country.

Go Huskies! Beat Felix the Cat!

Less common, but perhaps even more frightening, are Green Devils such as those found at the wonderfully welcomingly named town of Friendship, Wisconsin. Rarer yet are the Purple Devils of Franklin Central High School in Franklin, New York, and the Black Devils of Hettinger, North Dakota. Also in North Dakota, at Devil's Lake High School are the appropriately named Satans.[1]

There are Sun Devils at several sunny spots, including: San Diego Mt. Carmel and Apple Valley high schools in California, Scandia Prep in Albuquerque, New Mexico, El Dorado High School in Las Vegas, Nevada, and Rough Rock, Arizona, High School in the West. Across the continent they are also to be found at the Sea Island Academy, which is not on Sea Island, Georgia, but is in South Carolina near Charleston.

Page, Arizona, is where the dam was built that created wondrous Lake Powell in Glen Canyon. There are few excursions anywhere that are more fun or stimulating than a boat trip through the marvelous waters and rock formations of Lake Powell. Page High School selected Sand Devils for their mascot well before the lake came into being.

Also in Arizona, which can be extremely dry and dusty, are the aptly named Dust Devils of Mohave Valley and Santa Cruz Valley high schools.

At the high school in another wonderfully named town, Travelers Rest, South Carolina, are the not quite so welcoming Devil Dogs. How about a game between the Friendship Green Devils and the Travelers Rest Devil Dogs for nice sounding town names with mean sounding team names? Warren County High School in Georgia, which is due west of Augusta, has the even more frightening sounding Screaming Devils.

---

[1] Just as I concluded that Satans is an appropriate mascot for a town called Devil's Lake, I read the following in the August 31, 2002, *Indianapolis Star*: "Devils Lake Central High School in Devils Lake, North Dakota, has decided to drop the name 'Satans' for its athletic teams and come up with a less infernal description . . . 'It's hard to stand up and cheer for the Satans,' one parent/coach is quoted as saying."

I beg to differ. Perhaps she has never seen the "Cameron Crazies" stand up and cheer for the Duke University Blue Devils, on their feet for the entire game. Maybe they should change the town name if they take the Satans/Devils name that seriously!

Happy Halloween

At Gurdon, Arkansas, High School fans are rooting for the Go Devils, which may have something to do with the town's location near Poison Springs State Forest, a somewhat intimidating sounding locale. Closing out the devil theme is another one of my favorites, the Diablos of Mission Viejo, California: the Devils of the Old Mission. This sounds like a good movie starring Vincent Price or Boris Karloff.

In central North Carolina between Raleigh and Durham, are the Imps of Cary High School, the oldest in the state. I am told by Dr. Dave Coley, principal, that this team name was selected in admiration of the nearby Duke Univeristy Blue Devils, but with a desire for differentiation. The school's colors are green and white instead of Duke's blue and white

Just a bit farther west is the city of Winston-Salem. Originally settled by German Moravians who came to North Carolina from Bethlehem, Pennsylvania, the town of Salem was founded in 1766, soon followed by Winston, one mile away. Naturally, the two grew together. Winston-Salem prospered and became the headquarters city for the R. J. Reynolds Tobacco Company. The Demons of R. J. Reynolds High School in Winston-Salem, are a nice match for the Demon Deacons of Wake Forest University whose beautiful new campus was built when the school moved to Winston-Salem from the small town of Wake Forest near Raleigh.

There are also Demons at Washington, Iowa, and Des Moines, New Mexico. Des Moines means "The Monks," but I guess it sounds like Demons when the French is anglicized just a bit. There are Green Demons representing Manson, Louisiana, High School, and Blue Demons at Albia, Iowa. Duncan, Oklahoma, near Ft. Sill, also fields the Demons. The Duncan Demons, or, in basketball season, the Dunkin' Demons.

While discussing Demons, the adoption of the nickname Blue Demons by DePaul University is an interesting story. Before DePaul had any nickname they awarded letter sweaters to their varsity athletes, as many schools did, in the school's colors. They only had men's teams then and the sweater wearers were known as "D Men." Since the sweaters were white with a blue D, the wearers were referred to as "Blue D Men." This simply evolved into the Blue Demons and the devil motif, so familiar today, was added later.

Ghosts, Goblins, Spirits and Phantoms

The Passaic River flows from northern New Jersey into Newark Bay. Approximately eleven miles from New York City are the Great Falls of the Passaic with a seventy-foot drop, the most powerful waterfalls east of Niagara known to colonial America. Alexander Hamilton was the first to recognize the potential of these falls as a power source for American industry, and it was he who provided the impetus for the establishment there of America's first planned industrial city, Paterson. By the 1880s fully 80 percent of all of the locomotives in the country, fueling the young nation's insatiable westward expansion, were built in Paterson.

Paterson Eastside High School gained considerable fame from the movie starring Morgan Freeman chronicling the true story of its academic achievements in the face of some very difficult circumstances. Viewers may remember that their nickname was the Ghosts. What they may not have realized is that the name Ghosts was selected because the school's football stadium was situated on a former gravesite!

There are also Ghosts at Randolph, Vermont, and at Alexandria Bay, New York, high schools. There are Gray Ghosts at Chillicothe, Illinois Valley Central High School and at the Westford Academy in Massachusetts. Galloping Ghosts can be found at Kaukauna, Wisconsin, which produces marvelous cheese, and was purchased for five gallons of rum according to the first recorded deed in the state. Abington, Pennsylvania, a suburb directly north of Philadelphia, also fields the Galloping Ghosts. Shades (sorry about that) of Red Grange!

Proctor, Vermont, is near the source of the beautiful marble quarries of the state. The Vermont Marble Exhibit there is quite impressive. So, too, is

Happy Halloween

the eclectic, rambling Wilson Castle. Proctor High School teams are the Phantoms, and it doesn't require a great deal of imagination to envision some of them roaming the halls of the castle on a dark night. Phantoms also rise in Phoenixville, Pennsylvania, and are found at Phoebus High School in Hampton, Virginia—the Phoebus Phantoms has a nice, alliterative ring to it—and at Los Angeles Cathedral High School. The Phantoms of the Cathedral. Again, sounds like a good name for a scary movie.

The Grand Canyon of the Colorado River is truly a national treasure, undeniably one of the world's greatest natural wonders. Hikers who go to the bottom from the rim and up the other side traverse seven difficult miles. They are rewarded by a night's stay at the bottom in the famous Phantom Ranch, not exactly the Ritz-Carlton in accommodation, but a welcome respite in the middle of such efforts. The Grand Canyon High School teams are also the Phantoms.

Salinas, California, was founded in 1856 in the rich Salinas Valley and quickly became a center for the lucrative cattle industry of the area. In 1902 it was the birthplace of one of America's greatest writers, John Steinbeck. Salinas formed the setting for much of two of his greatest novels, *East of Eden* and *Of Mice and Men*. Notre Dame High School in Salinas fields the Spirits. Perhaps the Spirits of Steinbeck himself. Concluding our theme of specters are the Goblins of the marvelously named Wonderview High School in Hattieville in central Arkansas.

More Scary Stuff

The Catskills of New York is Washington Irving territory and many generations have been thrilled and horrified by his "Legend of Sleepy Hollow" and the frightening apparition known as the Headless Horseman. Two Catskills schools have done a marvelous job of carrying this theme forward. Sleepy Hollow High School teams are the Horsemen, presumably fully headed, and the teams from Ichabod Crane High School in Valatie are the Riders.

The Glynn Academy in Brunswick, Georgia, simply calls its teams the

Terrors. You might not wish to encounter the Terrors on the marshes of Glynn.

What would Halloween be without black cats? Every witch should have one. Traditional bringers of bad luck to those unfortunates whose path is crossed by one, the black cat is certainly a force to be reckoned with. Tell that to the opponents of Mexia, Texas, High School whose Blackcats are truly designed to bring misfortune to all those who dare contend with them. Goreville, Illinois, certainly has a Halloweenish sounding name. Their teams? Also the Black Cats. I'm not sure I would wish to schedule a game with them on October 31 either!

Witches

Salem, Massachusetts, was founded in 1626 to take advantage of the fine natural harbor there, not far north of Boston. The site selection was an inspired one and the town became one of the most prosperous in America through fishing and trade. Nathaniel Hawthorne's 1804 birthplace is there, as is the *House of the Seven Gables* that he made so famous in the novel of the same name. He wrote *The Scarlet Letter* while living there. The Salem Maritime Museum is a National Historic Site and the original settlement has been recreated as Pioneer Village. With all of this history it is perhaps a shame that Salem is generally first thought of in conjunction with witchcraft. There was a witchcraft hysteria in Salem in the 1690s. Nineteen women are known to have been hanged or crushed to death during this unfortunate phase. Arthur Miller's play *The Crucible* is based on this period. The people of modern day Salem have not turned their backs on the witchcraft period in their history. Far from it. Today one may explore the Witch Museum on the Salem Common. And of course, there are the Salem High School athletic teams. The Witches.

There is little more central to Halloween than witches, so we must make room for one more. That is in Greenwich, New York. Now what makes better sense than green witches? Remember the line from the movie

Happy Halloween

The Wizard of Oz: "I'll get you my pretty, and your little dog, too!" What color was the Wicked Witch of the East? Green, of course. The Greenwich Witches.

Now, how about the girls' teams? Well, interestingly, they both are the Lady Witches. Then I remembered more of the Wizard of Oz. The beautiful Glinda's first question to Dorothy was, "Are you a good witch or a bad witch?" Of course there are good witches. Like Glinda. And Ozma. And, of course, the girls' teams at Salem and Greenwich high schools.

Go Witches!

21
Some Nasties

SEVERAL SCHOOLS HAVE selected mascots that I would personally find somewhat distasteful. We are a people who like to shock and intimidate our opponents sometimes.

Scorpions and Spiders

Take Sedona, Arizona, for example, one of my very favorite places, nestled as it is in the beautiful red rock area of the state, an art colony, a pleasant place to stay, with the gorgeous Oak Creek Canyon just to the north. Why must their high school teams be the Scorpions?

Tarantulas describe more than one variety of spider. The most poisonous was the European version, in medieval times thought to be the source of a condition called tarantism, a dancing sickness, hence the tarantela. Gabbs, Nevada, is a town of some seven hundred located near Ichthyosaurus State Park, with a high school of only forty-seven students. They live in beautiful country, but they put the Tarantulas on the field.

Concord, North Carolina, was so named in 1775 when the Scottish and German settlers in the area finally decided to try to get along. It was the first place in North America in which gold nuggets were discovered and it was also the first place where placer mining for gold was done. With a history as rich as this, why did they settle for the Spiders for their high school mascot? Let's get the cobwebs out!

Some Nasties

Snakes

Fort Pierce, Florida, is a perfectly delightful place, right on the Atlantic Ocean, with broad, sandy beaches, plenty of golf courses and lots to do all year long. It was originally founded as an army base in 1838 during the Seminole Wars. Today there is a botanical garden in Fort Pierce, a Navy Seals museum, and a manatee observation point. So what does such a delightful place choose to call its high school athletes? The Cobras. Nice. Where is Rikki-Tikki-Tavi when you need him?

Tucumcari, New Mexico, was founded by the Rock Island Railroad in 1901 about 130 miles east of Albuquerque. It was named for a mountain often used as a lookout by the Comanches, which was in turn named for two star-crossed lovers named Tocom and Kari. Today Tucumcari is a town of about seven thousand close to two large reservoirs, the center of many water sports. They have named their high school teams the Rattlers. They probably have plenty of the real ones around, too.

In the Panhandle of northwest Florida, an easy drive to the Rattlesnake Round-Up Grounds near Wigham, Georgia, there is a pleasant suburb of Pensacola called Belleview. There you get the full treatment: their high school teams are the Diamondback Rattlers.

San Luis High School is near Yuma, Arizona. Their teams are the Sidewinders.

There are probably no pythons in New Hampshire, other than perhaps at a zoo. Nevertheless, the Pelham High School teams are called the Pythons, and I am sure they try to squeeze the life out of their opponents. There are also Pythons at the Padeira School in Atlanta, Georgia.

Mineral County High School in Hawthorne, Nevada, is about sixty-five miles southwest of Carson City in pretty rugged terrain. Likewise, Hawthorne is in a valley with a view of 10,500-foot Cory Peak. Walker Lake is just to the northwest of town and the Toyabe National Forest to the south and west. Sounds like a mighty nice place. However, the high school teams are the Serpents.

Go Huskies! Beat Felix the Cat!

Other Pests

Very close to Dallas is the city of Mesquite. Of all the pests that bother me when I am enjoying an otherwise pleasant evening cooking out or relaxing on my deck, the most persistent troublemakers are the mosquitoes. We have long known that they are much more than an irritation, as their bite can cause malaria, Yellow Fever, or West Nile Virus. Opponents, beware of the sting of the Mesquite High School Skeeters!

Progresso, Texas, is located on the Rio Grande River, about fifty miles west of Brownsville. It is a small town with a toll bridge to Rio Bravo, Mexico. If you want to play ball against Progresso High School you may get bitten some. Their teams are the Red Ants.

Fordyce, Arkansas, High School is, among other things, the alma mater of the great football coach who once was reported to have wrestled a bear, the man in the hound's tooth hat, long time headman of the 'Bama Crimson Tide, Bear Bryant. So, why are their teams called the Red Bugs? The story is that long ago the team played a game on the field when it had not been mowed for a considerable period of time (Where are the Fairlawn Cutters when you need them?) Anyway, the tall grass had apparently been infested with chiggers and the players were covered with the nasty red welts left by the bites of those unpopular little nuisances. Hence, the Red Bugs. How about a game between the Red Ants and the Red Bugs? I'm itchy already.

The Scarab was a beetle held sacred by the pharaohs of ancient Egypt. Cleveland East Tech, the high school that produced the Olympic hero Jesse Owens, calls their teams the Scarabs, as does St. Cecelia High School in Nashville, Tennessee.

Lizards

The bite of Gila monsters, the large orange and black lizards that live primarily in the Southwest is extremely poisonous. It is about an hour's

Some Nasties

drive from Phoenix to Gila Bend, Arizona, first west on I-10, then south into the Maricopa Mountains. Gila Bend, founded in 1699 by Father Francisco Kino, is a small town of around 1800 people close to the Gila Bend Indian Reservation. It is in a valley surrounded by mountains: the Sand Tanks, the Painted Rocks, and the Saucedas as well as the Maricopas. Today it is the center for a prosperous farming region. The Gila Bend High School teams are the Gila Monsters.

Dardanelle, Arkansas, is about sixty miles northwest of Little Rock on the Arkansas River. It is near several recreational lakes and the Ozark National Forest. A nice place, plenty of fishing, hunting, hiking and boating opportunities close at hand. The high school teams are the Sand Lizards.

22
LONG GONE . . . OR NEVER WERE

SEVERAL SCHOOLS HAVE taken their inspiration from prehistory, mythology, or more recent excursions into the realm of imagination.

Dragons

Many schools have chosen the dragon, a fearsome, evil beast, usually depicted as a huge, bat-winged, fire breathing scaly lizard or snake with a barbed tail, as their mascot. Such creatures obviously need slaying, just as maidens, which were often placed in the dragon's path in hope of appeasing him, obviously need saving. St. George, for whom the most distinguished order of knighthood in the British Isles is named, is generally credited with having slain at least one, has long been a hero to Englishmen and the English flag is comprised of his cross. Not surprisingly, St. George's School in Newport, Rhode Island, selected the Dragon for their mascot. This logical choice was echoed by another fine

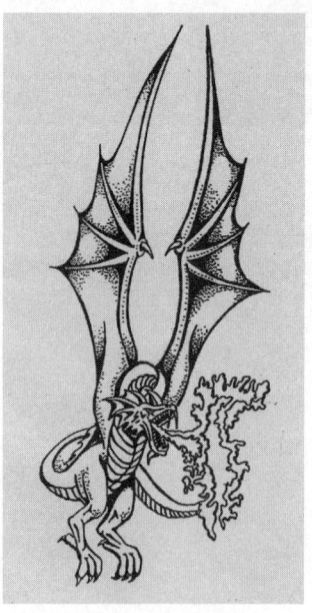

Long Gone... Or Never Were

school across the continent in Spokane, Washington. There also, we find the St. George Dragons.

The distinguished Dana Hall School in Wellesley, Massachusetts, was founded in 1881 by Henry F. Durant, who also founded Wellesley College. From his experience with the latter he had determined that many young women needed further preparation prior to attending college. The first building utilized by the young preparatory school was donated by Charles Dana. According to the Athletic Coordinator at the school the name Dragons (some would say Dragonesses) was adopted as a mascot fairly recently but the dragon had been central to an annual play given by Dana Hall students for many years. Some fourteen years ago a student, dressed in the dragon costume from the play in the school's royal blue rather than the more traditional green, showed up at an athletic event and from then on Dragons have been the nickname of all of the Dana Hall teams.

Pekin, Illinois, near Peoria, was the birthplace of Senator Everett McKinley Dirksen, and in its courthouse a young lawyer named Abraham Lincoln successfully defended the rights of a runaway slave called "Black Nance." There are Dragons at Pekin High School, but this also is a relatively recent development. Pekin's original nickname was the Chinks. This was abandoned in 1980 as being insensitive and inappropriate. People from Pekin tell me that there was never any intention to offend the Chinese by their choice of mascot. The town's name itself came from the fact that the original settlers thought that Peking (now Beijing) was exactly on the other side of the earth from where they were. The Chinese dragon was always the symbol of the school, and, although there was some thought given to selecting the Panda when the change from Chinks was under consideration, Dragon was the final choice. (Across the Illinois River from Pekin is the town of Canton, perhaps also having taken its name in the belief that it was directly opposite China on the globe. The Canton High School teams have been called the Little Giants, however, for as long as I can remember.)

There are not as many dragon slayers around as there are dragons, which has perhaps always been the case, but then one good dragon slayer such as St. George could probably be counted on to handle several dragons

Go Huskies! Beat Felix the Cat!

OTHER MYTHICAL CREATURES

The chimera of Greek mythology, a frightening combination of lion, goat, and snake, was female. It was slain by Bellerophon, son of the god Poseidon, who attacked it on the back of the winged steed, Pegasus. I can find no school whose mascot is Bellerophon, so the Chimeras of Willingboro High School in New Jersey must be slain by other means. One can, however, find the Pegasus' at the Cesar Chavez High School near Phoenix, Arizona.

The wyvern was a fabulous animal usually represented as a two-legged, winged, fire-breathing creature, resembling a dragon. Fortunately, there aren't too many around, but I did find some at Louisville St. Francis and at the Kingswood-Oxford School in Hartford, Connecticut. I could find no wyvern slayers anywhere. But that's probably all right, because the St. Francis Website assures us that Wyverns are not a threat to young maidens.

The griffin, frequently spelled gryphon, is another animal of song and story, typically having the head, forepart and wings of an eagle and the body, hind legs and tail of a lion. There are griffins in many places, including the Phillips Academy, in Exeter, New Hampshire. Gryphons are also a relatively frequently occurring phenomena, showing up at Holy Child Academy in Rye, New York, at Rocky Mount, North Carolina, and at Greenhills High School in Ann Arbor, Michigan, to name three.

Another fabulous animal, the unicorn, is essentially a white horse with a single horn, the hind legs of a stag and the tail of a lion. New Braunfels, Texas, was founded by Germans who sought to establish a colony in the New World in 1845. The

New Braunfels High School teams are the Unicorns. Unicorns have also been selected as the nicknames for the teams representing Keio High School in Purchase, New York, and the Columbus, Ohio, School for Girls.

Centaurs, half man and half horse, supposedly lived in the mountains of Thessaly in Greek mythology. The teams of Culver City, California, High School, Woodstock, Connecticut, Academy, and Buffalo, New York, City Honors High School are all Centaurs.

The legendary phoenix is a bird that supposedly lived for five hundred years, died in fire, then arose again from its own ashes to live another five hundred years. We find the Phoenix today at several schools, including Chicago Quigley and San Antonio, Texas, Health Careers high schools. The Fighting Phoenix are at McMichael High School in Mayodan, North Carolina. In a related choice, Firebirds can be found at the Lawrence, Kansas Free State High School, Scottsdale Chaparral High School in suburban Phoenix, Arizona, and at Phoenix, New York, High School.

American Indians believed the thunderbird to be the source of thunder and lightning. There are also Thunderbirds at several schools, including Zuni, New Mexico, and Anchorage, Alaska, East. An intriguing Thunderbird nickname is that of Edsel Ford High School in Dearborn, Michigan, because that is where the Ford Thunder-birds take the field!

There are Winged Lions at St. Pius High in Pottstown, Pennsylvania, and, very appropriately, at Salt Lake City Rowland Hall-St. Mark's School, reminiscent of the Cathedral of San Marco in Venice, Italy, with its own magnificent winged lions.

over a span of time. When one is needed today, you can find the Dragonslayers at Salt Lake Christian Academy in Sandy, Utah.

And you can find the Hunter Dragons at Ste. Genevieve, Missouri, a fascinating Mississippi River town south of St. Louis, the oldest French settlement in the state, with several well-preserved eighteenth-century buildings.

One of the first men in British legend to utilize the dragon on his shield and escutcheon as a symbol of his strength and daring was King Uther Pendragon. Uther was the father of the legendary King Arthur. Pender, Nebraska, keeps the legend and the glory of chivalry and honor alive. Their teams are the Pendragons.

Greek and Roman Gods

The Greek and Roman pantheons of gods also have not been overlooked. Vulcan, the Roman god of fire and metalworking, has been selected as the team name for Vassar, Michigan, High School. Mercury, the Roman god of speed and messenger of the gods, is the selection of McGregor, Minnesota, High School. Apollo, the Sun god, has been chosen by Houston, Texas, Sharpstown High and by Portland, Oregon, Sunset High.

The Titans, giants who ruled the earth in Greek mythology before the arrival of the Olympian gods, are the mascots and team names of Arcadia high in Greece, New York, Salt Lake City Olympus High School and at the Louisville, Kentucky, Collegiate School. Girls' teams at the latter are known as the Amazons, a race of female warriors in Greek mythology. Arsenal Technical High School in Indianapolis shares its impressive near downtown campus with an historic building that actually was an arsenal for the Union Army during the Civil War. Arsenal Tech teams are the Titans. The Titans are also the team name of T. C. Williams High School in Alexandria, Virginia, made famous by the movie *Remember the Titans*, starring Denzel Washington as the football coach of the recently integrated high school. Palos Verde High School in Tucson was opened in 1962 at about the same

Long Gone ... Or Never Were

time the United States Air Force was installing a number of the nuclear armed Titan missiles in the area. By student vote, the mascot Titans was selected and is depicted as a Greek giant straddling the globe holding a Titan missile and threatening to throw it earthward.

Valkyries

The Valkyries, maidens of the Norse god Odin, were beautiful, strong women, celebrated by Richard Wagner in his opera Die Walkyrie. Who has not thrilled to the musical "Ride of the Valkyries" as they conducted those heroes who had died in battle to eternal glory in Valhalla. Today we find Valkyries at Sacred Heart Academy, Louisville, Kentucky.

The Argonauts

When Jason went on his quest for the Golden Fleece, he recruited an impressive group of heroes to go with him on his hazardous journey. The name of his ship was the Argo and the members of his heroic crew were called the Argonauts. Today we find Argonauts representing the teams at several schools, perhaps most fittingly, at Argo Township High School in Summit, Illinois, a suburb of Chicago where cornstarch with that brand name was produced. (Anthropologists have recently discovered that sheep hides do, in fact, have an affinity for gold particles when placed in fast-moving streams and, when pulled out, are truly golden fleece.)

The Furies

The Furies in Greek and Roman mythologies were three terrible, winged goddesses with serpentine hair who pursued and punished doers of unavenged crimes. Today the Furies roam the playing fields of Forsythe High School in Lewisville, North Carolina.

Nike

On a happier note, Nike (not the shoes) was the Winged Goddess of Victory. A statue of the Winged Victory of Samothrace is beautifully on display at the Louvre, and she is well honored by the athletic teams of Burlington, North Dakota, High School. I must admit this strikes me as one of the better choices from mythology.

The Hodags

Another mythical beast is the hodag. I first became acquainted with the hodag when my boys enjoyed several summers at Camp Deerhorn, on one of the more than two hundred lakes near Rhinelander, Wisconsin. Tales of the hodag caused many a queasy stomach around the campfires in those days, especially when he was occasionally heard tromping and crashing around just beyond the fire's protective light. Bits and pieces of the horned monster had been found in the various forests around town since the 1880s when Rhinelander was a center of logging activity in that part of northern Wisconsin. Soon it was determined that these were merely wood and ox hide, left by the hodag's creator to chill the populace. Today the hodag, in all his glory, may be found on display in the Rhinelander Logging Museum. He may also be seen representing Rhinelander High School whenever the Hodags take the field. Mythical or not, the Hodag is no less fearsome to Rhinelander's opponents.

Lava Bears and Gold Bugs

Bend, Oregon, is a town of 20,500 people, beautifully situated next to the

Long Gone . . . Or Never Were

Deschutes National Forest at an elevation of 3,800 feet, with eye-catching views of the magnificent Cascade Mountain Range. The Cascades were formed by volcanic activity and Bend is just ten miles north of the Lava Lands Visitor Center with its interesting lava formations and myriad trails. Another modern creation is the Lava Bear, mascot of Bend High School, and also, one supposes, as daunting as any from ancient mythology.

For eerie thrills it is hard to beat *Tales of Mystery and Imagination* by Edgar Allan Poe. Fowler, Kansas, and Alva, Oklahoma, are apparently well acquainted with it, because their teams are both known as the Gold Bugs.

Wampus Cats

There is some dispute about just exactly what a Wampus Cat is. In Itasca, Texas, they tell me their Wampus Cat has no definite form. In Conway, Arkansas, however, it is six-legged and blue. The six legs, they say, are four to move with the speed of light, two to fight with all your might. One thing they might both agree on: they'll knock their opponents catty-wampus! I wonder what they would do to each other.

Cartoons

Several schools have selected cartoon characters for their team names and mascots. Let's begin with Elmira in south central New York. The Elmira Southside High School teams are the Green Hornets. Cartoon character or colorful insect? I guess you take your pick.

Madonna High School in Weirton, West Virginia, fields the Red Riders. Red Ryder was a comic book hero I well remember from my youth. Several schools have the Roadrunner as their mascot, including Sacred Heart Academy in Stamford, Connecticut.

Of course the premier cartoon character is the little black mouse created by Walt Disney: "M-I-C-K-E-Y M-O-U-S-E. Mickey Mouse, forever let us hold our banners high!" Yes, Mickey Mouse is the choice of Hallahan Catholic High School in Philadelphia.

Spoofhounds and Zizzers

Maryville, Missouri, is located in the far northwestern part of the state, home in fact, to Northwest Missouri State University. Maryville High School's mascot is a hoax, in part at least. They are the Spoofhounds. Also in Missouri, in the far south central part of the state, is the town of West Plains, close to the Arkansas line. Their team name is another bit of a spoof. They are called the Zizzers. No one at the school seemed to know what a Zizzer is. It was apparently an invented term, conceived by a teacher at the school many years ago, adopted and kept, proudly, right up to the present. The Spoofhounds and the Zizzers from the Show Me State!

Juggernauts

In Erlanger, Kentucky, the Juggernauts are the local high school's choice for their team name. A juggernaut is a massive, inexorable force that crushes everything in its path. Another good pick.

Gremlins

I have never seen a gremlin, but I have certainly seen the results of their presence all too often. Gremlins emerged from the troops in World War II to explain all of those things that go wrong for no apparent reason. Both Notre Dame High School in San Jose, California, and Karis High School in Karis, Pennsylvania, are the Gremlins. Hopefully, what goes wrong happens to their opponents!

Menehunes

The Menehunes, are little people in old Hawaiian lore, similar to fairies and gnomes in Europe. They often live in banyan trees and have been known to

Long Gone... Or Never Were

construct walls and perform other useful tasks at night. Waimea, Hawaii, on the big island, is the headquarters of the Parker Ranch, the largest individually owned ranch in America encompassing 225,000 acres and running a herd of 50,000 head of cattle. The Waimea High School teams are called the Menehunes. There are also Menehunes representing the Moanalua High School in Honolulu.

Martians

Now, I don't believe I have ever seen a Martian, but I would if I went to a game involving Goodrich High School where the Martians play. Goodrich, Michigan, is a small town of less than a thousand, just southeast of Flint.

Wizards and Magicians

From Merlin in King Arthur's Court, to the wonderful little man who defended himself to Dorothy in Oz when she said that he was a "humbug of a wizard and a bad man" by saying that he was "a good man, just a bad wizard," to Harry Potter, wizards have long captured our imagination and inspired our authors.

There are Wizards representing teams from schools on both sides of the continent: West Warwick, Rhode Island, and Washingtonville, New York, in the east and Windsor, California, in the west.

There are Magicians at several schools as well, including Marblehead, Massachusetts, Herkimer, New York, and Minot, North Dakota.

There are the Magic at Monticello, Minnesota and Barberton, Ohio.

Magic City

Colon, Michigan, just north of the Indiana line, bills itself as the Magic Capital of the World. When I asked Ms. Sherry Switzenberger of the high school the reason she was only too pleased to tell me. Years ago the great

215

Jeeps

Three schools have chosen Jeeps as their mascot. I have visited one, Northeast Dubois County High School in southern Indiana. There I met Dr. Keith Seger, who teaches history in the middle school in the town of Dubois. He told me his father, Ralph, was a member of the then Dubois High School basketball team before its consolidation into the county school and it was that team who gathered behind a local church one afternoon to seek a name appropriate to their conception of what they wanted their team to be. "After heated discussion, Jeeps was selected."

From the school's Website:

On March 20, 1936, the comic strip Popeye featured an imaginary little magical character known as Eugene the Jeep, supposedly the eighth wonder of the world.

But what is a Jeep? It's a complicated story and anyone who wants the full treatment should indeed go to the school Website, but, for our purposes, suffice it to say a Jeep is a creature from another dimension with supernatural powers. Back to the Website:

Long Gone ... Or Never Were

Alves J. Kreitzer, a local store owner in Dubois (who would later become the coach of the basketball team) purchased a miniature Jeep in St. Louis, and it became the team mascot. The first game played as Jeeps was played at Shoals on November 6, 1936. The Jeeps won the game 29–21 and went on to establish a 17–4 won-lost record that season. The 1937–38 season brought a mark of 18–5, and the Jeep mascot was here to stay.

Eugene the Jeep is a yellowish cat-like creature.

The only other school in the country that we know of with the JEEP as a mascot is South Webster High School in Ohio.

(However, Wheatland High School, also in southern Indiana, was also called the Jeeps before it was consolidated.)

I have also spoken with the administration at South Webster High School, which is near Portsmouth, Ohio, and they have confirmed that the source for their Jeeps mascot was also the Popeye comic strip.

magician, Harry Blackstone, would bring his troop to Colon for the summers. Blackstone's son actually attended Colon High School. Later, Blackstone's associate started the Abbott Magic Company, still in operation. The school's nickname, however, is not the Magic, as I expected, but the Magi, which at first brought to mind the Biblical story of the Three Kings from the Orient. Not so. The word magus, means wizard, or magician and magi is the plural of magus. The mascot for the Colon High School Magi is a rabbit coming out of a hat.

Dinosaurs

I must confess, with all the attention to the Jurassic age recently, I had expected there to be more references to dinosaurs than I was able to find. A clever one, however, is the Pterodactyl, a flying dinosaur, which has been chosen by the Marvelwood School in Kent, Connecticut. The only other reference I could find was across the country at Price, Utah, Carbon High School. Price is just north of the Cleveland Lloyd Dinosaur Quarry in the Castle Valley. In Price itself is the Prehistoric Museum, and at Price High School the Dinos play.

Saber-toothed Tigers and Mastodons

Saber-toothed Tigers still do roam the earth, around the St. Thomas More Academy, at least, in Champaign, Illinois. The saber-toothed tiger was a fearsome beast, extinct for many thousands of years now, but a true scourge in its time. Mark Randall, from the school, kindly informs me that the athletic teams of the Academy are usually just called the Sabers.

The mastodon was another mighty beast no longer in existence, related to the elephant. But today we can find Mastodons at Alpha, Michigan, High School, very much alive and well and far from extinct.

Long Gone . . . Or Never Were

Leprechauns

Two now-defunct high schools in Kansas belong in this chapter. Each was called St. Patrick, one in Parsons and the other in Walnut. These two towns are less than twenty miles apart in the far southeastern portion of the state. They also each had the same rather charming nickname and mascot, the Leprechaun. Leprechauns still prance in Ohio, at Toledo Central Catholic and Springfield Catholic high schools.

23

TOWN AND GOWN

MANY HIGH SCHOOLS near colleges or with similar names have selected team names related to those colleges.

Wildkits

Earlier I mentioned Wildkits and promised to explain later. This is later. Evanston, Illinois, is a north shore suburb of Chicago, on Lake Michigan, a lovely town, with many lake front mansions and nicely kept older homes throughout. Northwestern University chose Evanston for the site of its beautiful lakeside campus more than 150 years ago, moving northward from the original downtown Chicago location. When Northwestern started fielding athletic teams the name Wildcats was selected. Soon after, its crosstown neighbor, Evanston Township High School, selected the name Wildkits—baby wildcats—for their highly successful teams and so both names have been for these many years.

The Ivies

Farther east is another beautiful town, also located on a lake. Ithaca, New York, is the site of Cornell University, founded in 1865 by Ezra Cornell. Cornell's colors are carnelian and white, and for years her teams have been known as the Big Red. Ithaca High School, again in deference to her cross-

Town and Gown

town neighbor, is known as the Little Red, although I am told that their earlier nickname, in a period when they had some very powerful football teams that shut out many of their opponents, was the Skunks. However, in leaner years, I can see how this nickname could work against you. I guess I prefer Little Red.

Princeton University, the fourth oldest in this country, was founded in 1746. Its impressive Gothic campus is located in a lovely and historic section of New Jersey. Princeton's Tigers played the first intercollegiate football game against intrastate rival Rutgers in 1869. Throughout its storied history the tiger has been an integral part of the university, augmented by the traditional orange (chosen in honor of the Dutch House of Orange) and black jerseys worn by their athletes. Princeton High school teams are the Little Tigers. Princeton High Schools in several other states of the Union, including, Minnesota, Wisconsin, Indiana, and West Virginia, are also the Tigers. In addition, Woodrow Wilson High School in the District of Columbia calls its teams the Tigers. Before he became the twenty-seventh president of the United States, Woodrow Wilson had been the president of Princeton University. Camden High School in New Jersey, not far from Princeton, has dual nicknames, the Tigers and the Prexies.

Columbia University was founded in 1754 under a charter from King George II. The school was originally called Kings College, a name receiving somewhat less favor by the Colonists after 1776. The name Columbia was adopted in 1784, and at about the same time another Kings College was established in Halifax, Nova Scotia, by Loyalists who left the New York campus for the more receptive climate they found in Canada. England must have been forgiven, however, by early in the twentieth century because that

221

Go Huskies! Beat Felix the Cat!

is when Columbia adopted the Lions name for their teams and their lion also became the model for the MGM logo. Columbia Prep in New York City also fields the Lions.

Dartmouth College was founded in 1769 by the Reverend Eleazar Wheelock on the Hanover Plain above the Connecticut River in the wilderness of New Hampshire. His intention was to educate men for the purpose of bringing Christianity to the Indians of the region, thus the college's connection to Indians from its earliest days. For years Dartmouth College teams really had two nicknames, the Big Green, in reference to the distinctive dark forest green uniforms worn by Dartmouth athletes ever since the College's first intercollegiate contest, a baseball game, was played in 1866; and the Indians in reference to the school's original mission. Hanover High School chose Marauders for their nickname. Manchester Central, down the road a bit, chose the Little Green. And even farther away, Dartmouth High School in Massachusetts did, in fact, select the name Indians and has kept that name even though Dartmouth College dropped it in 1972 out of respect for those Native American students who preferred it that way. Deerfield, Massachusetts, also settled in 1769 down the Connecticut River Valley from Hanover, New Hampshire, is a stunningly attractive place with many seventeenth-century homes. Deerfield Academy, whose campus adjoins historic Old Deerfield, outfits its teams in dark green and calls them the Big Green.

Although Yale University, founded in 1701, is certainly one of America's treasured institutions of higher learning, I could find no evidence that any of the New Haven high schools had picked up on that by choosing the Bulldog as their mascot. However, the towns of Yale, in Michigan and Oklahoma, and New Haven, Indiana, have all done so. Yale, North Carolina, however decided upon the Tiger for their mascot, a somewhat schizophrenic selection it would seem.

Harvard is the oldest university in the United States and certainly takes

Town and Gown

its place among the finest institutions of higher education in the world. It was founded in 1636, just sixteen years after the Pilgrims first landed at Plymouth. A site on the Charles River just west of Boston was selected and the town was named Cambridge after the oldest university in England. In spite of this prestigious position, no high school anywhere seems to have selected Cantabs, as Harvard did in recognition of its location, or even the Johns as they are sometimes called in honor of their founder, John Harvard. However, Harvard is also often referred to as the Crimson, a nickname proudly worn by nearby Everett High School's highly successful athletic teams.

The Midwest

Iowa has several fine state schools, two of the most prominent being the University of Iowa in Iowa City and Iowa State University in Ames. The Iowa teams are known as the Hawkeyes and the Iowa City High School teams are the Little Hawks. Similarly, Iowa State teams are the Cyclones and the Ames High School teams are the Little Cyclones.

In Omaha, Nebraska, Creighton University teams are called the Blue Jays, and the teams at Creighton Prep the Little Jays. In Rockhurst, Missouri, a suburb of Kansas City, Rockhurst College teams are the Hawks and Rockhurst High School teams the Hawklets. Greencastle, Indiana, is the home of DePauw University, an excellent medium sized liberal arts school. Their teams are the Tigers. Across town at Greencastle High are found the Tiger Cubs. Franklin College in nearby Franklin, Indiana, another fine liberal arts school, a bit smaller than DePauw, is represented by the Grizzlies and Franklin High School, home of the storied "Wonder Five" teams of Indiana Basketball Tournament fame, by the Grizzlie Cubs.

Minnesota is justifiably proud of the University in Minneapolis and its Golden Gophers. The town of Cook, Minnesota, some miles north of the Twin Cities, has named its high school teams the Little Gophers.

The University of Illinois has its main campus in Urbana. Illinois teams have long been known as the Fighting Illini, led by mascot Chief Illiniwek,

CHICAGO

The University of Chicago once fielded powerful football teams under the leadership of their legendary coach, Amos Alonzo Stagg. The Maroons were founding members and frequent champions of the Big Ten, or, as it was then known, the Western Conference, and their tailback, Jay Berwanger, was the first Heisman Trophy winner. The University of Chicago was founded by John D. Rockefeller whose intention was to create a world class private college in the Midwest. The location chosen was the old Midway of the 1892 Columbian Exposition World's Fair on Chicago's South Side. The Chicago teams were truly the "Monsters of the Midway" long before George Halas brought the Decatur Staleys to Chicago and gave the city their beloved Bears. Those days are long past, following the de-emphasis of intercollegiate athletics by president Robert Maynard Hutchins in the late thirties. Interestingly, Stagg Field on the University's campus was the site of the first sustained nuclear reaction as part of the nation's Manhattan Project during World War II. When I was in high school I remember how nervous we were playing soccer against the University High School teams, also the Maroons, in the shadow of Stagg Field. Was there still radiation in the area? We were assured there was not, but who knew? Now Stagg Field is gone and Chicago teams compete in Division III, doing quite well there.

On the north side of Chicago, beautifully situated right on Lake Michigan, is Loyola University, the Ramblers, whose basketball team under coach George Ireland won the NCAA Championship in 1961 with a stunning overtime victory over the University of Cincinnati Bearcats. Loyola Academy in nearby Wilmette is also known as the Ramblers.

Town and Gown

whose authentic dance is the highlight, albeit somewhat controversial, of many a halftime in Memorial Stadium or University Hall. Urbana University High teams are the Illineks.

At one time the main shops of the Monon Railroad were located in Lafayette, Indiana, near the West Lafayette campus of Purdue University. In those days Purdue played Wabash College in Crawfordsville. The Wabash Little Giants fans were suspicious that some of the Purdue players might not have really been students at all and they accused them of being boilermakers for the railroad. Well, sure enough, Purdue liked that and they have been the Boilermakers ever since. Hail Purdue! Go Boilers! There are no Boilermakers in West Lafayette other than those wearing the old gold and black of Purdue, but not too far away, just across the Illinois line, are the Boilermakers of Bradley-Bourbonnais High School. Perhaps their players helped build boilers for the Illinois Central Railroad that ran through their towns.

Indiana State University is located in Terre Haute near the banks of the Wabash River, well remembered in native son Paul Dresser's song "Back Home Again in Indiana":

> *And it seems that I can see*
> *The gleaming candle light*
> *Still shining bright,*
> *Through the sycamores, for me. . . .*
> *When I dream about the moonlight on the Wabash,*
> *Then I long for my Indiana home.*

Indiana State University has chosen the Sycamores as its team name. The ISU Lab School, now closed, was known as the Young Sycamores.

The origins of the team name of St. Louis University Billikens are somewhat obscure. It is clear that the first Billiken was an imaginary little creature invented by a cartoonist early in the twentieth century, which for a while was a popular fad spawning toys and novelties. Someone, probably a sportswriter, apparently said the St Louis teams played like Billikens, or looked like them, or their coach did, or something, but anyway the name stuck. St. Louis University High is known as the Little Bills.

Marquette University in Milwaukee has gone through several team names. Initially they were known as the Hilltoppers, but that was considered too passive and a search for a new name and mascot resulted in the name Warriors. Shortly thereafter a student named Greg Huyette, later to become a valued friend and business colleague of mine, dressed himself up in an Indian costume and the mascot Willie Wampum was born. Both the nickname and the mascot were subsequently dropped and the university's teams are now known as the Golden Eagles. However, Marquette University High School teams remain the Hilltoppers.

The South

In New Orleans, Tulane University, founded in 1834, is a fine educational institution located in the beautiful Garden District of the city. Today Tulane's teams are known as the Green Wave, and their symbol is a breaking wave in the school's attractive blue and green colors. In an earlier era, however, they were represented by a strange little creature on a surf board called a Greenie. The name Greenie still exists at Isadore Newman High School in New Orleans, alma mater of Peyton Manning, the great quarterback for the Indianapolis Colts.

In Tallahassee is Florida A&M University, where retired President Fred Humphreys, a giant of a man both physically and intellectually, did such an impressive job of building the educational stature of the school, whose teams are called the Rattlers; FAMU High School's teams are the Baby Rattlers. The buttons?[1]

Grambling, Louisiana, is the home of the famous Grambling University Tigers whose longtime coach, Eddie Robinson, brought gridiron glory to the campus and sent numerous football players on to even greater success in

---

[1] See the section on clothing!

Town and Gown

the National Football League. Nearby, Grambling University High School teams are the Kittens.

Here are some other examples:

- The University of Hawaii Rainbow Warriors and the Honolulu University High School Little Bows
- The Penn State Nittany Lions and the State College High School Little Lions
- State University in Indiana (Pennsylvania) Indians and the local high school Little Indians
- The Washington and Jefferson University Presidents and the Washington High School Little Prexies
- The Duquesne University (Pittsburgh) Dukes and the Duquesne, Pennsylvania, High School Dukes
- The University of Pennsylvania Quakers and Philadelphia's William Penn Charter High School Quakers
- Florida State University and FSU High are the Seminoles (a name adopted, I am told, with the full blessing of the tribe)
- Eastern Tennessee State University in Johnson City is known as the Buccaneers while nearby ETSU High School are the Bucs

In Atchison, Kansas, are the Benedictine College Ravens, the Maur Hill Prep Little Ravens, and the Mt. St. Scholastica High School Lady Ravens. Shades of Edgar Allan Poe.

Louisiana State University is located in Baton Rouge. The LSU teams are known variously as the Tigers, or the Bayou Bengals. Locally, the Dunham School teams are the Tigers, and the Blair High School teams are the Bengals.

Southern University, also in Baton Rouge, has named its teams the Jaguars while the Southern University Laboratory School teams are called the Kittens.

Lindsborg, Kansas, is a charming town, very proud of its Swedish heritage. Bethany College there is known as the Swedes and Lindsborg High as the Vikings.

Nearby are the McPherson College Bulldogs and the McPherson High School Bullpups.

Finally we have Boston College and BC High School Eagles.

Notre Dame

The University of Notre Dame was founded in South Bend, Indiana, in 1842. One of the most beautiful campuses anywhere, Notre Dame is known for the Golden Dome and an enviable record of success on the gridiron as well as for the high quality of its educational offerings. There are few experiences more fun for a football fan than to attend one of Notre Dame's home games on a crisp autumn Saturday afternoon under a bright sun with a cloudless blue sky (or, as Grantland Rice saw it: "Under a cold gray November sky...") overhead. Whatever the weather, as a part of the magnificent pageantry before the game, the band is led onto the field by an honor guard of tall young men in Irish kilts and fur hats, the stirring Fight Song "Shakes down the thunder from the skies," the Leprechaun prances, the cheerleaders do a jig, and the team streams out of the tunnel to the cheers of the great crowd. Win or lose, it's a great day! Although no high school in South Bend has selected Fighting Irish for their nickname, many schools all around the country have, including Notre Dame Highs in Chattanooga, Tennessee, and in Lawrenceville, New Jersey.

Thomasville, Georgia

One last word on town and gown, from a slightly different perspective. In the early days of the railroad, the trains from northern cities such as Cleveland and Chicago terminated in Thomasville rather than going down to Florida as Henry Flagler's railroad would make possible sometime later. As a consequence many northerners took extended winter vacations there,

Town and Gown

some building palatial estates for the purpose. The town is nicely preserved, the Rose Garden is world renowned, and the environs are very attractive, particularly what is known as Plantation Row. There are two high schools in Thomasville, one named after the town, the other for Thomas County. There are also two prominent state schools in Georgia, the University at Athens, whose teams are called the Bulldogs, and Georgia Tech, in Atlanta, the Yellowjackets. These are also the nicknames of the two high schools in town, making their rivalry a microcosm of the state.

24
THE GIRLS TAKE THE FIELD

ONE OF THE greatest developments in all of sports in America has been the advent of organized interscholastic and intercollegiate sports for girls and young women. Not only has this been good for the many participants, but it has also been fun for spectators as the fifteen thousand-plus fans at the Indiana girls' state basketball tournament, among other examples, bears witness.

Coed Schools

In many cases the girls' teams came about forty or fifty years after team names and had been selected and established for the boys' teams. Thus, it is very common that, if the boys' teams were known as the "Blanks," the girls' teams became either the "Lady Blanks," or the "Blankettes," at those schools or even merely used the same nicknames without feminizing them. However, that has not always been the case. In fact, there are some extremely clever nicknames for girls' teams around the country, some at coeducational institutions, some at all girls schools. Let me begin with those combinations of boys' and girls' teams at the same school that are particularly fun. (My personal favorite I am saving for later. If you must peek, check out Centralia, Illinois, in the End Game chapter.)

One of my favorites is from Alaska, the town of Metlakatla, located on Annette Island in the far southeastern part of the state. The town was founded in 1887 by an Anglican missionary and four hundred Tsimshian Indians who had migrated there from Canada, naming their new town after the one they had left. The boys' teams at Metlakatla High School are the Chiefs. The girls' teams are the Miss Chiefs.

Moving to Iowa, the town of Liberty Center, south of Des Moines, we find another nickname that appeals to me. There, the boys' teams are the Comets, the girls' teams are the Belles. Thus, when the girls take the court the fans are cheering for the Liberty Belles.

In Monroe, Michigan, at St. Mary's High School, the boys' teams are the Falcons. The girls' teams are the Kestrels. The kestrel is America's smallest falcon. Interestingly enough, as I learned on a recent visit to the fascinating Vermont Raptor center near Woodstock, the females of the falcon family are generally much bigger than the males, the female peregrine usually fully one third larger than her male counterpart.

In Enka, North Carolina, near Asheville and the exquisite Biltmore Estate and Gardens, the boys' teams are the Jets. I love the girls' nickname: the Sugar Jets.

Another pairing that I find attractive is to be found in the pleasantly named town of Comfort, near San Antonio. In Comfort the boys' teams are the Bobcats, but the girls' teams are the Deers.

Several schools have had boys' teams with horses of some kind as their team identifier, sometimes Mustangs, sometimes Broncos, Colts, or Chargers, and the girls' teams have often been the lady version of the same. There is, I think, a better solution, more imaginative. Barrington, Illinois, a northwestern suburb of Chicago, is an example of Broncos, and their girls' teams are the Fillies. Similarly, other hooved pairings include:

Casper, Wyoming, the Mustangs and the Fillies
Colstrip, Montana, the Colts and the Fillies
Willow Creek, Montana, the Broncos, and the Bronco Ponies
Yankton, South Dakota, the Bucks and the Gazelles.

And some other good pairings:

Bunker Hill High School in southern Illinois fittingly selected the

Minutemen for their nickname. The girls' teams are delightfully the Minute Maids. Orange juice, anyone?

In Chicago, Washington's Minutemen have been joined by the Minutewomen. Also in Chicago, Dunbar High's boys' teams were known for years as the Mighty Men. Now the girls teams are the Mighty Women.

In Flora, in southern Illinois, the Wolves have been joined by the Wolf Gals. Sounds more like fauna than flora to me.

At the marvelously named town of Ladysmith in the vast forests of northern Wisconsin, the boys' teams have long been known as the Lumberjacks and the girls' teams are now the Lumberjills.

At Lakeview, Nebraska, High School, the boys' teams are called the Vikings, due in part to the Scandinavian heritage of the town. Now the girls' teams are the Viqueens.

Another favorite of mine is in Cairo, Illinois. Cairo is right at the junction of the Ohio and Mississippi rivers and has a storied history of river boating. In 1837 it is reported that more than thirty-seven hundred steamboats docked at Cairo. The boys' teams of Cairo High School have been known as the Pilots for many years. More recently the girls' teams have become the Co-pilots for their male counterparts. In a similar vein, the Pirates of Valmeyer High School, also in Illinois, on the Mississippi River south of St. Louis, have been joined by the First Mates.

Chicago's South Shore High School, as befits its lakeside location, selected Tars as their nickname years ago. When the girls needed a nickname, they chose Tarettes.

Southern High School in Stronghurst, Illinois, has two interesting nicknames. The school was the second consolidation in Henderson County, a narrow stretch along the Mississippi River with a population of eighty-five hundred. The first was in Biggsville, in the northern part of the county. This consolidation was named Union High School and they selected Yanks, fittingly enough for their nickname. Southern, sensing the rivalry that was bound to develop between the two schools located some nine miles apart on Illinois Route 94, equally appropriately selected Rebels for theirs, thus leading the way to numerous reprises of the Civil War over the years

The Girls Take the Field

It takes two

Fort Sumner, New Mexico, the Foxes and the Vixens.

Sutton, New York, the boys' teams are the Sammies, and the girls' teams are the Suzies.

Pleasant Hill, Missouri, the Roosters and the Chicks.

In Nashville, Illinois, the Hornets have been joined by the Hornettes.

Ronan, Montana, just south of beautiful Flathead Lake, the Chiefs and the Maidens.

Jourdanton, Texas, the Indians and the Squaws.

Waynesboro, Pennsylvania, the Indians and the Maidens.

West Sudbury, Pennsylvania, Moniteau High School, the Warriors and the Squaws.

Crescent City, Illinois, the Golden Eagles and the Golden Girls

North Harrison High School in Ramsey, Indiana, the Cougars and the Lady Cats.

Avon Lakes, Ohio, the Shoremen and the Shoregals.

Christopher, Illinois, the Bearcats and the Lady Cats.

Clarion, Pennsylvania, the Bobcats and the Lady Cats.

Lovejoy, Illinois, the Wildcats and the Wildkittens.

Falfurrias, Texas, the Bulls, and, no, not the Cows—the Belles.

Carthage, Illinois, the Blueboys and the Bluegirls.

West Philadelphia, the Speedboys and the Speedgirls.

Poteet, Texas, High School, the Aggies and the Agates.

Archbishop Ryan High School in Philadelphia, Pennsylvania, the Raiders and the Ragdolls.

Ridgefield, Washington, the Spudders and the Sweet Potatoes.

whenever the two Henderson County schools met on the athletic field. When it was time to add girls' teams to the mix there was much discussion about what their nickname should be. Finally Belles was settled upon, making them the Southern Belles.

In Hawaii, the entire island of Lanai was bought in 1922 by James Dole. Although attempts to grow sugar cane on the island had been made by Europeans as early as 1802 with limited success, Dole had a different idea. Pineapples. His idea met with great success and today most of the island's inhabitants have jobs involving pineapples. More than one million pineapples per day are loaded into ships to leave the island. Every day. The Lanai High School teams recognize this. The boys' teams are called Pinelads and the girls' teams are the Pinegals.

All-Girls Schools

Up to this point I've been dealing entirely with girls' nicknames at coed schools that fielded boys' teams, in most cases, before they had girls' teams. How about names chosen by all girls schools? Here again, I'm sure I don't have them all, but there are some very clever ones among those I do have.

One of my favorites is that of the Buffalo, New York, Seminary. They are the Sem-Sirens. One definition of sirens is temptingly beautiful women, but a second, from mythology, refers specifically to temptresses who lured sailors onto rocky shoals.

Another favorite, full of life and originality, are the Vivettes of Visitation Academy in St. Louis. Also in the St. Louis area are two rival Catholic girls high schools with intriguing nicknames. Webster Grove's Nerinx Hall teams are the Markers. Why? Because Nerinx girls make their mark wherever they go. Their biggest rival, albeit a friendly one, is Ursuline Academy. The Ursuline teams are officially the Bears, but the Nerinx girls often refer to them as the Liners. So whenever they play it's the Markers versus the Liners. Toe that mark! Hold that line! Tote that barge! Lift that bale!

Many of the all girl schools have selected somewhat milder team names and mascots than their male counterparts. Like these: The Daisies of the

The Girls Take the Field

Dallas, Texas, Hockaday School, and the Honeybears of Harpeth Hall in Nashville, Tennessee. Maria High School in Chicago is represented by the Mystics, while the Skylarks and Doves fly at San Antonio, Saint Francis, and Covington, Louisiana, Saint Scholastica respectively. Three schools in Philadelphia with mild team names are the Bambis of Saint Hubert, the Lambs of Saint Maria Goretti, and the Pandas of Nazareth Academy. Not to be taken too seriously are the Jesters of Saint Joseph's High School in Lakewood, California. In New York City at Saint Jean Baptiste High School are the Jewels. The Angels of Buffalo Holy Angel Academy and Miss Hall's School in Pittsfield, Massachusetts, round out this section.

Certainly, not all of the girls schools have mild nicknames. Noteworthy exceptions:

Valkyries of Louisville, Kentucky, Sacred Heart.
White Bears of the Baldwin School in Bryn Mawr, Pennsylvania.
Panthers of Brooklyn Catherine McAuley.
Bruisers of Chattanooga, Tennessee, Girls Prep.
Gators of Mother Guerin, River Grove, Illinois.
Pride of Queen of Peace, Burbank, Illinois.
Sting of Seton Academy, South Holland, Illinois.
Fighting Tigers of Immaculate Heart of Mary, Westchester, Illinois.

And in Chicago:

Mighty Macs of Mother McAuley.
Marauders of Madonna.
Cougars of Josephenium.
Lions of Lourdes.
Panthers of Notre Dame.
Stingers of Saint Scholastica.

Turning our attention to New York, Staten Island Notre Dame teams are also the Cougars while Buffalo Mount Mercy Academy fields the Magic.

235

Go Huskies! Beat Felix the Cat!

Opponents of Mount Saint Mary's in Kenmore hear the Thunder, shaken down from the skies, no doubt. Brooklyn's Fontbonne Hall Academy fields the Elephants and their neighbors at Our Lady of Perpetual Peace teams are the Dolphins. Dobbs Ferry is on the Hudson River north of New York City: the teams of Our Lady of Victory Academy there are simply called Victory.

Sag Harbor was founded in 1707. In 1789 the United States Congress determined that there would be two principal ports of entry into the country. These were designated as New York City and Sag Harbor. Sag Harbor developed into the principal whaling port on Long Island and became quite prosperous. As befits such a nautical environment, the all girls Catholic high school in town is called Stella Maris—Star of the Sea—and their teams are the Flippers.

Oldenburg Academy is located in a charming southeastern Indiana town known for its beautiful spires. The town is well worth a visit, but perhaps not on certain spring days as it is in an area sometimes referred to by Hoosiers as "tornado alley." The Oldenburg Academy teams (now coed) are appropriately called the Twisters.

In Honolulu, Hawaii, there are three girls high schools worthy of mention: Saint Andrews Priory teams are called the Priory Pride, Saint Francis fields the wonderfully and uniquely named Troubadours, and La Pietra Academy is represented by teams known as the Kaimana, a native word meaning Diamonds. What a great choice for a school practically in the shadow of beautiful Diamond Head!

Bryn Mawr High School in Baltimore has a nickname that has a special appeal to me: they are the Mawrtians. Saint Mary's High School in Inglewood, California, has a nickname that rings particularly true. They are the Belles, so their teams are the Belles of Saint Mary's, which I think would make Bing Crosby proud. Mount Saint Mary's, in Little Rock, Arkansas, has also selected Belles as their nickname.

My final selection in this category is that of Rosary High school in Aurora, Illinois, a suburb of Chicago. Although their official nickname is the Royals, *The Chicago Tribune* frequently refers to them as the Beads.

25
Indian Team Names

If Columbus had known that there was a continent between his New World and the Indian subcontinent he would not have referred to the natives he found there as "Indians" and we might now be referring to them by some other, perhaps more appropriate name. Some prefer "Native American," but others think that should be reserved for all people who were born here. Whatever they are called, however, should be said with dignity and respect, and, we might still have the issue in front of us as to the propriety of using any mascot or team name that is racially specific to define the names of the teams we cheer for.

The argument for doing so, in most cases, revolves around the concept that no one actually chooses a team nickname that they consider to be pejorative. Surely Notre Dame does not denigrate the Irish by selecting "Fighting Irish" as their mascot. So, the argument goes, how can Illinois be seen to denigrate Indians by selecting the "Fighting Illini" as theirs? Those opposed say that by doing so you stereotype us as a group and that interferes with your ability to know us as individuals.

Clearly Indiana University does not insult its residents by calling their teams the "Hoosiers" nor does the University of Oklahoma do so to its citizenry by choosing "Sooners" as their nickname. Equally clearly, however, Indiana's student body contains a preponderance of Hoosiers, Oklahoma's many, many Sooners, and Notre Dame's at least a liberal sprinkling of persons of Irish ancestry whereas the University of Illinois has relatively few tribal members in its classes. Notre Dame, Indiana, and Oklahoma have, if not formal consent from those whom they have chosen as their mascot, at least implied consent, but Illinois, perhaps, does not. The argument rages.

When schools as prestigious as Dartmouth College, Stanford University, Miami University, and others go to the trouble of changing their mascots from something involving at least a reference to Indians, it is reasonable to pause at the very least and ask why. My personal experience with Indians has been somewhat limited, but those I have known have actually been proud to be associated with places like Dartmouth, which, particularly, has a pronounced Indian heritage dating from the College's founding in 1769. I once was dining with my wife at the restaurant in Mesa Verde National Park and I happened to have a Dartmouth baseball cap on when I arrived. The hostess who seated us was an Indian, I'm not sure which tribe, probably either Navajo or Ute. At any rate, she asked about my connection to Dartmouth. When I told her I was an alumnus with degrees in Engineering and Business she told us that she had been accepted to

> **IT HAS** also recently come to my attention that some students at the University of Northern Colorado in Greeley (whose intercollegiate athletic teams are the Bears) have established an intramural team known variously as the Fighting Whites, or the Fightin' Whities. This they say they have done both to have a little fun as well as to call attention to the issue of stereotyping that emerges when a racial nickname is used to portray an athletic team, however well intentioned. There are both Caucasian and Indian students on this intramural team and the questioned begged by this development is How do I, as a white male, or other Caucasians in general, react to a team called the Fightin' Whities? Are we honored? Amused? Annoyed?

Indian Team Names

Dartmouth and hoped to major in Engineering Science. This pleased me immensely and of course I congratulated her and welcomed her into the Dartmouth family. I eventually asked her if she knew our mascot had once been the Indians and that it no longer was and what did she favor. Her ready response was that she thought it was great to have the Indian mascot and she wished we had not dropped it, but she could understand why some people might object to it. When I asked her the mascot of her high school she said they were the Chieftains, so maybe she was Navajo from Shiprock, Arizona.

Anyway, the Indian mascots are ubiquitous in this country at the high school level and, although there is a move afoot to banish all such references in at least New York State, I think it will be some time before it is done, if ever, everywhere. Interestingly enough, I very recently met a Seneca from near Binghamton, New York, who told me quite forthrightly that he had no objection to Indian mascots for any teams as long as they did not use caricatures in their portrayal.

The use of the Indian mascot is an important segment of our quest to determine who we are. Perhaps a good place to start in our exploration of Indian-related mascots is in the West, with the Tribal Schools themselves. Many Tribal Schools, in fact, proudly use Indian mascots for their teams, and I doubt if anyone would seriously object to that. Here are some:

> The Santa Fe Indian School calls its teams the Braves and the Ladie Braves.
> The Ethete, Wyoming Indian High School teams are the Chiefs.
> The Salem Oregon, Chemawa Indian School also fields the Braves as does the Sherman Indian School in Riverside, California.
> The Kickapoo Nation School in Powhattan, Kansas, has selected Warriors as their team name while in Ft. Hall, Idaho, the Sho Ban School calls their teams the Chiefs.

The state of South Dakota has several Indian schools. In Flandreau are the Indians, in Marty the Braves, and in St. Francis the Warriors. The Chieftains represent the Crow Creek Reservation High School in Stephan.

Go Huskies! Beat Felix the Cat!

I particularly like the team name chosen by the Tiospa Zina Tribal School. They are the Wamdis, which means Eagles in their language. In Vernal, Utah, is Uintah High School, home of the Utes.

Many Navajos live in the Four Corners area of New Mexico, a culture well described in the enjoyable novels of Tony Hillerman. Tohajilee High School in Canon City fields the Navajo Warriors and Shiprock offers the Chieftains, as mentioned previously. Shiprock is a wonderful place to stay as a taking off point for viewing the spectacular scenery in the area including the impressive monolith that looms from the desert like a clipper ship from the sea thereby giving the town its name. At Fort Defiance Window Rock High School, just over the line into Arizona but still within the Navajo Reservation, are the Fighting Scouts and at Teec Nos Pos Red Mesa High School, even closer to Shiprock, are the Redskins. Just to the south, and back in New Mexico, are the Zuni High School Thunderbirds. We stopped at the Zuni Pueblo on our way to the fascinating "Sky City" of the Acoma Pueblo, rearing itself 357 feet high on a precipitous mesa. Acoma comes from the Indian words "ako" for "white rock" and "ma" for "people." Coronado described it in 1540 as the best defensive position in the world. A New World Masada, perhaps. Anyway, it is a spectacular place with its many adobes and the impressive church of San Esteban Rey, completed in 1641.

Farther south in Arizona is the Fort Apache Indian Reservation. Fort Thomas High School, on the Gila River at the southern edge of the reservation, has aptly named its athletic teams the Apaches. A bit west of there is Ajo, near the Papago Indian Reservation. The Ajo teams are the Red Raiders. Bullhead City is in far western Arizona, near the Nevada and California state lines. Located in the Mohave Indian Reservation the Bullhead City Mohave High School teams are the Thunderbirds. Tuba City is near the Hopi Reservation in north central Arizona. My niece, a nurse, and her husband, a physical therapist, spent several rewarding years in Tuba City ministering to the health needs of the Hopis and Navahos of the area. The Tuba City High School teams are the Warriors.

Jim Thorpe was chosen in 1950 by vote of sportswriters and broad-

Indian Team Names

casters as the greatest American athlete of the first half of the twentieth century. He was also an American Indian of the Sauk and Fox tribes. Born in the Oklahoma Territory in 1888 he burst on the national scene while playing football for the Carlisle, Pennsylvania, Indian College. Coached by the legendary Glenn "Pop" Warner, Thorpe's Carlisle teams took on the best teams the country had to offer, winning the lion's share of those games. Thorpe was declared an All American by Walter Camp in both 1911 and 1912. He was also an accomplished track and field star. At the Stockholm Olympic games in 1912 he won Gold Medals in both the Pentathlon and Decathlon, a truly incredible accomplishment. The Decathlon winner alone of any Olympics is often described as the world's greatest athlete, and it is quite probable that Jim Thorpe was indeed that in 1912 at the very least. However, football and track and field were not the sum total of Thorpe's remarkable athletic abilities. From 1913 until 1919 he was a Major League outfielder with the New York Giants, Cincinnati Reds and the Boston Braves. He returned to football in 1919, playing professionally for eight years in what would become the National Football League. Although his medals from the Olympics were stripped from him because of what today would not have been considered a problem, they have finally been restored and his name is once again deservedly in the Olympic Record Book. In his memory, two towns in Pennsylvania have merged and renamed themselves Jim Thorpe. The nickname they have chosen for their teams? The Olympians. Also in memory of this wonderfully gifted yet tragic American Indian athlete are the teams representing Pine Ridge High School in South Dakota. They are proudly called the Thorpes.

Many tribes are specifically honored by high schools around the country. Some examples:

- In San Antonio, that historic city of the Alamo and with the beautiful Canal Walk, is Sam Houston High School, home of the Cherokees.
- New Hampton, Iowa, and Blytheville, Arkansas are represented by the Chickasaws.

Go Huskies! Beat Felix the Cat!

West Tallahotchie High School in Webb, Mississippi, fields the Choctaws.
Somerville, Texas, teams are the Yequas.
Shawsville, Virginia, High School teams are the Shawnees.
In Doylestown, Ohio, at Chippewa High School, are the Chipps.

Watkins Glen is located in the Finger Lake region of upper New York State. There is a spectacular gorge with dramatic waterfalls flowing through the center of the village and into Lake Seneca, named after the Seneca Tribe, which is still very prominent in south central New York. The teams representing Watkins Glen High School are the Senecas.

The Apaches are known in part because they were fierce warriors, brave, proud, and skilled horsemen. The names of their chiefs are legendary in American history: Cochise, Geronimo, Victorio. It is not surprising that many schools have chosen to identify themselves with these brave men. Apaches are found representing Vallejo, California, and, in Booker, Texas, are the Kiowas, a subgroup of the Apache nation.

Mohawk, New York, teams are the Mohicans.
Shoshone, Idaho, fields the Indians.

The towns of Seminole, Comanche and Cherokee, all in Texas, call their teams the Indians. North Miami High School in Denver, Indiana, teams are the Warriors.

The Comanches, a powerful tribe of Southwestern plains Indians and one of the first tribes to obtain horses from the Spaniards and to breed them has bequeathed its name to Canyon High School in Anaheim, California.

The wonderful writings of Louise Erdrich grant significant insight into the history and present day plight of the Lakota Sioux, a tribe that once dominated the area now occupied by North and South Dakota. Several schools in these states honor the Sioux as their mascot. These include Solen, Stanton and Westhope in North Dakota, and Wakpala, South Dakota.

Honoring another tribe is the town of Iroquois, South Dakota, whose teams are the Chiefs, while Iroquois High School in Pennsylvania fields the Braves.

Indian Team Names

Roger City, Michigan, teams are the Hurons.

Pontiac, Michigan, leant its name to a famous automobile and their high school teams are the Chiefs.

Several towns in Oklahoma are deserving of mention. The first is the town of Cherokee. The Cherokees were originally located in the Southeast portion of the country and their tragic move to the Oklahoma Territory was aptly named the "Trail of Tears." The town of Cherokee calls their high school teams the Chiefs. In Calumet, deriving its name from a tribe originally from the Chicago area, are the Chieftains while the town of Comanche fields the Indians as does Mohawk High School in Marcola. In Rogue River we find the Chieftains and the Indians represent Scapoose. In Seminole, named for another Southeastern tribe generally identified with what is now Florida, are the Chieftains. Sequoyah High School in the town of Tahlequah also fields the Indians and Tecumseh, named for the valiant Shawnee Chief, who might properly object were he able to, calls their teams the Savages.

Pocahontas, Virginia, also uses Indians as their nickname, in honor of the beautiful Indian princess whose name was given to their town.

Shamans were, of course, Indian medicine men, and we have learned through recent pharmaceutical reasearch that many of their treatments and nostrums have validity today. Shamans is the team name for the high schools in Chefurnak and Caputnuaq, Alaska.

The word Sachem was frequently used instead of chief by certain tribes, primarily those originally in the Northeast. Laconia, New Hampshire, located in a beautiful part of a beautiful state, calls their teams the Sachems as does Rahm High School in Hebron, Connecticut.

Piqua is a town of twenty thousand people in western Ohio, built on the site of a one time important Miami Indian village. In 1780 the Shawnees took control of the area and the word Piqua is derived from a Shawnee creation myth meaning "A man formed out of the ashes." Piqua High School teams are known as the Indians.

Carrollton is a town of three thousand people in eastern Ohio. It was the home of the Fighting McCooks, a family that had sixteen men who fought with the Union army in the Civil War. Their house, on the south edge of the village square, is now a Civil War Museum. Perhaps the nickname Warriors for Carrollton High School may have something to do with the McCooks, but the full-feathered chief's headdress on the sign at the edge of town leads me to believe otherwise.

Illinois, itself an Indian name as derived from the French (home of the Illini), had several other tribes also located within what is now its borders. The Sequoits are now representing Antioch, a town located on the far northern shore of Lake Michigan, near Wisconsin. At almost the opposite end of the state is Collinsville, a suburb of St. Louis, located near the well-preserved Kahokia Mounds. Collinsville High School teams are the Kahoks. At Iroquois West High School in Gilman are the Raiders and at Nokomis in the center of the state, a small town with a recent State Champion girls' basketball team, are the Redskins. Lemont, near Chicago, fields the Injuns, a mascot perhaps on the fringe of being unacceptable to many, although not, I am sure, offered in a disrespectful way by the good townspeople. The Sauk tribe with the legendary chief Blackhawk is a genuine source of pride to most of the citizens of Illinois and in Pittsfield are the Saukees.

Gold was discovered in Dahlonega, Georgia, in the early nineteenth century, providing after that the predominant share of all gold mined in the United States as well as most of our gold coinage until the discoveries in California in 1849. There is something of a tale around Dahlonega gold. It was originally the property of the Cherokees who, when their claims were usurped, went all the way to the United States Supreme Court seeking recovery. Although they won their case, they never got their gold. Nevertheless, in their memory, Dahlonega High School teams are called the Indians.

The legendary Chief Joseph led his Nez Perce tribe. If you enter Yellowstone Park by the Northeast route, through Montana, you are treated to quite a bit of Nez Perce history. Although the tribe was granted a large reservation by treaty on what had generally been the lands they had roamed before Lewis and Clark, the discovery of gold on the land soon led to the treaty's abrogation. Chief Joseph fought a brave series of delaying battles as

INDIAN TEAM NAMES

he strove to march what were left of his people into Canada. Chief Joseph was a Christian and well admired by the soldiers against whom he fought, only to be finally defeated within forty miles of the Canadian border. Both Nez Perce and Shoshone high schools in Idaho are the Indians.

In Salisbury, Maryland, we find Wicomico High School, home of the Wi-Hi Indians. In the towns of both Yuma and Kiowa, Colorado, Indians are the team names as is the case in Palm Springs, California, where the springs themselves that provide the water to nourish this otherwise desert valley still belong to the local tribe.

Hiawatha, Kansas, teams were originally called the Indians. Hiawatha was a legendary chief of the Onondagas and Henry Wadsworth Longfellow's poem lifted the name to almost mythical status, along with his bride, the beautiful Minnehaha. For some reason unknown to me, their school's team name was changed from Indians to Redskins. More recently, for reasons I think I do understand, yet a third iteration took place and the teams are now called the Redhawks.

A similar story took place in Sigourney, Iowa, as related to me by a friend and colleague, Hal Schimmelpfennig, who attended Sigourney High many years ago. At that time the school's nickname was the Savages and their uniforms carried the portrait of a war-painted Indian brave. Subsequently the portrait has been replaced by a king cobra, coiled, ready to strike. The nickname is still the Savages, sometimes the Savage Cobras.

Chief Osceola was the famed chief of the Seminole tribe in what is now the state of Florida. He led the tribe in the Second Seminole War that took place mainly in the Everglades in the 1830s. The town of Osceola, Arkansas, fields the Seminoles as do many high schools in Florida, including Osceola High School in Largo and Bradenton Southeast High School. The town of Seminole, Texas, has selected Indians as their team name.

Two high schools in Medford, New Jersey, make an interesting pair. Medford Shawnee High School teams are the Renegades and Medford

Go Huskies! Beat Felix the Cat!

Lenape High School (the Lenapes are also known as the Delawares) teams are the Indians.

We recently visited two towns in New York where the Indian name had been changed under pressure, or such change was being debated. The first was New Lebanon, just across the line from Vermont, southeast of Albany. A high school sophomore with a cheery smile, who served us ice cream cones in the little roadside eatery in New Lebanon informed us that the teams were now the Tigers, no longer the Indians, and she thought that was fine. Two of the patrons in the shop disagreed, feeling that the change was unfortunate, as the school had been known as the Indians for a long, long time.

A day later we were having a wonderful breakfast at the unsurprisingly crowded Bill's Deli in the town of Owego in south central New York where the sentiments were not at all divided. "We're the Indians and always have been," declared our vivacious waitress, Mary. "Owego (and she said it the way they cheer it: Oh, we go!) is an Indian name, we're in Tioga County and that's an Indian name, and we're on the Susquehanna River, another Indian name. Why can't we be the Indians if we want to?" No one in Bill's disagreed.

Spirit Lake, Iowa, is in the northwest corner of the state. Several lakes, including Spirit Lake, were formed by the glaciers and were originally discovered by the Sioux who considered them sacred. When white settlers were drawn to the beauty of the lakes they were resented by the Indians, but tolerated by all but a few. One of these, outlawed by his own tribe, led a raid in March of 1857 in which thirty settlers were killed in their cabins and remained undiscovered for several weeks. This is known as the Spirit Lake Massacre. The citizens of Spirit Lake have quite clearly forgiven the renegade Indian perpetrators of this crime, for their high school teams are the Indians.

Fort Davis, Texas, is in the Davis Mountains of the Big Bend section of the state. Both were named for Jefferson Davis in 1845 when he was Secretary of War, well before the establishment of the Confederate States of

Indian Team Names

America. Fort Davis is noteworthy for several reasons, one of which was the posting there of a Regiment composed entirely of black Americans known popularly as the Buffalo Soldiers. One of their officers was the first black graduate of West Point. Today the Fort Davis high School teams are the Indians.

Two final selections that appeal to me: In Bold, Minnesota, at Olivia High School, are the Bold Warriors—certainly the best kind—and in the town of Tomahawk, in far northern Wisconsin, are the Hatchets. Perhaps the Tomahawk Hatchets should play the Bad Ax Hatchets some day. Someone would get chopped down to size!

26

ALL THE SMALL SCHOOLS

UNTIL RELATIVELY RECENTLY we were a rural society with small schools located in small towns dotting an essentially agrarian countryside. The names given to these small schools are wonderfully descriptive of what was important, or fun, or part of the hopes and dreams of those who lived there. Many of these schools have been lost to consolidation, and those illuminating team names lost with them. I am sure this is true all over the country, but it is only in Indiana that I have been able to capture them all. I hope publication of this book will spur interest in saving all of these names all over the country.

Over the years there have been something in the neighborhood of 1,000 high schools in Indiana. In the 1938 state basketball tournament, 787 schools were entered in a single class championship and as many as 710 played in the tournament as late as 1959. Now there are fewer than 400 teams entered in what has become a four-class tournament. Most of the closed schools were tiny, serving only the town that bore their name and the surrounding farms, graduating classes often numbering in the single digits. Basketball was the perfect sport for these small schools, requiring only five players and a gym. Hoops hung on the sides of barns covered, and still do, the Indiana countryside.

The names chosen by these communities to honor their school, its teams and, in fact, the entire town, are marvelous indicators of what was important to the people who lived there, what amused them, or, even,

All the Small Schools

perhaps, what their dreams were. Many of these names would have been lost were it not for the scholarly work of the Indiana High School Athletic Association, which preserved them for posterity and kindly shared them with me. I wish I could find similar records for other states.

Toward the end of the movie *Hoosiers*, as the Hickory team is preparing to take the floor for the state championship game, one of the players, in the locker room far beneath the court, says "Let's win this for all the small schools that never had a chance to be here." Schools like tiny New Ross, the Blue Jays, who went 21–1 in the regular season, only to be upset in the sectionals in 1959. The Blue Jays were led by a 6–2 sharpshooting guard, Russell Nichols. "Rusty" went on to play at Wabash College and became the highly respected President of Hanover College. Or schools like equally tiny Alamo, aptly nicknamed the Warriors, whose highly successful teams were led by another sharpshooter, Charles Bowerman, also a Wabash "Little Giant" who went on to become a senior executive for the Phillips Oil Corporation. Here, then, are some more of those small schools.

Knightstown is a short drive east of Indianapolis on the old National Road, U.S. 40. It is well worth the trip. Just north of the downtown stores and antique malls is the beautifully restored Knightstown Academy that once housed all of the grades from kindergarten through high school for the community. The old gym was on the top floor and had to be abandoned when the pounding shoes of many years of basketball players of all ages threatened to weaken the structure of the entire building to the point of danger to its occupants. Thus the "new" gym was built in 1931 and recently marvelously restored. The Knightstown Falcons no longer play there, the Academy having been replaced by a modern scholastic and athletic plant and a new nickname, the Panthers. But the memories remain. The memories are strong. There are trophies in the trophy case and the ticket booth in the corner. Though there hasn't been a game there for perhaps fifty years, it is easy to imagine that there might be one tonight.

One of Indiana's glories is to be found under the earth in the form of immense oolitic limestone deposits. Ninety percent of the country's architectural grade limestone comes from Indiana. Many of America's most treasured buildings have been faced with limestone from the quarries in south central Indiana, including the Empire State Building in New York City, the United States Capitol, the National Cathedral and many state capitols and county courthouses. Recently, in a large old shed of a factory in Ellettsville, workers cut and polished the stones that were used to replace those destroyed by the cowardly attack on the Pentagon of September 11, 2001. They were horrified by the deed that led to their work, but were proud to be doing it. They wrote the words of President George W. Bush on the inside of many of the stones, the words that so ably rallied the country in the dark days immediately following the attack: "We will not tire. We will not falter. We will not fail . . . may God bless America." These words were spoken at that very National Cathedral faced with that very Indiana limestone. Many of these men would have graduated from Ellettsville High School, before its consolidation. They would have been Ellettsville Eagles.

Three other small towns in the limestone region also provided many workers for the quarries and factories of which they are justifiably proud. St. Paul's teams were the Blasters, Stinesville's were the Quarry Lads and Bedford's were the Stonecutters. Locals in Bloomington, home of the Indiana University Hoosiers, were for years known as the 'cutters' as all realize who enjoyed the movie *Breaking Away* in which the local bike team of that name carries the day at the Little 500.

Agriculture was and is extremely important to Indiana life. Corn and beans, wheat and tobacco grow abundantly from Lake Michigan to the Ohio River. Apple and peach orchards testify to other crop specialties in the state. Cory is located just southeast of Terre Haute. When there was still a Cory High School the teams were known as the Apple Boys. There is an amusing double entendre here, too, the Cory Apple Boys, unlike Crabby Appleton, were definitely not rotten to the core.

Another clever double meaning is found at the town of Hayden, located between Seymour and North Vernon. The town was originally called Hardenberg but, after it was realized that the surrounding area was perfect for growing forage crops, the name was changed to Hayden and the teams were called the Haymakers, partly because that is what they did on their

ALL THE SMALL SCHOOLS

farms and partly because that was what they laid on their opponents! Hayden provided the state with Governor Ed Whitcomb in the 1960s and I am fairly sure most of the state was unaware of his role as a onetime Haymaker on the Hayden High basketball team.

Dana is a small town in the far western part of the state, near the Illinois line and the birthplace of Ernie Pyle. It is on the great prairie, the land flat as far as the eye can see in all directions, dotted with barns and silos. This is marvelous farming country, the rich black topsoil being measured in feet rather than inches. The train ran through the south side of Dana, and the feed mills and storage bins are still in evidence. The high school's teams were known, very appropriately, as the Aggies.

Monroe City, in southwestern Indiana, near Vincennes, was the home of one "Blue Jeans" Williams, a real down-home politician. His popularity is attested to by the fact that the high school's teams were named the Blue Jeans after him.

Shawswick was even more straightforward: they were the Farmers, and Farmersburg, due south of Terre Haute were the Plowboys. I particularly like the town of Wheatfield's selection: the Shockers, which again spoke to what they did most for their livelihood and also to what they expected to do to opponents on the athletic fields, yet a third double meaning.

Many mills were located on the rivers and streams that run through the state: sawmills and gristmills, rolling mills and oil mills. Several towns selected Millers as their teams' nicknames. Among them were Millersburg and Milltown, in the south central portion of the state, and Union Mills, just south of LaPorte.

Windmills throughout the state provided water for livestock and other farming needs. Between the 1870s and the 1930s there were, in fact, seventy-six companies within a 150 mile radius of Kendallville in northeastern Indiana producing windmills. Today this heritage is commemorated in the fascinating Mid-America Windmill Museum. This museum is located on 16 acres east of Kendallville and displays more than 100 windmills, the nation's largest collection. Butler, also east of Kendallville, fielded the Windmills as their mascot. Opponents were thus placed in the unenviable

INDIANS IN INDIANA

Indiana, of course, derives its name from the Indians who once lived there. Many towns also identified themselves with this Indian heritage. Tiny Advance was known as the Osceolans, in honor of the famous Seminole chief. Alquina teams were known as the Blue Arrows and Blackhawk, named for another famous chief, of the Sauk Nation, were the Chieftains. The Flint Arrows took the field for that small town in the far northeastern part of the state while Monticello honored the Tioga Indians. Metz, in the northwestern part of the state, near the Ohio line, selected Mohawks for their mascot. To the east, were the Fair Oaks Cherokees. Owensville is just north of Evansville and their teams were the Kickapoos.

Thorntown, which won the state basketball championship in 1915, is a small farming community northwest of Indianapolis. Thorntown was built on the site of a former Indian village at the juncture of the Sugar and Prairie creeks. The original Indian name translated as "place of thorns" due to the many thorny bushes there. One story has it that a grieving Indian maiden pierced her heart with such a thorn, killing herself when her lover was killed in combat. The Thorntown high school teams were known as the Kewasakees.

Hymera, though settled by Sicilians and named for a town on that island, chose to honor a one-time local tribe, the

Shakamaks, with their mascot. Winslow teams, for reasons quite unknown to me were the Eskimos. Perhaps the most interesting Indian team name belongs to the town of Battleground, near the spot where the Battle of Tippecanoe was fought in which Indiana Territorial Governor and soon to be President William Henry Harrison defeated a coalition of several Indian tribes led by the famous Shawnee chief, Tecumseh, and his brother who was known as the Prophet. No less than ten of Indiana's ninety-two counties bear the names of men who fought in this battle. The Battleground High School teams were called the Tomahawks.

position of having to joust with windmills whenever they played Butler High School. Cervantes would have been proud!

Because there were two towns in Indiana pronounced the same and one was already spelled Circleville, the other town spelled their name with an "S" to differentiate it. Thus the Scircleville Ringers took the field, just east of Frankfort.

So many Irishmen came to America during and after the potato famine that their offspring here may even outnumber those still in "the auld sod." Ireland, in western Indiana, called its teams, wonderfully, the Spuds.

Although it was not really much colder in Chili than in the rest of Indiana, their teams were nonetheless the Polar Bears. The following towns showed a knowledge of history in selecting their team names:

Raleigh fielded the Sir Walters.
Lincoln teams were the Railsplitters.
Lexington offered the Minutemen, as did Bunker Hill.
Jackson Township High School were the Stonewalls.
Remington presented the Rifles.

At Klondike, although there may not have been any gold fields there, the teams were the Nuggets.

Near Princeton, in the far southwestern part of the state, is the town of Fort Branch, well represented by the Twigs.

Michigan City Rogers teams were the Raiders, after the famous Rogers Raiders of the French and Indian Wars from 1754–1763, with famous victories at Fort Ticonderoga and Montreal.

Ladoga had a canning factory that was the town's largest employer and the Ladoga High School teams were known as the Canners.

The town of West Point took pride in the fact that their name was the same as the New York State home of the beautiful United States Military Academy, and named their teams the Cadets. Perhaps they sometimes played the Middlebury Middies.

Cadiz, just west of New Castle, is where the Spaniards played and the

All the Small Schools

Aztecs represented the town of Montezuma on the other side of the state. When the Aztecs won rematch games with their opponents, was it Montezuma's revenge? Perhaps. Just south of Montezuma is the town of Mecca, which fielded the Arabs. The town of Russiaville, almost blown away by a deadly tornado in 1965, was represented by the Cossacks. There were also the Scotland Scotties, the Rome City Romans, the Holland Dutchmen and, down by the Ohio River, the Troy Trojans.

Oakland City, in the southwestern portion of the state were the Acorns, while the towns of Oakland and Oakton were each the Oaks. I don't know whether or not either of the Oaks ever played the Acorns, or which came first!

Rivers were very important to the early commerce of Indiana, particularly the Ohio, which forms the entire southern boundary of the state. Thus it is not surprising to find the Pilots in Mauckport, the River Rats in Newberry, and the Rivermen in both Leavenworth and New Amsterdam. There were also the Blue River Echoes in DePauw.

One of the most beautiful and historically intriguing sections of Indiana is in the south central part of the state where sulphur springs with supposedly curative powers were discovered in the latter part of the eighteenth century. This area, known as Springs Valley, attracted many visitors, first for the waters and later for the casinos that blossomed along with two fabulous hotels, one in French Lick and the other in nearby West Baden Springs. The hotel in West Baden is particularly noteworthy. Built in 1899 it was an engineering marvel. Its design was crowned by the largest free standing dome ever built in the world up until that time. Although the structure fell into considerable disrepair over the years since its heyday, thankfully it has been recently restored and is a most impressive sight.

When my wife and I were there on a balmy summer day we stopped in the local café for lunch and noticed several pictures of graduating classes of West Baden Springs High School, long before its consolidation. The nickname of their teams was the Sprudels. I asked our waitress if she knew why. She said she had not gone there, but she pointed out a man who appeared to be about my age at another booth who had, and perhaps he would know. Pretty soon he and I were having coffee together and comparing notes on a wide variety of topics. After solving the world's problems, he told me that the name Sprudels derived from the waters with their supposed curative powers. But why Sprudels? He thought for a moment before replying that "down in French Lick they had Pluto water and up here in West Baden we had Sprudel water," and he had always assumed it was because if you drank the water, known for its rather pronounced cathartic properties, you surely got the sprudels!

Of course, there's a bit more to it than that. Many of the original settlers in southern Indiana came from Germany. This from my classmate Bob Mackay, who has lived over there for many years:

> *The word* Sprudeln *means "to bubble up"—like a bubbling spring. So* Sprudelwasser *is bubbly water. They even use it for taxes: When the economy is good, the* Finanzminister *is happy with bubbling (tax income). If you choose* Sprudelwasser *in a restaurant, you will get it with bubbles;* Mineralwasser *is without.* Leitungswasser *is tap water, which they don't like to bring you because they can't charge you for it, I suppose. . . . Come on over and we'll drink some. Cheers!*

Those Pluto waters from French Lick were labeled with a small logo of a red devil with a pitchfork, which makes sense because Pluto was the Greek god of the Underworld. It also makes sense that the French Lick High School athletic teams were called the Red Devils.

Trinity Springs has similar waters, but not the great hotels and exotic past of West Baden Springs or French Lick although at one time as many as six smaller hotels did exist there to serve the needs of people wanting to bathe in and perhaps even drink the waters. The people of Trinity Springs were pretty straightforward when it came to selecting a nickname for their high school teams. They were known as the Little Sulphurs.

Stendal, a small town just west of Huntingburg in southern Indiana, was the birthplace of long-time United States Senator Vance Hartke. The Stendal teams were enthusiastically known as the Aces.

All the Small Schools

Ferdinand, named for an Archduke of Austria, is another town in Southern Indiana well worth a visit. It is nestled at the base of a fairly large hill rising dramatically from the flat lands that surround it, with a convent and a cathedral crowning its summit and another church part way up the hill with a tall spire. The convent and its related properties serve the needs of one of the largest concentrations of Benedictine nuns in the country, if not the world. When Ferdinand had its own high school the teams were nicknamed the Crusaders. The consolidation has left a high school in Ferdinand with the new name of Forest Park. The Forest Park teams are, appropriately enough, the Rangers.

The word "creek" is often pronounced "crick" by Hoosiers, so it is not surprising to find the Deer Creek Crickets south of Logansport and the Sugar Creek Crickets near Frankfort. However, the Mill Creek Creekers represented their town just a bit farther north. Were the good people of Mill Creek "high-hatting" their neighbors with their pronunciation? Prairie Creek avoided controversy and settled for the Gophers.

Rockport, on the Ohio River, once fielded basketball teams wearing uniforms that had black on one side and white on the other leading someone to refer to them as "zebras," a name that was shortly afterward officially adopted as their mascot.

Elnora was originally called Owl Town because of the abundance and variety of owls on the prairie in the area. The name was changed to that of the wife of a William Griffith who platted the town prior to its incorporation. However, the Elnora High School teams were happily called the Owls.

A restaurant in Fontanet once served wonderful bean soup and other bean dishes. The Fontanet High School teams were called the Beantowners.

Lynnville, just north of Evansville, may have selected their team name at about the time Charles Lindbergh gained fame for crossing the Atlantic

Many nicknames just flow off the tongue

The Boston Terriers.
The Buffalo Bisons.
The Poseyville Posies.
The Pittsboro Burros.
The Roll City Rollers, sometimes called the Red Rollers. (I wonder if the Rollers ever played the Scircleville Ringers?)
The Star City (sounds like a Soviet cosmonaut base now) Stars.
The Pine Village Pineknots.
The Kingsbury Kings.
The Beaver Dam Beavers.
The Cynthiana Annas.
The Graysville Greyhounds.
The Huntingburg Happy Hunters.
The Clarks Hill Hillers.
The Concannon Cannons.
The Mount Olympus Mountaineers.
The Michigantown Ganders.
The Mulberry Berries.
The Oil Township Oilers.
The Otter Creek Otters.
The Indianapolis Wood Woodchucks.
The Wolf Lake Wolverines.
The Lyons Lions.
The Poling Polecats.
The Mount Ayr Ayrdales.

Southeast of Terre Haute, where enormous deposits of bituminous coal were found near the surface, were the Coal City Colts.

The town of Twelve Mile is just about twelve miles from Logansport; their teams were called the Milers.

All the Small Schools

alone in the Spirit of St. Louis. Whether this telling is accurate or not, they were certainly known as the Lynnville Lindys.

Near Evansville were the Yankeetown Yanks, a name also selected by the town with the intriguing name of Young America, south of Logansport.

Railroads have long been important to Indiana. When one of the early lines from the Ohio River to Lake Michigan crossed another connecting Indianapolis with Chicago the intersection was destined to become an important one. This happened in 1878 at a little town bearing the Potawatomi Indian names of Big and Little Monong (swiftly flowing) Creek, later shortened to Monon. The railroads led to the growth of a thriving, prosperous town and soon there were repair shops, a roundhouse with the capacity for eighteen engines, a depot that saw as many as thirty-six trains in every twenty-four-hour period, and a large freight house. The railroad became known as the Monon Line, but it truly was the "Hoosier line." A popular song of the time was called "Up and Down the Monon" and well known Indiana humorist George Ade said it this way: "The traveler who wishes to see Indiana best must go riding on the Monon. It was the first iron trail to be pushed from one end of the state to the other . . . it links the Ohio with the Grand Calumet and . . . all its trains are 'Hoosiers.' " At one point all of the Monon Line's passenger trains were painted in the Cream and Crimson of Indiana University and all of its freight trains in the Old Gold and Black of Purdue.

Jack Hughes, editor and publisher of the *Monon News*, a tall, erudite, engaging man in his late sixties kindly shared this history of his town with me. We talked about the high school, now consolidated into North White County along with his own high school, the Buffalo Bisons. He agreed with me that the nickname of the new school, the Vikings because it is, after all, in the north, was not even close to being as meaningful as that of the now-closed Monon High School, which was located exactly where I thought it would be, just east of the tracks. Those early Monon High School teams were called accurately and proudly, the Railroaders.

Garrett is another railroad town of significance in Indiana. When the Baltimore & Ohio decided in 1874 to extend its line west to Chicago, a site

Hoosier Hysteria

Several towns obviously had basketball on their minds when it came time to selecting nicknames. Fancy that—basketball on their minds in Indiana!

Union Township in Huntington County, near Fort Wayne, and the town of Milton, located between Knightstown and Richmond, were the Sharpshooters.

Warren, northeast of Marion, fielded the Lightning Five.

Swayzee, which bills itself on the sign just outside of town as "The only Swayzee in the World"—a claim that I have never seen disputed—and also calls attention to the fact that Swayzee won a nine overtime game against Liberty Center in 1964, believed to be the longest high school game ever played, were the Swayzee Speedkings. Nearby Urbana's teams were also called The Speed Kings so, while there may only be one Swayzee, there were at least two Speed Kings.

Rosedale, north of Terre Haute, offered the Hotshots.

Dunkirk is near Logansport on the Wabash River, not the English Channel, and it has never been made famous by a massive, high speed evacuation. But it could have handled the speed part, apparently: the Dunkirk teams were the Speed Cats.

Kirklin (and I may be reaching a bit here to associate this name with basketball) teams were called the Travelers—perhaps their opponents chose this one! Or perhaps they were simply admirers of Robert E. Lee's horse.

Edwardsport, in south central Indiana, had teams originally called the Powerhouse Gang, later shortened to the Powers.

All the Small Schools

was selected just south of Auburn on which to build shops, a roundhouse and yards. Almost everyone who lived in Garrett was associated with the railroad. At its peak of traffic, sixteen passenger trains a day stopped at the Garrett station, which was still active until just after World War II. Today the main line of CSX passes through Garrett. Garrett still has a high school and the teams are called, as they always have been, the Railroaders, and their gym is decorated not only with the colors and mascots of their traditional athletic opponents, but with the logos of the great railroads of the country as well, such as the B & O, Union Pacific, and the Santa Fe.

There are more covered bridges in Parke County, Indiana than in any other county in America. At last count there were thirty-two and every effort is made to preserve and sustain them. Rockville, the seat of Parke County, hosts a very popular covered bridge festival every October. The Rockville high teams were known as the Rox.

Several covered bridges also may be found in adjacent counties. My own particular favorite is in Putnam County, just southwest of Greencastle. Built in 1886 it is known as the Houck Bridge. Several of the bridges, such as the one at Bridgeton, also have mills and are very popular places for picnickers and photographers. The Bridgeton Bridge crosses Big Raccoon Creek and the high school teams there were known as the Raccoons. Probably the Big Raccoons, at that.

Colfax, between Indianapolis and Lafayette, was known for years as the best place around for a catfish dinner. After a Purdue home football game, the town would be overflowing with hungry fans, anxious to get at the all you can eat, hickory smoked catfish dinner. Or was it deep fried? They still celebrate Hickory Days every October in Colfax and every old timer recalls the glory days of the Colfax High School Hickories.

For some reason unknown to me, the town of Arlington chose the Purple Breezes to be the name of their teams. Perhaps they helped carry the

Go Huskies! Beat Felix the Cat!

Purple Eagles of Terre Haute Garfield High School aloft to ever-greater glory. In New Market they had the Purple Flyers, which I thought must refer to Martens. I have it authoritatively, however, from a prominent New Market alumna, Mrs. Patricia Nichols, that the symbol used was that of a purple airplane, not a bird at all. Purple Breezes, Purple Eagles and Purple Flyers!

Very close to Knightstown was Spiceland, which derived its town name from the abundance of wild spice bushes growing there. These plants must have attracted many bumblebees, wasps or hornets because the Spiceland Academy teams were the Stingers. Again close to Terre Haute was my very favorite bee nickname. That would belong to the Honey Creek High School Honey Bees. And that was before the days of girls' teams!

I know there are no kangaroos in Indiana except in some zoos, but Kirkland teams were once called the Kangaroos. Equally unexpected are the Zebras of Jonesboro, a small town near Marion.

Just west of Seymour, the town of McKinley selected Presidents as their team name for reasons readily understandable. Equally clear is the choice of Cavemen for the teams from Marengo, located adjacent to the largest series of caves in Indiana and a favorite spot for the many spelunkers in the state. Just north, in Bloomington, were the University High Univees. For aptness, you have to love the Craftsmen, from the Masonic Home High School, near Franklin.

Clay Township, near Kokomo, called its teams the Brickies. Mellott, northwest of Crawfordsville, fielded the Derbies. Perhaps they once had a hat factory in town, or maybe a special horse race was held there. If that is the case, perhaps the Montpelier Pacers came over to compete.

Some small towns recognized their size in their selection of team names. Perry Central, Plainville and Wanatah were all called the Midgets. Hartford Township High School rebelled a bit, however. They decided to call their teams the Gorillas. I don't know how it came out if the Gorillas ever tangled with the Midgets on the sports field.

West Lebanon is located on the western edge of the state, near the town of Williamsport. Williamsport announces itself as the spot with the tallest

All the Small Schools

waterfall in Indiana. We did go there to see it, and it is fairly tall, although most of the other states in the Union have little to fear from it as competition for their own tallest waterfalls. Anyway, the West Lebanon teams were called the Pikers, which probably had nothing to do with Williamsport's waterfall, and nothing to do with the townspeople's generosity either, and more to do with the road that passed through town. The Williamsport teams, by the way, were interestingly known as the Bingy Bombers. Bingy? I don't know.

Summitville's selection is even more mysterious. This hamlet northwest of Muncie may have had a haunted house or two at one time because their teams were the Goblins. However, relatedly, the Literary Prize for this section goes to the town of Banquo, a tiny farm community northeast of Marion. Someone in Banquo must have been well acquainted with Shakespeare. Just for the record, Banquo was a friend of Macbeth's, also a general, who conspired with Macbeth to kill King Duncan. Later, in part to cover up his own role in these dastardly doings, Macbeth also kills Banquo. In Act IV, however, Banquo returns as a ghost and torments Macbeth unmercifully. These happenings must have been known to every citizen of Banquo at one time. Their choice of nickname for their high school teams? The Banquo Ghosts. There is no longer a Banquo High School: only Ghosts remain.

Unfortunately, the Literary Prize for Opportunity Missed is shared by the towns of Hamlet and Tennyson. Both fielded teams called the Tigers. I would have preferred either the Princes or the Danes for the former and the Lords, of course, for the latter. Oh well, I guess the tide in the affairs of man is not always taken at the flood.

Just east of Lafayette is the town of Monitor. In remembrance of the famous Civil War ironclad warships, the *Monitor* and the *Merrimac* (or the *Virginia*, as it was then called), the teams of Monitor High School were cleverly called the Commodores. Southwest of Peru is the small town of Onward. With perhaps an eye on the Revolutionary War, the Onward teams were the Redcoats. One hopes they were more successful on the athletic fields than were their British namesakes on the battlefield.

Go Huskies! Beat Felix the Cat!

My wife was pleased to learn that there is a small town in northern Indiana named Hanna, for that is her maiden name. (One day, our granddaughter named Hanna will undoubtedly also share that sentiment.) Hanna is apparently located near some good fishing holes because their high school's nickname was the Fishermen.

Smithville was a small town, south of Bloomington, which has turned into a prosperous resort area with the creation of man-made Lake Monroe. When there was a Smithville High School the teams there were called the Skibos. I hope one day someone will be able to tell me why. Can it possibly be named for Skibo Castle, located in the Highlands of Scotland? I like to think so.

The town of Petroleum in Wells County was so named because of the oil fields there and nearby Gas City because of the abundance of natural gas in the area. Both Gas City and nearby Fairmount, later to gain fame as the birthplace of the talented young actor James Dean, became sites for many glass manufacturers who found the natural gas advantageous to their production. Petroleum High School teams were originally known as the Zippers. This name was adopted because the basketball team, the only interscholastic team fielded by this tiny school at the outset, used uniforms with the newly invented devices known as zippers while most others still used the older more conventional fasteners, and also because the team wanted to be known for its speed on the court. So Zippers they were for some thirty plus years until, perhaps, the novelty wore off and a new nickname was selected, the Panthers, in about 1947. Fairmount teams were known as the Quakers and Gas City, somewhat unimaginatively, as the Tigers.

A significant number of Swiss immigrants settled in Indiana and they did not forget their origins when it came time to select their high school team names. The city of Luzern (or Lucerne), Switzerland is located on a beautiful glacier-fed lake. One of the treasures of Luzerne is the magnificent sculpture near the Glacier Gardens called the Lion of Luzerne, honoring the Swiss Guards. The town of Lucerne is in north central Indiana and the teams that represented their town were known as the Lions. The Lions of Lucerne.

ALL THE SMALL SCHOOLS

Vevay is located in far southeastern Indiana, bordering the Ohio River. It is the principal town in Switzerland County and its teams, perhaps with a recollection of the fierce Swiss Guards, were known as the Warriors. Berne is the capital of Switzerland and is also the name of one of the four forest cantons. The symbol of the city and canton of Berne is the bear. The town of Berne, in northern Indiana near the Ohio line, also chose the Bear to be the mascot of their high school (as did Lake Zurich High School in Illinois).

Tell City, on the banks of the Ohio River, is named, of course, for the famed Swiss archer who shot an apple off of his son's head. On the grounds of the City Hall there is a statue of William Tell with his crossbow in hand and his son at his side, which is similar to the one in his home town and Tell City's sister city, Altdorf, Switzerland. The athletic contests at Tell City High often find the pep band playing Rossini's "William Tell Overture" to get the teams and fans fired up for their beloved cream-and-crimson clad Marksmen.

The town of Bowers fielded teams called the Blackshirts. I have never seen their uniforms, but can easily imagine what they must have looked like. The town of Kingman once fielded the Black Aces. Black Aces up the sleeve of Blackshirts?

The town of Orange, Indiana, is located near Connersville. In deference, perhaps, to the house of Orange, Old Nassau, and Princeton University far to the east, the Orange High School teams were the Tigers. Haubstadt is in the far southwest part of the state in beautiful Gibson County. The unabashed, prideful nickname for their teams was the Elites. The town of Pimento is located just south of Terre Haute. As most people know, whether or not martinis play a role in their lives, pimentos are sweet red peppers often used to stuff green olives. Pimento's teams were wonderfully known as the Peppers. Epsom is a small town in the south central part of the state. You have to love a town called Epsom, which had the foresight and courage to call their teams the Salts, don't you? They went through their opponents like a dose of . . . well, you get the idea.

27
OTHER HEROES

OUR SCHOOLS HAVE honored many other men and women with their selection of names and nicknames than those mentioned elsewhere in this book. Here are some more.

New York City's Borough of the Bronx is a good place to start, and Al Smith High School is, perhaps, as New York as you can get. Alfred Emanuel Smith was born and died in the city he loved. He was elected as Governor of New York State four times and in 1928 became the first serious Catholic candidate for the Presidency of the United States. His campaign featured the song "Sidewalks of New York" and he was referred to, in part because of his love for campaigning and more so for his constant smile while doing so, as the Happy Warrior. Al Smith High School teams are the Warriors. Happy, I hope.

Nearby is Adlai Stevenson High School. Stevenson, from Illinois, had also been a successful governor and unsuccessful Democratic candidate for the presidency. Extremely erudite, Stevenson was perhaps at his most eloquent and effective self in the halls of the United Nations, which he was instrumental in founding and where he served our country with distinction as Ambassador. Adlai Stevenson High School teams are, appropriately, the Ambassadors. (Lincolnshire, Illinois, Stevenson High School also honors Adlai: their nickname is the Patriots.)

OTHER HEROES

DeWitt Clinton was Governor of New York for all but two years of the period 1817–1828. Clinton's vision for the Erie Canal, which would connect the Hudson River to the Great Lakes, and his energy and drive to get it accomplished, ensured that New York City would be the primary port on the east coast for Midwestern trade with the eastern United States and with Europe. DeWitt Clinton High School teams in the Bronx, New York, are the Governors.

Thomas Edison was perhaps the world's most prolific inventor, with the incandescent electric light bulb, the phonograph and the basis for motion pictures among his world-leading total of 1,093 patents. Edison also established the world's first industrial research laboratory and the foundations of the electric industry. Edison Vocational Technical High School in New York City appropriately calls its teams the Inventors.

Two of America's greatest World War II generals are honored by high schools in Decatur, Illinois. Douglas MacArthur graduated with highest honors from West Point and was later to return to the Academy as its commandant. He is remembered primarily for his vow to return to the Philippines after the islands were lost to the Japanese in the early days of World War II, and for his inspired leadership of Japan during the occupation following the war. Decatur MacArthur High School teams are the Generals.

The other great World War II general honored in Decatur is Dwight D. Eisenhower. Another West Point graduate, "Ike," as he was familiarly known, was the commander of all of the Allied forces in the European Theater of Operations. He masterminded the forbidding logistics and tactical problems involved in the Normandy Invasion. Following the war, Ike made the successful transition to civilian life as President of Columbia University and as two-term president of the United States. Decatur Eisenhower teams are the Panthers.

A third great American military leader of World War II who also was a highly successful civilian leader was George C. Marshall. Following his distinguished career in the Army, Marshall became Secretary of State under President Harry Truman. His innovative European Recovery Plan, more commonly referred to as the Marshall Plan, was in large measure responsible for enabling Germany, our former enemy, and other nations of the devastated continent, to restore democratic governments and rejoin the western powers as vibrant economic entities. In 1953, Marshall was awarded the Nobel Peace Prize. Falls Church, Virginia, Marshall High School teams are the Statesmen.

Webster Grove, Missouri, is a western suburb of St. Louis. Their high school remembers the accomplishments of Dartmouth graduate Daniel Webster with the same nickname. They, too, are the Statesmen.

Other honorees:

Robert Taft, by the Cincinnati Taft High School Senators.
James Sparkman by the Harvest, Alabama, Sparkman High School Senators.
Robert Byrd by the Clarksburg, West Virginia, Byrd High School Eagles.
James Bowie by the Arlington, Texas, Bowie High School Volunteers.
Sam Houston by the Arlington Houston High School Texans.
Daniel Boone by the Boone High School in Gray, Tennessee, Trailblazers.

Henry Clay was considered a great orator and his abilities to reconcile differences between groups with opposing viewpoints earned him the appelations of "Great Compromiser" and "Great Pacificator." Henry Clay High School in South Bend, Indiana, fields the Colonials.

Several presidents of the United States, in addition to those mentioned elsewhere, are honored as well. Warren G. Harding, who had owned a profitable daily newspaper in Marion, Ohio, ran his successful campaign for the presidency in 1920 from his front porch. His home is still there in this pleasant central Ohio railroad town and Harding High School teams are called the Presidents.

Hyde Park, New York, was the home of President Franklin Delano

Other Heroes

Roosevelt, a highly effective leader who guided our country through the final days of the Great Depression and the dark days of most of World War II, and who reminded us of the Four Freedoms that are our birthright, and whose ringing words following Pearl Harbor declared unambiguously that December 7, 1941, was "a day that will live in infamy." Roosevelt High School in Hyde Park calls its teams, so very appropriately, the Presidents.

There are also Presidents at Grover Cleveland High School in Buffalo, while cross-town William McKinley High School teams are more familiarly known as the Macs.

Captains

One of America's great inventors was Charles Franklin Kettering. Born in Loudonville, Ohio, in 1876. Kettering invented the first electric cash register and the first automobile electric starter, installed on the 1912 Cadillac, as well as several other significant innovations. He became Vice President and Director of Engineering for the General Motors Corporation and a leading American philanthropist. Charles Kettering was truly a "Captain of Industry" and Kettering High School in Waterford, Michigan, acknowledges that in the nickname they have chosen, the Captains.

Semper Fi

Short for *Semper Fidelis*—"Ever Faithful"—is the motto of a fellowship I have long admired, the United States Marine Corps. Several schools seem to share that admiration. Hamilton, Indiana, is a town of fewer than seven hundred citizens in the far northeastern corner of the state. It is near Lake Hamilton and the high school teams are the Marines. There are also Marines representing the attractive lakeside town of Marinette, Wisconsin. With a more obvious connection to the Corps is the Marine Military Academy in Harlingen, Texas, home of the Leathernecks. Finally, there are Lejeune, North Carolina, and Quantico, Virginia, two places where the

Go Huskies! Beat Felix the Cat!

Marines have definitely landed. Lejeune Prep's nickname is the Devil Pups, junior to the Corps itself whose members are often called the Devil Dogs, and the Quantico High School teams are the Devil Warriors.

The Caissons Go Rolling Along

For years the field artillery has moved its heavy ordinance with caissons. In Waynesboro, Virginia, at the Fishburne Military School the teams are the Caissons.

28
Religious Schools

WE HAVE LONG had a tradition of strong religious schools in our country along with our equally strong and well-conceived separation of church and state. Surely our founding fathers were wise to prevent the establishment of a state religion. Theocracies and democracies are an unhappy union, doomed, I think, to failure. We should, however, rejoice that we have considerable diversity of thriving religious thought in this country and I am convinced that our founders would also be pleased that this is so. Many of these religious schools have selected team names that speak to their value system, or the source or practice of their faith.

Here are some examples:

Portland, Oregon, Jesuit teams are the Crusaders, as are those of Belleville, Illinois, Authoff.
Youngstown, Ohio, Calvary teams are the Sons of Thunder.
Grandville, Michigan, Calvin Christian Schools are the Squires and, also emphasizing the value of service to others, is nearby Mattawan Christian, the Footmen.
Madison Heights, just south of the magnificent sweep of the Mackinaw Straits Bridge and close to beautiful Burt Lake, is Bishop Foley High School, home of the Ventures. Nothing ventured, nothing gained.

Paraclete High School in Lancaster, California, is represented by the Spirits—but not the scary kind, the holy kind.

Detroit St. Gabriel High school teams are the Trumpeteers.

Milwaukee Pius XI High School recognizes their heritage by choosing Popes as the name for their boys' athletic teams while the girls' teams are, perhaps optimistically, the Lady Popes.

In Alabama, Jacksonville Christian teams are the Thunder and Montgomery Calvary Christian teams are the Watchmen.

Christian Brothers High School in Albany, New York, simply calls their teams the Brothers.

Merion Station Episcopal in Pennsylvania fields the Churchmen.

Denver Lutheran High School teams are the Lights.

Shanley High School in Fargo, North Dakota, presents the Deacons.

Across the country in the wonderfully named Panorama City, California, is St. Genevieve High School, and they field the Valiants.

Syracuse Living Word and, down in Texas, Laredo Christian Academy share a nickname that I just love. They are both the Lions of Judah.

In Champaign, Illinois, is the Judah Christian School. Their teams are the Tribe.

Rye Cathedral Preparatory School, in Westchester County, New York, is a place where they take religious law very seriously. They are the Canons.

St. Mary's High School in Bay City, Michigan, are the Shillelaghs. I guess they enforce the law!

Wichita Cathedral High School teams are the Micks.

St. Peter's Church on the Rock High School in St. Louis fields the Champions. Optimistic, sure, but Champions for St. Peter, always, win or lose on the athletic field. Perhaps a worthy opponent would come from Villa Marie Academy in Erie, Pennsylvania. Their teams are the Victors.

Jersey City St. Anthony High School has a storied athletic history, particularly in basketball where they have sent many graduates on to great success in college and the NBA. Mr. Robert F. Kanaby is executive director

Religious Schools

of the National High School Federation in Indianapolis and an alumnus of St. Anthony. The St. Anthony teams are the Friars.

Providence High School in New Lennox, Illinois, a Chicago suburb, has also had an enviable record on the athletic fields for years. Their team names are the Celtics, but they were beaten to it by St. Patrick High School in Elizabeth, New Jersey. St. Pat's teams are the Original Celtics. Also in New Jersey, the Hawthorne Christian School teams are the Defenders. Of the faith, I am sure, as well as of the honor of their school. Nearby, New Monmouth Mater Dei ("Mother of God") High School, has about as mild a nickname as I can imagine, short of cherubim, which I did not find anywhere. They are the Seraphs.

Many religious schools have chosen Angels as their mascot, of course. Two examples are St. Joseph Academy in St. Louis, and Hosanna Christian School in St. Joseph, at opposite ends of the state of Missouri.

At Chesapeake, Virginia, Great Hope Baptist High School, and at Huntington, West Virginia, Grace Christian High School, the teams are the Soldiers. "Onward, Christian Soldiers" and "Soldiers of Christ, Arise"—two of my favorite hymns—spring to mind when I think of their choice. They would go well with the Faith Warriors of Tampa Bayshore. Or, with Charleston, South Carolina, Bishop England's Battling Bishops. Or, perhaps, with the Stormin' Saints of Carrolton, Texas, Christian Academy.

A paladin was once the name given to the champion of a medieval prince or potentate, but can also be used to describe the champion of any worthy cause. We find Paladins representing Paramus Catholic High School.

Johnstown, Pennsylvania, Bishop Accore teams ask no quarter and give none. They are the Crushers. Neither does St. Andrew's Parish High School in Charleston, South Carolina. They field the Rocks. How about a game between the Rocks and the Crushers? Maybe the Nazareth Academy teams from Rochester, New York, could handle either one with their scientific approach. They are the Lasers.

At Mountain Mission High School in Grundy, Virginia, are the

Go Huskies! Beat Felix the Cat!

Challengers and at San Francisco Mercy Academy are the Skippers. The Spirits represent Salinas Notre Dame and, also in California, at West Hills West Valley Christian School are the Seekers. Seekers after truth and beauty, I believe. Continuing in California, we have the Victorians of Downey St. Matthias, the Heralds of LaHabra Whittier Christian School, and the Valiants of Panorama City St. Genevieve.

The Eastern Orthodox Church is well represented by Encino Holy Martyrs Armenian School: the Armens. Park Hill Christian School in Pueblo, Colorado, fields the Chargers and Sacred Heart Academy in Waterbury, Connecticut, teams are simply the Hearts. In Van Buren, Arkansas, Christian Academy teams are the Miracles, and the Jacksonville, Florida, University Christian teams are straightforwardly the Christians. Also in Florida, the Melbourne Central Catholic teams are the Hustlers, the Plantation Broward Christian school teams are the Ambassadors, and the Riviera Beach Headley Christian teams are the Disciples. Ambassadors for, and Disciples of, Christ. There are also Ambassadors at the marvelously named Azalea Garden Christian School in Norfolk, Virginia. How could you not be inspired to learn in such a setting?

Many Christian high schools all over this country have selected the Eagle for their mascot. I think this speaks volumes about the value system they have adopted, combining patriotism with a favorite selection from Psalms: "They shall mount up as eagles."

St. Augustine

St. Augustine was born in 354 A.D. in Tagaste, Roman North Africa, and died in Hippo, where he was the bishop, in 430 A.D., as the Vandals were sacking the city. While he lived he had the reputation of being something of a recluse. Perhaps the chief order that emerged from the Augustinian period would be the Augustinian Hermits or Friars, often simply called the Augustinians, which came into existence as a single body in 1256. This order is devoted to the cure of souls and the advancement of learning through teaching and research. In Richland, New Jersey, St. Augustine Prep School fields the Hermits.

St. Sebastian

Toledo, Spain, is a marvelous place to visit, a well-preserved medieval wonder. A Greek artist who came to Toledo to paint was called El Greco by his new neighbors, as do we. Many of El Greco's paintings are on display in his house in Toledo. One that struck me in particular was his oil of the Christian martyr, Saint Sebastian, riddled with arrows. He had been slain by the Roman Mauretian archers. Thus there is a good sense of history in the selection of Needham, Massachusetts St. Sebastian Country Day School: the Arrows.

29
A Few More Good Ones

WE ARE A nation of such diverse interests and experiences that not all of the good team names fit conveniently into the categories I have selected. On the following pages are some of those too good to omit.

For openers

For sheer energy, we can start with the Dynamos of the German School in White Plains, New York. That might be disputed, I suppose, by the Buckaroos from the marvelously named town of Smackover, Arkansas. Don't you love it, the Smackover Buckaroos?

For historical significance, how about the Praetorians of Heritage Prep in Orlando? The Praetorians were elite troops with considerable political power and influence who guarded the Roman Emperors stretching from Augustus Caesar to Constantine, a span of close to three hundred years.

Of more recent historical import we can cite the Cajuns of Park Country Day School in Metairie, Louisiana. You would expect Cajuns in Louisiana, certainly, where the Acadians from New Brunswick, Canada, settled after being driven out of the north-country. Longfellow's poem, "Evangeline," recounts much of this tale.

East Greenwich, Rhode Island, enjoys a beautiful setting overlooking Narragansett Bay with the oldest house there dating from 1679. Another home in town, built in 1773, was that of General James Varnum, the first

A Few More Good Ones

commanding officer of the Kentish Guards. The East Greenwich High School athletic teams apparently have something that they need to get even with their opponents about: they are the Avengers.

Also in Rhode Island is the mill town of Woonsocket. Many of the workers in those mills originally came down from Quebec. Woonsocket was their new home and, perhaps with this and their French heritage in mind, the Woonsocket High School teams are the Villa Novans.

The Kent School in Connecticut was founded by an Episcopalian priest in 1906. Their teams are usually referred to as the Blue and Greys, but I have seen references to them as the Fighting Episcopalians as well.

Prophetstown, Illinois, is located on the Rock River in the western part of the state. The high school teams may have the ability to foresee the future: they are the Prophets.

John Deere

When John Deere came to Illinois from his native New England, he discovered that the plow he had brought with him would not work on the rich, deep Midwestern topsoil that clumped and stuck on the blade. Deere solved that problem by carefully polishing his blades and in the process he created "the plow that broke the plains." This he did in Dixon, Illinois, but success soon caused him to move his burgeoning young company to the better transportation afforded by the Mississippi River in what is now Moline. The Deere Corporation is still headquartered there and, although the official listed name of the Moline High School teams is the Maroons, they are also often called the Plowboys.

Yoemen

A yeoman is variously defined as an officer or an attendant in a royal or noble household or as a person who owns and cultivates a small farm. The yeomen of the guard in Great Britain, however, are those marvelously costumed gentlemen one finds today at the Tower of London, the repository

A few others

Alexandria, Alabama, the Valley Cobs.
Chillicothe, Ohio, Unioto High School, the Sherman Tanks.
Lincoln, Nebraska, High School, the Links. As strong as the weakest . . . ?
Walla Walla, Washington, the Wa-His.
Seattle Franklin High School, the Earthquake.
Broxton, Georgia, the Gold Nuggets.
Silver Grove, Kentucky, the Big Train.
Newcastle, Oklahoma, the Racers.
Cherryvale, Kansas, the Cherries.
Blissfield, Michigan, the Sugarboys.
Utica, New York, Notre Dame, the Jugglers.
Naples, New York, the Big Green Machine.
Graham High School in Bluefield, Virginia, the G-Men.
South Beloit, Illinois, the SoBos.
Roman Catholic High School in Philadelphia, the Cahillites.
Fiorello LaGuardia High School in New York City, the Athletics.
Chicago Mt. Carmel High School, the Caravan.
Carthage, Illinois, High School, the Blue Boys and Blue Girls (not Blue Belles, regrettably).
East Chicago, Indiana, Washington, the Senators.
Wilbraham and Monson Academy, in Massachusetts, the Coachmen.
Marion, Indiana, the Giants.

The high school in Waterford, New York, with the marvelous name of Half Moon, fields the Fordians. (I wish they were the Crystals. Or else the Henry Hudsons.)

Sand Springs, sounding like an oasis in the Sahara, is located in Oklahoma, and their teams are the Sandites.

Perhaps the alliteration award should go to a school in southern Georgia. That would be the Valdosta Valwood Valiants.

A Few More Good Ones

for the crown jewels. So, the yeomen do, in fact, have some serious guarding to do. These yeomen are also more commonly known as beefeaters—their uniforms may be seen on the gin of the same name—and, one suspects there is plenty of beef eaten in and around Cameron, Texas, where Cameron-Yoe High School fields the Yoemen. (And that is the way they choose to spell it!)

Watersmeet

The small town with the intriguing name of Watersmeet is located in the Upper Peninsula of Michigan and is inhabited by 450 people, many of whom love to hunt and fish. Watersmeet is in the Ottawa National Forest, south of Lake Superior. The Watersmeet High School athletic teams are the Nimrods. Now, at first I assumed that a nimrod was perhaps some kind of fish. A little research quickly proved otherwise. Nimrods are descendants of Ham, a "Mighty hunter before the Lord" and King of Shinar. I do believe that there are many, many mighty hunters in Watersmeet.

The Tarblooders

In the 1940s, the Glenville High School football team in Cleveland, Ohio, developed a pregame ritual that included a cheer that they would "knock the tar and blood" out of their opponents. They became known as the Tarblooders. Their colors? Red and black, of course! The mascot appears to be a cross between a robot and Dorothy's Tin Woodman.

Hoosiers

A word about the nickname of those of us who live in my adopted state is in order. What exactly is a Hoosier? Here are some of the theories, with thanks to columnist Dave Barry:

> The name of a contractor who worked on the Ohio River in the early nineteenth century.

Go Huskies! Beat Felix the Cat!

A word meaning "highlander" or "hill dweller."

A word referring to anything large of its kind.

"Who's there?" being asked after a knock on a cabin door or "Who is ya?" from a riverbank.

"Who's yours?" from mothers, referring to the children, asking each other at family reunions.

"Whose ear?" being asked in the aftermath of knife fights in Indiana taverns.

It will be left to greater historical scholars than I to determine which of these, or some other theory is the correct one. In a sense it really doesn't matter. We who live in Indiana are Hoosiers, the Indiana University teams are Hoosiers and we're happy with that.

Surprisingly, there is only one high school in Indiana with Hoosiers in its nickname. That is the Indiana School for the Deaf, in Indianapolis, once the Orioles, now proudly the Deaf Hoosiers.

30
NICKNAMES, MASCOTS, AND SYMBOLS

AT THIS POINT a word concerning the difference between nicknames, mascots and symbols might prove useful. We define ourselves and present that definition to others in a variety of ways. The best of these are clear, reinforcing and unifying.

Nicknames, or team names, are the most obvious. As has been clear, I hope, in this book, these are the names on our athlete's jerseys in addition to those of the schools themselves. "Go, Panthers, go Pirates, go Poets." Mascots are defined as "a person, animal or object adopted by a group . . . to bring them good luck, such as the Fourteenth Indiana Regitment did when they "adopted a goose which happened by" needing all the luck they could get as they were headed toward the grim battlefields of Antietam, Chancellorsville, and Gettysburg.

Mascots, at the high school level at least, are usually costumed people, prancing along the sidelines, dressed like Cavaliers, Rhinos, and Devils, but they may be more dramatic than that, particularly at places that can afford the real thing, such as many Division I colleges. When the buffalo comes charging into the stadium, you know the University of Colorado is in town; when the Prairie Schooner pulled by its four strong horses charges across the field the University of Oklahoma team is surely somewhere near; when the

Go Huskies! Beat Felix the Cat!

leprechaun starts doing his Irish jig, Notre Dame is in the house; and when Uga shows up the pugnacious bulldog is a sure sign that the University of Georgia has come to play. Some mascots are quite different from the team nickname. Thus the Army Cadets (also called the Black Knights on occasion) bring their Mule to their annual encounter with the Navy Midshipmen with their Goat; the Crimson Tide of Alabama has an elephant for a mascot and the North Carolina Tarheels have a ram for theirs. High schools, of course, use both mascots and nicknames, too. That the desire to use these names to solidify our affiliations begins at an early age is attested to by the fact that my grandson (the world's only other Emerson Houck, as far as we know), a second grader, already owns a T-shirt with Woodbrook School Lions on it, and his sister, Hanna, in preschool, is a proud Butterfly!

We also use symbols, something that stands for or suggests something else, as the lion is a symbol for courage, to bind ourselves together and to tell the world who we are. The Florida State Seminole spear thrown in the ground before the opening kickoff is a pretty powerful visual symbol, and others, less dramatic but equally potent, also exist.

Shortridge

As promised, here is the story of my wife's beloved Shortridge High School. It nicely delineates the difference between a mascot and a nickname.

According to Laura Gaus' fine book, *Shortridge High School 1864–1981*, the mascot came first, in 1925, when a female student placed a cat in the center circle of a basketball game after the opponent's red-clad dog had gone out there before the second-half tipoff. At this point, the underdog Shortridge team was losing, but as they went on to win an upset victory; the students were convinced the cat had indeed brought them good luck. They adopted the cat as their mascot and, Latin scholars that they were, named it Felix.

The Shortridge nickname came three years later when the school paper held a contest to select one. The winning entrant was from a student who remembered a group of French soldiers who had stayed at his home while

Nicknames, Mascots, and Symbols

on an American fund-raising trip during World War I. They had belonged to a regiment known as the Blue Devils and thus it was that the Shortridge High School Blue Devils were born. Blue Devils and Felix the Cat, nickname and mascot.

Logansport, Indiana, has a similar story, perhaps deriving from the Shortridge experience. Long known as the Berries, Logansport's mascot is actually also Felix the Cat, adopted in 1926 when the basketball captain, in an effort to inspire his teammates, took from his locker a Felix doll that the coach had earlier given him and placed it in the center circle at the halftime of an important game. Again, when the Berries went on to win that game, the school adopted Felix the Cat as their good-luck piece and mascot.

Some schools go even farther and adopt school symbols. The following schools demonstrate the significance of symbols, as opposed to nicknames and mascots:

The Sextant

The sextant is a navigational device that measures the angle of elevation of heavenly bodies as an aid to determining latitude. It was used by early sailors as an important component of determining their location and proper course. When the Belmont Hill School was founded in 1923 in suburban Boston the first Headmaster, Reginald Heber Howe, was searching for a symbol to define the purpose of the new school as he saw it. He selected the sextant, feeling it was representative of the course to be chartered by the young men now in his responsibility. His words are clear and telling: "The sextant is a symbol of orientation ... for it is only by finding ourselves, by discovering our capacities and aptitudes, that we can be of service to the community." From that day to this the sextant has been the symbol of this

Go Huskies! Beat Felix the Cat!

fine preparatory school for young men. *The Sextant* is the name of the school newspaper and adorns the letterhead of all official school writings. The school seal has the sextant at the center and the Latin words *providentia, studium, fidelitas* around it. Although the Belmont Hill School teams, noted particularly for their prowess in hockey, are known as the Hillies—"There was a vision of it, 'standing high on a hill, excellent, aspiring, a lighthouse school' "—the Sextant is more truly the symbol of the orientation and direction in life that these men will take. Thus the Hillies is the team name of the Belmont Hill School and the sextant is their symbol. (I am indebted to George Ferguson, former hockey player and coach of Belmont Hill, and to Harold Prenatt, school archivist, for this information.)

The Lamp of Knowledge

Similar in philosophy to the Belmont Hill School and also near Boston, in Brookline, on the grounds of the original Longwood Cricket Club, is the Winsor School for girls. The Winsor School also does not really have a mascot. Their symbol is the lamp, in depiction somewhat like those that when rubbed are apt to send forth a genie willing to grant three wishes. In this case the lamp depicted is the Lamp of Knowledge, bringing light into the darkness of the uneducated, untrained mind. It strikes me that the paired symbols of the lamp and the sextant provide a strong metaphoric insight into the purposes of education: light, knowledge, orientation, direction.

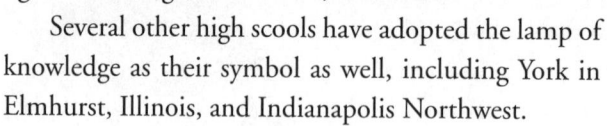

Several other high scools have adopted the lamp of knowledge as their symbol as well, including York in Elmhurst, Illinois, and Indianapolis Northwest.

The Sundials

The Ethel Walker School was founded in 1911 in Lakewood, New Jersey, and moved to its present six-hundred-acre campus on a former Dodge

Nicknames, Mascots, and Symbols

family estate in Simsbury, Connecticut, six years later. It was founded as a college preparatory school for women when most of the secondary schools of the era were considered "finishing schools" for women not intending to go further but wishing to learn the finer aspects of social life.

The symbol of the Ethel Walker School is the sundial. This one had me stumped until I heard the engaging full story from Dr. Susanna Jones, head of the school. The name has come down from the very earliest days of the school. At the first dinner for the new students, after their parents had dropped them off and departed, the new faculty, new staff, and Miss Walker herself were all together, somewhat nervous, everyone a bit uncertain of their relationships and roles, all wanting this exciting venture to succeed but none knowing precisely how to insure that success. At a time when a somewhat awkward hiatus in the conversation had occurred one of the students, unfamiliar with a pepper grinder, saw one on the table and asked if it were a sundial. After a bit of a pause a burst of general laughter eased the tension and everyone decided that the school now had a symbol. They have been the Sundials ever since.

From those very early days there have been two clubs on campus, non-exclusive, open to all, the Suns and the Dials. With their own colors, cheers, and periodicals, the *Sun Rays* and the *Time Pieces*, as well as friendly but intense competition of all kinds between the two for these eighty-five years now.

Recently the school commissioned a Millennium Sundial to be built and placed on campus such that the time could be read from inside or outside of one of the main buildings. The sculptor selected for this project was Danielle Langford and her resulting work represents the convergence of mathematics, art and science. A sundial for this fine school whose teams and, indeed, all students are the Sundials.

Some Others

At Indianapolis North Central the Panthers are the mascot and the team name both, but the symbol is a crest with "NC" on a scroll and the Torch of the Future burning brightly at the top. This is indicative of the light educated North Central graduates are expected to shine into the darkness of ignorance as they make their way through life.

Oak Park High School had its symbol in 1907, some twenty years before it had the Huskie mascot and team name. The symbol is the town crest with oak leaves, an acorn, and the words *Ta Garista,* Greek for "The Best." All Oak Park students are expected to give their best in all endeavors throughout their lives, in school and out.

At Glenn's Ferry High School in Idaho the team name is the Pilots and the symbol is a ship's wheel. Education is meant to provide a sense of direction, but we are all at the helm of our own lives.

At Monticello, Illinois, High School, the team name is the Sages, the symbol a wise old owl. Education and knowledge are not all that is required for a successful life, wisdom must also be acquired.

Cathedral High School in Indianapolis was founded in 1918 by Bishop Joseph Chartrand. From the beginning, the school had an extremely close relationship with the University of Notre Dame. Cathedral teams have long been known as the Fighting Irish, perhaps predating even Notre Dame in that regard,[1] and their version of the leprechaun mascot bears a remarkable resemblance to that used by the university. Cathedral, however, also uses both the shamrock and a Celtic cross as symbols of their school, as well as the shield of Bishop Chartrand with its Latin inscription: *IPSA DUCE NON FATIGARIS*—WITH HER LEADING YOU SHALL NOT TIRE. (With thanks to Chris Kaufman of Indianapolis Cathedral High School.)

---

[1] In its earliest days, though known even then as the Irish, the Notre Dame mascot was not the leprechaun, but an Irish terrier!

31
AMERICAN HISTORY 101

As we have seen, our choice of nickname, or mascot, or school name, is often very instructive as to our shared history as a nation and as a culture. Here are some more.

Explorers

Several schools are named for Christopher Columbus. One is in Nebraska, west of Omaha. Their team name is the Discoverers. (Interestingly, Columbus is not far from Colon. Cristobal Colon is the Spanish name for Christopher Columbus.) There is also a Christopher Columbus High School in the Bronx. Their teams are the Explorers.

Frenchman Rene Robert Cavalier, Sieur de LaSalle, was one of the first white men to sail down the St. Lawrence River and was known to be the first to build a boat and sail it on the Great lakes. He saw Niagara Falls and continued west into what is now Illinois. The town of LaSalle, at the juncture of the Illinois and Vermillion rivers, is named for him. LaSalle continued on down the Mississippi to the Gulf of Mexico, again, the first European to do so, and claimed the entire area for his king, Louis XIV, naming it Louisiana. LaSalle-Peru High School in LaSalle, Illinois, fields the Cavaliers in his honor. LaSalle High School in Niagara Falls teams are the Explorers.

Henry Hudson, a skilled navigator and explorer, discovered Hudson Bay, and was the first European to navigate up the river that bears his name. He sailed at least as far as the site of present day Albany in his vessel the *Half Moon*, and went beyond by smaller craft in 1609. Henry Hudson High School in Highlands, New Jersey, fields the Admirals. In Montrose, New York, using the name Hudson was given during his explorations for the Dutch East India Company, Henryk Hudson High School fields the Sailors.

Pere Jacques Marquette was another French explorer whose travels included the areas from Green Bay, Wisconsin through most of Illinois. He is mentioned extensively elsewhere in this book (see Piasa Birds). Marquette High School in Ottawa, Illinois, teams are the Crusaders. In the Mississippi River town of Alton in southern Illinois, Marquette High School teams are the Explorers.

The Lost Colony

Roanoke Island, between the Pamlico and Albemarle Sounds off of the coast of North Carolina, was the site of the first attempt at a permanent settlement in the New World by the English, begun in 1585, fully twenty-two years before Jamestown and thirty-five years before the Pilgrims landed at Plymouth. The attempt was made by Sir Walter Raleigh and Sir Richard Grenville and at first involved one hundred men who stayed on the island and constructed a fort on the northern shore. The "Roanoke Hundred" were apparently killed by Indians. A second expedition arrived two years later, in July of 1587 and also encountered many hardships. When help finally arrived at Roanoke Island in 1590, Fort Raleigh had been abandoned and the word "Croatoan" had been carved into a tree. Croatoan was an Indian word for Hatteras, but no trace of the Lost Colony was found there or anywhere else. Today, the town of Manteo, North Carolina, site of the reconstructed Fort Raleigh of the Lost Colony calls its high school athletic teams the Redskins.

American History 101

Peter Stuyvesant

Peter Stuyvesant was born in 1592 in Friesland, the Netherlands. In 1643, while the Director General of the Dutch West Indies Company with responsibility for the island colonies of Aruba, Bonaire, and Curacao, he was severely injured in a fight on the then Portuguese island of St. Martin. His injury resulted in the amputation of his right leg below the knee. He was fitted for a peg leg, covered with filigrees of silver, of which he became exceedingly proud. People would come from miles around just to see it. Stuyvesant was soon given the larger responsibility for Dutch possessions in the New World, headquartered in New Amsterdam. Although he successfully dislodged the Swedes from those possessions that bordered the Delaware River and made peace with the Indians there, he eventually was forced to surrender New Amsterdam to the English forces led by the Duke of York, hence changing the name to New York. Peter Stuyvesant High School, located in lower Manhattan, not far from the site of Stuyvesant's farm, the Bouwerji (the Bowery now), is one of the crown jewels of American public education. It is also close to the site of the World Trade Center, Ground Zero. Its halls were utilized during the horrendous days following September 11, 2001, by the search and rescue teams. The nickname of Peter Stuyvesant High School? The Peg Legs!

Drums Along the Mohawk

A fascinating area of upstate New York, formed as a triangle by the Mohawk River and Lake George, is filled with history. The western point of this triangle is composed of the towns of Johnstown and Gloversville. As the latter name would indicate, this was a center for the glove trade. The Gloversville teams, though officially the Huskies, are frequently referred to as the Glovers by local newspapers and fans.

Johnstown is notable, in part, for being the site of the last battle of the Revolutionary War fought on New York soil, an American victory, on October 25, 1781—six days after the surrender of General Cornwallis in Virginia. Johnstown is named for Sir William Johnson, a British general and hero in the French and Indian Wars, knighted after he won a significant victory at Lake George and constructed Fort Henry on the southern end of the lake. Upon his retirement, he built a magnificent Georgian mansion in Johnstown, now a state historical site, open to the public. In honor of Sir William, the high school teams are called the Sir Bills.

Another important strategic location was at the northern end of Lake George, controlling as it also did the southern portion of the larger body of water, Lake Champlain. Fort Ticonderoga, nicely restored and a very interesting site to tour, was built there and several significant battles occurred around it. In 1775 Ethan Allen and his Green Mountain Boys recaptured the fort during the American Revolution, but it again changed hands when General Burgoyne and his massive army marched southward from Lake Champlain. The Ticonderoga High School teams are well designated as the Sentinels. The Lake George High School teams are equally well named, the Warriors.

Burgoyne was somewhat surprisingly defeated in perhaps the decisive battle of the war (at least up to that time, when American victories had been few and far between) by General Horatio Gates and his American troops at the Battle of Saratoga in 1777. A monument to this victory has been built at the site of this battle, which is somewhat outside of the present town of Saratoga Springs. Saratoga Springs, as the name suggests, was known for its curative waters and was to become a favored resort town. Horse racing became an important addition to the Saratoga Springs scene and many wonderful homes and hotels, built in the nineteenth century, are still there and make for a very interesting visit. Everyone loved the waters, the gambling, and of course, the horses. The present day Saratoga Springs High School athletic teams are called the Streaks and nearby Schuylerville High School teams are the Horses

A bit to the north and east is the town of Whitehall, which calls itself

American History 101

"The Birthplace of the American Navy" because General Benedict Arnold put the Colonials' first fleet into the water there, leading them down river to Lake Champlain. The construction of those first ships may be seen on display today in Whitehall. Later, Whitehall became a significant railroad town and their high school teams are called the Railroaders.

The Colonials

Morristown, a town of sixteen thousand people in central New Jersey, was an extremely important site throughout the Revolutionary War. Much of the iron needed by the Continental Army was forged in Morristown and much of the equally essential gunpowder was produced there. This made Morristown an irresistible target for the British, but the defensible nature of the site resulted in repeated redcoat frustrations. George Washington utilized Morristown for his headquarters during three different years of the War at which times the Continental Army was also stationed there. Washington's headquarters were in the Ford Mansion, now a National Historic Site. Can it be any surprise that the Morristown High School athletic teams are proudly known as the Colonials?

The Patriot

The stirring movie *The Patriot*, starring Mel Gibson, was, with a considerable degree of artistic license, based upon the life of Francis Marion, who was born in South Carolina in 1732 and died in Berkeley County in 1795. During the Revolutionary War his elusive tactics and escapes into the swamps of his native state after leading his militia in effective strikes against the redcoat regulars, earned him the epithet "The Swamp Fox" from his British adversaries. By the end of the war Marion had been commissioned a brigadier general, and afterward he served his state in their Senate. The town of Marion is located near the North Carolina line just east of Florence. The Marion High School athletic teams remember General Marion, the Patriot well: they are also the Swamp Foxes.

Go Huskies! Beat Felix the Cat!

Who was Molly Stark?

Weare, New Hampshire, a small town about fifteen miles southwest of Concord, is the home of John Stark Regional High School. It is named for a native son who rose to the rank of general during the Revolutionary War and distinguished himself at the Battles of Bunker Hill and Bennington. Starke has been described by historian John Elting as "a combination of New England cantankerousness and Scots-Irish contentiousness." At the Battle of Bennington he is remembered for having told his troops before the fray: "There my boys are your enemies. We'll beat them before dark or Molly Stark will be a widow!" Beat them they did, and Molly Stark still had her husband. And John Stark Regional High School had its nickname: the Generals.

The Bullets

The small town of Topton, Pennsylvania, between Reading and Allentown, though somewhat north of the actual site of the Brandywine Creek Battlefield, remembers that near disaster for General Washington and his troops in September 1777 with its choice of a school name. Brandywine High School in Topton remembers the battle itself with the nickname they have chosen, the Bullets.

The Little Noises

When I first saw that the Moodus, Connecticut, High School athletic teams were called the Little Noises, I had to wonder what that was all about. Not particularly the kind of name you would expect in the sometimes raucous world of sports. The story as it was told to me, however, makes it one of the very best I have heard.

Moodus is located near the Connecticut River as it wends its way to Long Island Sound south of Hartford. The entire area has long been one of considerable seismic activity. Probably this was why the Indians called it Morehemoodus, their name for "Place of Noises." The largest earthquake ever to occur in Connecticut since being settled by Europeans happened on May 16, 1791. The quake was of Level 7 intensity and was felt as far away as Boston and New York City. Stone walls and chimneys were toppled, a fissure several meters wide opened up and more than a hundred aftershocks were recorded during the next twenty-four hours.[1] Anyone who has ever been in a major earthquake knows how it feels and sounds. No wonder the area was called Place of Noises. Hearing this it became clear why Nathan Hale-Ray High School[2] in Moodus calls their athletic teams the Little Noises!

Lockport

In 1848 a plan to enable water transportation to be possible from the developing port of Chicago on Lake Michigan all the way to the Gulf of Mexico was put into effect with the engineering of what was called the Illinois and Michigan Canal. The canal was ninety-seven miles long and went from Chicago to LaSalle, where it emptied into the Illinois River, which in turn flowed into the Mississippi. The canal portion of the trip took twenty-two hours and the charge for a passenger was four dollars, but the primary purpose was to move merchandise. The main locks were at the point where the company that built and operated the canal established a town and made it their headquarters, calling it Lockport. The canal closed with the advent of railroad traffic between Chicago and LaSalle, but today the locks and the area around them are a well preserved historical attraction. The nickname of the Lockport High School teams, perfect for a port, for a place that carries people and things, is the Porters.

---

[1]Seismicity of the United States 1569–1989, Stover and Coffman, U.S. Geologic Survey Paper 1527.

[2]Nathan Hale once taught school there.

Go Huskies! Beat Felix the Cat!

Pioneers

St. Charles, Missouri, on the banks of the Missouri River, was the first capital of the state and the original capitol building has been nicely restored along with a number of other eighteenth- and nineteenth-century homes and public buildings in this historic town. St. Charles was founded seven years before the Declaration of Independence, by French fur traders who had come there in need of a river port. In 1798 Daniel Boone came to St. Charles and in 1804 the Lewis and Clark expedition to explore the newly acquired Louisiana Purchase began from the docks of St. Charles. It was not to be an auspicious start, however, as leaving in a driving rain rather late in the day and against a strong current the travelers made it only three miles upstream before their first night's encampment. Well, a journey of two thousand miles begins, I guess, with a single stroke of an oar. Mother Phillipine Duchesne, founded the first free school west of the Mississippi River and the St. Charles Duchesne High School teams are fittingly called the Pioneers.

Boomers

The area of the United States acquired from France in the 1803 Louisiana Purchase now known as Oklahoma was first called Indian Territory as its exclusive use was for the resettled Eastern American Indian tribes. Following the Civil War and the Territory's alliance with the South it was placed under military rule during Reconstruction. Those who coveted Oklahoma land and came into it despite the Indian's claims were called Boomers. Then came the famous Homestead Act and the land rush of April 22, 1889. Those who jumped the noon starting gun in an effort to get particularly attractive parcels were called Sooners. Today all Oklahomans take pride in both of these sobriquets. The state is the Sooner State, the University teams are the Sooners, and the songs and cheers refer to Boomer Sooners: "Boomer Sooners, Boomer Sooners, Boomer Sooners, OKU!" Woodward, in the western part of the state, is home to the Plains Indians and Pioneers

American History 101

Museum. It is also home to the Woodward High School Boomers. Interestingly enough, there are also Boomers in the town of Toledo, Oregon. Perhaps some Oklahomans took the Oregon Trail out west and brought the name Boomers with them. (Or, possibly I should relate Toledo more to Glendale, California. Their teams are the Dynamiters.)

Back to the pioneer theme. Many of those who raced across the Oklahoma countryside in a desire for their own plot of ground, and many of those on the Oregon Trail or other trails traversing the west, did so in those wonderful Conestoga wagons, sometimes in trains of three hundred or more wagons stretching out over thirty miles in length. These wagons were homes for weeks and months for many a family trekking across those vast spaces, often beset upon by hostile Indians and renegade white men. In Berwyn, Pennsylvania, near Philadelphia, is Conestoga High School and their teams are the Pioneers. There are also Pioneers at Pilgrim Academy in Egg Harbor, New Jersey.

Quakers

The Society of Friends, known more frequently as the Quakers, is generally associated with William Penn, eastern Pennsylvania and Philadelphia. However, in 1858 they built their Western Meetinghouse in Plainfield, Indiana, a suburb of Indianapolis on the old National Road that is still visible there, including one of the original bridges, next to what is now U.S. 40. For the period from 1881–1919 the Friends established and ran the Central Academy, since superseded by Plainfield High School. The nickname of the Plainfield High School athletic teams: the Quakers. Well actually, it's the Fighting Quakers, about which the young waitress—a recent grad now studying art—who served us lunch said wryly, "Kind of an oxymoron, isn't it?"

Pathfinders

Lieutenant Colonel John Chase Fremont, known as "The Pathfinder" for

New Harmony

The town of New Harmony, Indiana, is located in the far southwestern portion of the state, on the Wabash River near its confluence with the Ohio. New Harmony was originally settled by the German idealist, Georg Rapp, who had come to Pennsylvania from Wurttemberg, Germany, to found a millenial community. He was attracted to the commercial opportunities afforded by the two rivers near his chosen Indiana site and purchased thirty thousand acres in 1815 that he called Harmonie. Soon his community was prospering. More than 150 homes were built as well as a grist mill, an oil mill, and a saw mill, a grand granary, a silk factory, brick kiln, dye works, a distillery, and a brewery. There were orchards, a vineyard, and fields for a variety of crops.

Unfortunately, as was true for virtually all such communes historically, this prosperity did not last and the site was sold to a Scotsman named Robert Owen and his friend, scientist and philanthropist William McClure. Their vision was to create a Utopian community of scholars, educators and scientists and they were initially quite successful at luring many great thinkers from Europe to enjoy the fruits of a society less encumbered by the restrictions on thought they had encountered in the Old World.

There was indeed freedom of thought in the town Owen renamed New Harmony and, although the Utopian ideals of a communal society failed rather rapidly, the mark of the great thinkers was indelibly left on the American scene. New Harmony became a center for scientific thought, educational innovation, and the feminist movement in the New World. Linkages were made to the Philosophical Society in Philadelphia and New Harmony became a dominant force in the fields of geology, zoology, botany and chemistry. What was later to become the United States Geological Survey had its roots in New Harmony.

New Harmony is truly an American historic gem, well worth a visit by anyone interested in understanding and unraveling the mysteries of the past. There is, in fact, a small high school in New Harmony. With the new class based tournaments they are now occasionally winning their sectional and when I was there I saw spray painted in many a store window "Go Rappites," harkening back to their original founder. What a marvelous nickname for a truly marvelous place.

his trailblazing activities, captured the Mexican garrison at Sonoma, California, in 1847, at the close of the Mexican War. He then declared the California Republic, a short-lived entity that lasted only about a month. The bear flag designed by Fremont, however, did provide the inspiration for the present-day state flag. The city of Fremont, south of Oakland, bears his name, as does Fremont High School in Los Angeles, whose teams are the Pathfinders.

Chincoteague

Most of us are familiar with the Island of Chincoteague, Virginia, and its ponies from the series of books by Marguerite Henry, the first of which is *Misty of Chincoteague*. Local lore has it that the ponies on Chincoteague and its sister island, Assoteague, are descended from Spanish mine horses that survived a shipwreck in the sixteenth century and swam to shore. More likely is that they are the descendants of horses brought over by the first English colonists of the islands some years later. On the last Wednesday and Thursday of July each year the foals and yearlings swim at slack tide from Assoteague to Chincoteague and are sold at auction. Those unsold swim back and roam the island with the other ponies. The Chincoteague High School athletic teams are the Ponies.

Kentuckians

Abraham Lincoln, our Civil War President, was born in a log cabin just south of Hodgenville, Kentucky. Jefferson Davis, President of the Confederacy, was born in similar circumstances in Fairview, Kentucky, just east of Hopkinsville, on the Todd County line. These two birthplaces are marked by monuments. Interestingly, as the crow flies, they are probably no more than ninety miles apart. Many schools have honored Lincoln's memory; unfortunately Hodgenville did not, selecting the name Hawks. Todd County High School does remember Davis as they are known as the Rebels. Hopkinsville High teams are the Colonels.

American History 101

Ashland

Ashland, Wisconsin, is due east of Duluth, Minnesota, at the base of the harbor formed primarily by the Bayfield Peninsula as it juts out into Lake Superior. Interestingly enough, one of the best preserved of all the ore docks used so extensively until the deposits of the rich Mesabi Iron Ore Range vein were depleted, is the one at Ashland. This dock extends far out into the water and can be seen from several vantage points along the shore including the lakeside inn where we enjoyed an excellent whitefish lunch and could easily imagine seeing train after train pull their cars out on the dock and tip their contents into the enormous waiting ore boats. The people of Ashland have preserved this dock and this phase of our country's history with the name they selected for their high school teams: The Oredockers, and the Dockerettes.

Hambletonian

Hambletonian, foaled in 1847, is the name of the standard bred horse that is the ancestor of almost all of the harness race horses in America today. His original owner, a hired man named Rysdyk, became wealthy after it was noticed that Hambletonian's first several foals ran exceptionally well and the horse became popular at stud, siring well over a thousand foals. The Hambletonian Stakes, named in his honor, were run for many years in the town of Goshen, New York. Four miles away, in the town of Chester, is the Chester Union Free School. Their teams are called the Hambletonians.

Fox Valley High School in Milton, Iowa, and Rutherford B. Hayes High School in Delaware, Ohio, are kindred spirits to the Chester Union Hambletonians. They are both the Trotters. So, too, with a different gait, are the teams of Sacramento Grant High School in California. They are the Pacers.

Watervliet

During the War of 1812 an arsenal was constructed in Watervliet, New York, a Hudson River town near Troy, to provide cannons for the American Army as Great Britain sought to reacquire her former colony. That arsenal, America's oldest, has been in continuous operation ever since, still making the large gun barrels needed for our twenty-first century military. There is an excellent museum of military history and cannon construction in the arsenal. The Watervliet High School teams are appropriately and proudly called the Cannoneers.

The Woolies

When we lived in Australia we were reminded on a cold day in Sydney, which admittedly did not happen too often, to put on our "woolies." We had pullovers, cardigans and jumpers to choose from, but it was clear that wool was needed whenever the temperature dropped. This was also, of course, necessary to the American Colonists in the seventeenth century. Millbury, Massachusetts, was, as you may have guessed, a mill town, and an important center for the manufacture of both wool and the machinery needed to process it. The citizens of Millbury recognized the importance of wool to their own history in selecting the nickname for their high school team, which, again, you have guessed: The Woolies.

The Bell Ringers

East Hampton, in central Connecticut, was founded in 1767 and soon became the leading center for the manufacture of bells in the world. Bells made of various metals and alloys and even of wood have been formed, shaped and stamped since as early as 1808. The Bevin Bell Company is believed to be the oldest bell manufacturing company in continuous operation in the world, having been established in East Hampton in 1832. Bells of all sizes and uses have been made in East Hampton, for churches, schools and boats, for toys, rickshaws and some early versions of the automobile. No wonder the town of East Hampton proudly calls itself the Bell Town. No wonder the East Hampton High School teams are called the Bell Ringers. (I had hoped the girls' teams would be the Belle Ringers, but I am told they are not, they are the same as the boys' teams.)

The Canalmen

Bourne, Massachusetts, is situated on Cape Cod, at the west end of the present day Cape Cod Canal. When it was built in 1914, the canal was an engineering feat of considerable significance and value. The 17.4-mile waterway from Bourne to Sagamore, linking Buzzards Bay and Rhode Island Sound to Cape Cod Bay, changed the Cape from a peninsula to an island and reduced the shipping distance from Boston to New York City by 135 miles. The Bourne High School teams are called the Canalmen.

The Hatters

Danbury, Connecticut, is located in the far western part of the state. Danbury was founded in 1684 and the first hat shop was opened there in 1780. By 1784 it was turning out hats at the rate of three a day. There has been a Dodd Hat Shop in Danbury since 1790 and for over two hundred years the city has been the center of the hat industry in the world, known universally as the "Hat City." Can it be any surprise that the Danbury High School athletic teams are the Hatters?

The Tanners

Two towns in Massachusetts have very interesting stories to tell. Peabody is now a Boston suburb, some thirteen miles northeast of the capital. From the time of the Revolutionary War, tanning has been the chief industry of Peabody. As late as the mid-twentieth century, Peabody was the largest tanning center in the nation for both leather and sheepskin. It can come as no surprise then that the Peabody High School teams are called the Tanners.

Woburn, also a Boston suburb, has enjoyed an equally long history as a leader in the tanning industry and in the manufacture of leather tanning machinery, beginning as long ago as the 1640s. The Woburn High School teams are also called the Tanners. I wonder whose hide gets tanned when Peabody and Woburn meet on the field of athletic competition.

Wausau

Locals like to point out that while Wausau, Wisconsin, is in the middle of the USA, the USA is also in the middle of Wausau. The area was once an Indian settlement and the name means "Far away place," which is not as true now as it may once have been. The first white settlement on the site of the present day city was a logging camp called Big Bull Falls. Today Wausau East High School remembers that settlement with its nickname, the Lumberjacks, and Wausau West remembers the earlier Indian presence with its nickname, the Warriors.

Old Abe

Eau Claire, Wisconsin, is located at the confluence of the Chippewa and Eau Claire rivers, the latter so named by French trappers and loggers in the area who appreciated the clear water, free of rocks and rapids that they found there. Few schools have selected a mascot with as much American historical significance as has Eau Claire Memorial High School. The mascot's name is Old Abe. The story is rich and wonderful.

Early in 1861 a Flambeau Indian rescued an orphaned eaglet from its nest and traded it for food to a family who had homesteaded on the future site of Eau Claire. The bird quickly grew into an impressive creature with a broad wingspan, a fierce cry, and apparently some martial inclinations, because whenever the violin was played "the bird would rise up, flap its wings, and hop and dance during the fast parts of the 'Bonaparte's March.'"

The family gave the bird to the commander of the Civil War Eighth

Wisconsin Regiment, who named him "Old Abe" in honor of Abraham Lincoln and the Eighth Wisconsin began to be called the Eagle Regiment. The eagle was sworn into the United States service as "Old Abe, the Mascot," and decorated with red, white, and blue ribbons and rosette.

Whenever the regiment went into battle, Old Abe was at the front, on a perch and "the royal bird was borne with the regiment on all its marches into every battle in which the gallant Eighth was engaged. . . . In the midst of the roaring of the cannon, the crack of the musket, and the roll of smoke . . . the appearance of Old Abe was perfectly magnificent . . . he would spring up, spread his wings, uttering a startling scream, heard and felt, and gloried in by all of the soldiers. The fiercer and louder the storm, the fiercer and louder were his screams." Old Abe was at the front for some twenty-two battles and sixty skirmishes, and it is reported that not a single color or eagle bearer of the Eighth Regiment was ever shot down. The soldiers were convinced that the eagle led a charmed life.

The Confederates called him the "Yankee Buzzard" and one general ordered his men to capture or shoot him, adding that he would sooner capture Old Abe than a whole regiment.

Whenever the American flag passed by, Old Abe would rise "to his full height, spread his broad wings and (flap) them three or four times. . . ." Old Abe now resides in a glass case on an elegant pedestal in the rotunda of the State House in Madison.

Can anyone question the choice of Old Abe, magnificent eagle, protector of the Wisconsin Eagle Regiment, bane of the Confederacy, honored in the state capital, as the choice for the mascot of Eau Claire Memorial High School? Certainly not this writer. (Thanks to Pat Harvey and Julie Lowy of Memorial High School for this history.)

Brush High School

The Charles F. Brush High School is located in Lyndhurst, Ohio. Lyndhurst is a close-in east side suburb of Cleveland, between Euclid to the north and University Heights to the south. The school is named for Charles Brush who was a pioneer in electricity, a contemporary of Thomas Edison. Brush was an inventor almost on a par with Edison. Upon graduation from the University of Michigan Brush determined to turn the electric arc lamp, first discovered by Sir Humphrey Davy, into something more than a laboratory curiosity. He was imminently successful in doing so and founded the Brush Electric Company to commercialize his invention. Its first practical application was the lighting of Wanamaker's Department Store in New York City in 1878. The following year he introduced the first electric street lighting in America, installing his arc lights on the Cleveland Public Square, and one year later did so in New York City. The arc light was a great success both in America and in Europe, and the Old Lamplighter of songdom was needed no more where Brush's invention was installed. Although Edison's discovery of incandescent lighting led to the replacement of Brush's arc lights they should still be remembered as the first. Cleveland has, in fact, done so by reinstalling the arc lights on that public square in 1974, and there they may be seen today. The high school that bears his name was dedicated in 1927. Their nickname? Why, the Arcs, of course. Their mascot? Arcy, a lucky student who gets chosen annually to wear the Arcy suit and help lead the cheers for the Brush High School Arcs.

(Thanks to Ms. Robinson of the Brush High Alumni Association and Mr. John Huth for the above material.)

32
END GAME

ALTHOUGH I HAVE certainly scattered some of my personal favorite nicknames throughout this book, this chapter is a selection of several particularly meaningful ones, deserving of emphasis and reflective of the rich variety of our American heritage.

Centralia

Centralia, Illinois, is located in the south central portion of the state. The town was founded by the Illinois Central Railroad, hence its name. (The 1960 census placed the center of population of the United States six and a half miles northwest of Centralia adding further to the appropriateness of the name!) Coal is also mined in the area around Centralia and corn and soy beans are farmed there. Centralia is not a wealthy town, but it is a proud town and one of its sources of pride is the local high school and it's highly successful basketball teams, both boys' and girls'. Recently, *USA Today* listed Centralia as the nation's leading high school boys basketball program in terms of overall victories. The nickname of the boys' athletic teams at Centralia High School is the Orphans, and thereby hangs a story.

In the twenties Centralia had an excellent basketball team. They won their way to the State Championships in Champaign. Because of the economic conditions in the town the school could not afford new uniforms for all of the players. The seniors got the new ones, the juniors had last year's and the underclassmen got whatever was left. Up until that time Centralia

Go Huskies! Beat Felix the Cat!

High School had no official mascot or nickname. Apparently a sports writer for the Champaign newspaper who watched Centralia's games in the tournament wrote "The boys from Centralia play like wonders but they look like orphans" with reference to the variety of uniforms. It turned out that Centralia's citizens liked that description and from that day to this the Centralia High School boys' athletic teams have been proudly called the Orphans.

I mentioned in an earlier chapter that I would withhold mention of my favorite girls team name until later. Now is later. In the early 1970s girls' teams became common in interscholastic sports around the country, and, of course, Centralia needed a nickname for its girls' athletic teams. Would it be the Lady Orphans? Perhaps the Orphanettes? No, with an inspiration of imagination they selected the Annies. The Orphans and the Orphan Annies. What a great combination!

But there's more. When I was recently escorted through the impressive red-and-white-trimmed basketball arena at Centralia High School (located on Dike Edelman Drive) by athletic director Roger Stieg, I not only noticed the large sign counting the nation's greatest number of boys' basketball victories changed, of course, after each win, but also the name given to the student rooting section: The Or*fan*age.

Amarillo, Texas

Amarillo is a west Texas town whose name means yellow in Spanish. It is located in an area that can get pretty dry and windblown. I cannot improve on the words of my Dartmouth classmate, Joe Obering, who provides the following description of the derivation of Amarillo High School's nickname, which I believe he got from a local paper: From Savages to Sandies.

> *On a windy spring day in 1922, the Amarillo High "Savage" baseball team was practicing in the windblown sand of the old professional baseball stadium of the now-defunct Amarillo Grays. Coach Astayanax Saunders Douglas shouted encouragement to his team. According to the*

End Game

former shortstop, Winfield "Windy" Nicklaus, Douglas barked, "Come on you golden sandstormers, come on now, bear down." The team immediately adopted the new name and became the Amarillo High "Golden Sandstorm" aka the "Sandies." Later that school year, at a ceremony during a Downtown Rotary Luncheon, coach Douglas christened the AHS teams. Sprinkling a football with sand, he said, "As from now and henceforth, all the athletic teams of Amarillo High School will be known as the Golden Sandstorm."

This, of course, is often reduced to the Sandies. The sophomore team is called the Stormies and the Jayvees are the Yannigans. A Yannigan, I am told, is a person who substitutes for another.

Nickname Evolution I

Two schools in southern Indiana—Huntingburg and Jasper—have been rivals from the early days of the twentieth century when they each fell in love with Dr. Naismith's magical game and started throwing round balls through round hoops of exactly twice the diameter. From almost the beginning the two schools played for a trophy called the Little Brown Jug, as important to them as was the more famous Old Oaken Bucket prize contended for by Indiana and Purdue Universities in football. At (or near) the beginning, the Jasper teams were called the Giants. The prevailing school of thought on this is that Jasper, which has always played excellent baseball, was enamored of the New York Giants and their great success in the National League under Manager John McGraw. Huntingburg's teams were called the Lions. This eventually led the Jasper faithful to desire a new nickname, one designed to have a better chance of beating a lion. They settled on the wildcat. The wildcat, it was believed, was quicker than the lion and speed was so important on the basketball court that the Jasper Wildcats were created, a name they still answer to. This, in true Newtonian fashion, prompted a reaction by Huntingburg. They decided to become the Hunters, confident that they could thus slay the Wildcat. Today the rivalry

Go Huskies! Beat Felix the Cat!

is just as fierce, even though Huntingburg High School has been replaced by Southridge High School. The Southridge teams still go after the Jasper Wildcats, as the Raiders.

Nickname Evolution II

Milton, Massachusetts, ten miles from downtown Boston is adjacent to the Blue Hills Reservation, a seven thousand-acre hilly oasis of forests, wetlands, trails and open green space that some farsighted officials saved many years ago for the enjoyment of all. Some years after that, Milton High School had an excellent basketball team. They compared themselves to the University of Illinois Whiz Kids, made of up Andy Phillip, Gene Vance, Dwight Edelman, and their fine teammates who were doing so well in Champaign at about the same time, and adopted Whiz Kids as their own nickname. Some years later, however, it was determined that Whiz Kids either did not fit the then prevailing sentiment of what would constitute a suitably awe-inspiring mascot for the school, or perhaps the basketball team was merely not doing so well. At any rate, the nickname was changed, a new one selected, and the teams began to be called the Bobcats, perhaps because of those roaming the Blue Hills Reservation. Personally, I prefer Whiz Kids. It's more distinctive.

Nickname Evolution III

Ralph Hayne, assistant principal at Washington High School in southwestern Indiana, points out that their teams were not always known as the Hatchets. From 1896 until the early 1920s, they were known simply as the Old Gold and Black after their school colors. In 1922 the star player came from a family who ran a local funeral parlor and fans began calling them the Undertakers. This was not a name that was likely to last, and, when a particularly strong team came along in the 1924–1925 season, sportswriter Edward Brouilette wrote after one game that "the team had cut through its opponent like George Washington's hatchet had cut through the

End Game

cherry tree." Fans loved it, and began taking black and gold hatchets to their games. The nickname stuck

The Jesters

No discussion of the education of women in the United States would be complete without mention of the pioneering work done by Emma Hart Willard. Emma Hart was born in Berlin, Connecticut, near Hartford in 1787. Her father was probably related to the man for whom the capital of the state was named. Fortunately he was an enlightened man who encouraged the full development of the lively intellect and inquiring mind presented to him by young Emma, an uncommon stance for the time. As her own learning widened her horizons, Emma determined to provide other young women with similar opportunities and established a small school to do so in Middlebury, Vermont. By 1818 Emma, now Emma Willard, had created a plan for the broader schooling of young women that she sent, with some apparent misgivings, to then New York State Governor Clinton who not only approved of her plan but shared it with such notables as President James Monroe and former presidents Thomas Jefferson and John Adams.

In 1824, the Marquis de Lafayette, on his trip up the Hudson River, stopped to pay a visit to Emma Willard and her new school in Troy. We are told that the marquis presented his hostess with a bouquet of pink roses to mark the occasion, and for years pink was the official color of the school. More recently it has been changed to the rich red worn by Willard's present athletic teams. Their mascot is the Jesters, chosen from a popular character in one of the school's annual student theatrical performances. According to the school's website, the Jester represents "an aggressive yet playful love of the game."

Mitchell

Mitchell, South Dakota, was originally a railroad town, named for the president of the Chicago, Milwaukee, St. Paul and Pacific, Alexander Mitchell.

Go Huskies! Beat Felix the Cat!

Corn is grown in great abundance in the area around Mitchell and in 1892 it was decided to have a Corn Exposition in Mitchell. The centerpiece was to be a large building, the Corn Palace, that would be faced with corn and other locally grown products, but mostly just good old corn. It was expanded in 1921 and completed in its present form with Moorish towers in 1937. Every year the façade of the building is completely redone with new ears of corn in a variety of colors, as many as eleven, augmented by local grasses, and depicting a timely theme.

At any time, in any year, the Corn Palace is a sight to behold. A variety of goods and services are offered inside and, astonishingly enough, in the center of the Corn Palace is an ultra modern, very impressive basketball arena where the highly successful Mitchell High School teams play their home games. John Gillis, now a vice president of the National Federation of High Schools in Indianapolis and a man who provided me with valuable assistance in the data-gathering of nicknames for this book, once played his high school basketball in that very Corn Palace. He was a Mitchell High School Kernel.

A Great Rivalry

One of my favorite rivalry stories comes from the capital city of Alabama, Montgomery. Montgomery is a place filled with history, an extremely interesting and friendly place to visit with its capitol building, the fascinating First White House of the Confederacy, and the home occupied by Scott and Zelda Fitzgerald, the famous literary couple.

There are two high schools in Montgomery with interesting names and a longtime rivalry. One is Sidney Lanier High School, named for the great American poet who wrote such words as the following:

End Game

As the marsh hen builds on the watery sod
I will build me a nest on the greatness of God.

The nickname of Lanier High is, very appropriately, the Poets. Their rivals are Robert E. Lee High School, named for the revered leader of the Confederate armies. Lee High's mascot is, equally appropriately, the Generals. One time, some years back, when these two schools were playing a football game, the Lee cheerleaders came with a large sign that they held up for all to see. It said "We're fighters, not writers." By halftime the Lanier cheerleaders had their response in the form of an equally big sign that they held up. Their sign said "The pen is mightier than the sword." I'm told those signs show up for games to this very day. The Poets versus the Generals. Montgomery, Alabama.

Refreshments, Illinois Style (or "The Cola Wars")

Back in the days when it was truly a pleasure to travel by rail, the passenger line from southern Illinois to Chicago run by the Illinois Central Railroad, had stops at several smaller towns on the swing north. A friend of mine was riding that line one day when he heard an amusing interchange between the conductor and a fellow passenger. The train had just stopped in Arcola when the conductor announced "Next stop, Tuscola." The passenger said "Arcola, Tuscola—I suppose the next one after that is Coca-Cola." The conductor answered back, "No, actually it's Champaign."

Tuscola and Arcola have an intense rivalry in all sports. They have been playing football against each other for over a hundred years. Whenever the two play it is referred to as another installment of the "Cola Wars." Long before Pepsi-Cola and Coca-Cola, these Cola Wars commanded the attention of almost everyone in these two towns separated by only eight miles of lush farmland along U.S. Highway 45. I was told by the students I spoke with in Arcola that "we almost always win." Curiously, the Tuscola students said the same thing. I was assured by a more objective person that it's actually been quite even over all of these years in most sports. Johnny Gruelle, the originator of the Raggedy Ann and Andy stories and dolls, was born in Arcola and there is a museum dedicated to his creations in the town. The Arcola High School's basketball stadium is astonishingly large for a school with a graduating class in 2002 of thirty-seven seniors. The shields and colors of all the teams in the conference are displayed at the west end of the arena, with Tuscola enjoying a prominent place. It is a rivalry based on mutual respect. The Arcola teams are called the Purple Riders, a name bestowed by a writer for the *Champaign News-Gazette* in the mid 1930s in recognition of the football team's thirty-three game winning streak. I had thought perhaps there was some connection to Zane Grey and his "Riders of the Purple Sage" but could find no evidence of that. The Tuscola teams are the Warriors, so there is a definite Wild West tone to the Cola Wars. One of these days I'll have to drive over there and see one for myself. The one hundredth battle of the Cola Wars, which began in 1895, is scheduled to be played in 2004. I'd like to see that one.

The Artists

One of the most beautiful beaches in Southern California is Laguna Beach. Long a favorite place for artists, the town is located on a bluff overlooking the Pacific and the tops of the bluffs are filled with pretty little parks so that everyone can enjoy the magnificent views and the glorious sunsets. No wonder this little town, nestled between the foothills to the east and the waters to the west was early on destined to become an artist's colony. Today, artists are celebrated in a variety of ways in Laguna Beach. There is a Festival of the Arts held in a canyon setting that highlights the work of 160 Southern California artists every summer; there is the Laguna Art Museum with a permanent collection of works of Laguna artists and photographers, and there is the annual Pageant of the Masters, where actors and local townspeople portray famous classical and contemporary works in living tableaux. When I was last in Laguna Beach I enjoyed seeing several young artists atop the cliffs in one of the parks working on their creations in oil and

End Game

water colors. With all of this around, can it be any surprise that the Laguna Beach High School athletic teams are the Artists?

The Pretzels

Freeport, Illinois, was first settled in 1835, after the Black Hawk Indian wars. It was little more than a stage coach stop between the burgeoning community of Chicago and Galena, but began to grow with the lead mining based economy of the region. Freeport got its name from a kindhearted man by the name of William "Tutty" Baker who operated a ferry across the Pecatonic River. He never charged for this service, and was generous in many other ways. Finally his wife told him, "If you're not going to charge a fare and you keep giving things away from our store we might as well call this place a free port." And so they did. I was still in high school when I first learned that the Freeport teams were called the Pretzels. I later was informed that that name was selected because in the 1920s there were two major industries in town, a brewery and a pretzel factory. Sounds like a great combination to me! Anyway, the suggestion that the name Brewers be selected was rejected by the more temperate-minded citizens in favor of Pretzels. (It was left for Vassar College, then an all-girls school and one of the prestigious "Seven Sisters" to adopt the Brewers in honor of the manner in which their major benefactor had amassed his fortune.) I think Pretzels is a wonderful nickname, but it is not quite a unique one. Also in Illinois, in the smaller town of New Berlin, are to be found the Pretzels.

The Literary Prize

In spite of strong competition from the Poets of Sidney Lanier High School in Montgomery, Alabama, as well as the Poets from Paul Laurence Dunbar High School in Baltimore, the Literary Prize is awarded to Sauk Center, Minnesota, High School. Sauk Center was the birthplace of Harry Sinclair Lewis in 1885, better known by his middle and last names only. Following his graduation from Yale in 1907 Sinclair Lewis hit the top with the publication of his highly successful novel, *Main Street*, in 1920, excoriating small town life. Sinclair Lewis followed *Main Street* with four other well-known novels examining the American psyche and value system. In 1930 he became the first American to be awarded the Nobel Prize for Literature. The nickname of Sauk Center High School is the Mainstreeters.

An honorable mention citation goes to the golfers' mecca of Pebble Beach, California. There we find the Robert Louis Stevenson School. Perhaps my earliest introduction to literature came when I read Stevenson's stirring novels of swashbuckling adventure, *Treasure Island* and *Kidnapped*. How pleased I was to learn that the Stevenson School nickname is the Pirates.

Another honorable mention goes to Tennyson High School in Heyward, California. In a bloody battle of the Crimean War, on October 25, 1854, the British Light Brigade led by Lord Cardigan, was annihilated near Balaclava after their misbegotten charge into the teeth of superior Russian forces. Alfred, Lord Tennyson, immortalized this tragedy with his poem "The Charge of the Light Brigade":

> *Half a league, half a league,*
> *Half a league onward,*
> *All in the valley of Death*
> *Rode the six hundred.*

Tennyson High School remembers the six hundred. Their nickname is the Lancers.

A final honorable mention goes to Greensboro Grimley High School in North Carolina. Greensboro is named in honor of General Nathanael Greene who commanded the American Revolutionary forces at the nearby Battle of Guilford Courthouse in 1781. It was also the birthplace of William Sidney Porter, better known by his penname of O. Henry. In 1910 he published *Whirligig*, a collection of short stories including one of his funniest and most enduring, "The Ransom of Red Chief." Today the teams at Greensboro Grimsley High School are the Whirlies.

End Game

The prize for opportunity lost goes to the town of Byron, Illinois, some ten miles southwest of Rockford in the valley of the Rock River. Byron was settled by New Englanders who originally named it Bloomingvale. Later, however, the townspeople became so enamored by the poetry of Lord Byron that they renamed their town in his honor. Unfortunately, they did not carry this theme through when they selected the nickname for their high school teams. They are the Tigers. Perhaps they should have named their town for William Blake.

Clippers IV

Heretofore the nickname Clippers I had encountered had always referred to ships and the sea. Thus, I was surprised when riding through eastern Ohio, far from any large body of water, to see the sign at the entrance to the town of Columbiana to read "Home of the Clippers." So we stopped and I made some inquiries. We found out that the high school was in a new facility just a few blocks away, so off we went. I was welcomed into an impressive facility by the Superintendent, Dr. Patty Hura, an energetic young woman who, as I got to know her during my tour, struck me much as the Superintendent of Oak Park High School, my alma mater, Dr. Sue Bridge, had, as an outstanding educator. Dr. Hura cleared up the Clipper question for me very quickly. A star football player named Dick Fisher had gone on from Columbiana in the 1930s to lead the Paul Brown-coached Ohio State Buckeyes to Big Ten Championships and Rose Bowl victories. At that time Pan American Airways had just introduced the China Clipper, the world's most impressive airplane to date. Dick Fisher reminded one of the Columbus newspaper's sportswriters of that airplane because he, like the plane, was big, strong, fast, and able to cover considerable distances without the need to stop for rest. The townspeople liked the sound of that and adopted the Clipper as their school's teams name as well. The new facility was built in 1998 and is both attractive and functional with the interior brightly painted in the school's red and white colors. The basketball arena has an enormous two-dimensional model of the famous China Clipper

Go Huskies! Beat Felix the Cat!

flying through a red C on the wall at the east end of the court. Before I left the high school, Patty Hura gave me a lapel pin with a white China Clipper superimposed on a large red C, making me an honorary Columbiana Clipper, which I'm proud to be.

The Wingate Spartans

The 1913 and 1914 Indiana State basketball tournaments were won by tiny Wingate. Photos of those Wingate teams show the seven players wearing somewhat strange uniforms. On closer inspection they are apparently wearing football pants. In fact they were. Wingate had no gym and practices got pretty chilly in wintertime Indiana. Then, too, the court was dirt covered by cinders and football pants were appreciated whenever anyone had to dive for a ball! Eventually a gym was built, after those two championships were won. The gym is simply a barn, seats on both sides where the cattle would have their heads, and court down the center. It was actually heated by wood and coal burning stoves, whence the term "barn burner" used now to describe any exciting, closely fought game. Small wonder the Wingate teams were known as the Spartans.

The Hebron Story (Short Version)

Hebron is in the far northern part of Illinois, a rural community, surrounded by lush farmland, mostly corn. The water tower in Hebron is painted brown, with black curved lines. On closer inspection it is a basketball. A sign proudly states that Hebron won the Illinois State Basketball Championship in 1952, a feat no one in town is likely not to know or ever forget. This was accomplished by a school with a student body of less than one hundred, and a team that seldom played more than the starting five, a school that triumphed over opponents with student bodies

End Game

ten, twenty, even thirty times as large. It could have been the model for the movie *Hoosiers*, had not Milan, Indiana's similar story been selected. The Hebron team's nickname, very appropriate for a farming community, was the Green Giants. Jolly, particularly, in March of 1952. (For the full treatment, see Appendix II, page 363.)

Tuskegee

Our quest to discover who we are took us to the historic city of Tuskegee, Alabama. Tuskegee is an adaptation of the Creek Indian name for the site, Taskigi, in the east-central part of the state, selected by Booker T. Washington for the institute he founded in 1881. Washington was a freed slave who had the vision to understand the importance of education, including the skilled trades, if African Americans were to take their rightful place in our society. He began with those trades but, in 1927, the Institute became a full-fledged university. The campus is very impressive with 160 buildings on the fifteen hundred acres it occupies. Many of the older buildings and Washington's own home were built with bricks produced by his students. His home, the Oaks, was designed by the first African-American graduate of MIT and is open to the public. Washington was later joined by another great African-American, the chemistry and horticultural genius, George Washington Carver, who came to Tuskegee in 1896. Carver's pioneering study of the peanut went a long way toward saving the economy of the South following the precipitous decline of "King Cotton." This and other significant accomplishments earned him his fellowship in the Royal Academy.

But that's not all that happened in Tuskegee. In World War II a group of African Americans wished to become pilots in what was then the United States Army Air Corps so that they could apply their flying skills to the winning of the war. There were many barriers placed in their path, but they overcame and proved their worth after receiving training at an airfield just outside of town under the inspired leadership of General Benjamin Davis (1913–2002). These men became known as the "Tuskegee Airmen" and their story has been nicely documented in the film of the same name. That airfield is still there.

Tuskegee High School's athletic teams recognize all of this in their choice of a mascot. No bird more greatly signifies America than does the eagle, and that's exactly what they chose. The Tuskegee Eagles. What could be more fitting?

The Goldbacks

Newburgh, New York, is a Hudson River town about fifteen miles north of the majestic campus of the United States Military Academy at West Point. Newburgh is a town rich in history. It was the headquarters town of General George Washington for more than a year during the Revolutionary War and was the place from which he ordered an end to that war and the subsequent acceptance of British General Cornwallis surrender. The town was also a center of the whaling industry and other seafaring trade after the whales were depleted. As was true of so many schools, Newburgh had no mascot at the time of World War I. Their colors were gold and blue. During the Battle of the Hindenburg Line in Belgium, on September 29, 1918, a handsome and brave young soldier named Walter Allison was killed while trying to save the life of his company commander, Captain Harry Hayward. The extent of Allison's wounds made it impossible to identify his body, but it was soon discovered that he had been wearing a blue football jersey with a gold "N" on the front and a gold back. When the colonel heard what had happened he said something like "Who is that Goldback? I want to give him a medal." One of his teammates heard of the uniform and quickly determined that it was the high school football jersey from the Newburgh Free Academy. Eventually that jersey was returned to the school. From that

End Game

day to this, as I am informed by the present athletic director and third-generation Newburgh graduate, Chris Townsend, all Newburgh teams have been known as the Goldbacks. And that football jersey worn by Private Walter Allison in World War I is proudly and reverently on display just outside of Chris Townsend's office for all to see, and at the annual awards banquet he recounts the tale of the Goldbacks so that all will know it and remember the sacrifices that are made by men like Walter Allison so that we may live in freedom. (I am indebted not only to Chris Townsend but to Mr. Richard Durbin for this.)

Let's Roll

On September 11, 2001, two planes struck the soaring twin towers of the World Trade Center in New York City. To the horror of onlookers in person and on television the fiery inferno brought these elegant buildings crashing to the ground. Twenty-eight hundred innocent people died. Another plane struck the Pentagon. More dead. More grieving families. A fourth plane crashed in a field in western Pennsylvania. The passengers, crew, and hijackers died in that impact. More than likely that plane, United Air Lines Flight 93, was headed for Washington, D.C., and the White House. But several passengers, led we're told, by Todd Beamer and Mark Bingham, two athletic young men with a great love of family and country who knew what the other three planes had done were resolved that this one, at least, would not have a similar result. Leading the charge with the words, "Let's roll," Beamer, Bingham, and equally brave and determined crew and passengers, stormed the hijackers and the plane crashed in the Allegheny wilderness near the town of Shanksville in western Pennsylvania.

Some months later, nine coal miners were trapped underground in a mine near Somerset, also in western Pennsylvania. They had broken through a wall into a previously flooded shaft improperly located on the their maps. The cold water poured in. There was no way to get them up or to get down to them. All were feared lost. However, through ingenious, dedicated, engineers and other rescue workers, warmed oxygen was pumped down. While a shaft was being bored through the rock large enough to send down a cage for the men, families above held their vigil, hoping for a miracle. For nine miracles. A nation joined them in prayer. Finally the cage descended and, beginning around two A.M. on July 28, 2002, one by one the men were lifted out of their potential grave. Black with coal dust, exhausted, cold, mentally and physically spent, these nine miners were reunited with wives, parents, children, friends. All were safe and remarkably healthy, considering their ordeal. Their resolve and strength of spirit and the resolve and resourcefulness of the rescuers had turned a nightmare into a celebration of life. The nation rejoiced, but no place more so than the town of Somerset. Shanksville and Somerset, these two towns with such dramatic happenings in less than a year, such disparate endings but such commonality of spirit, are no more than ten miles apart. I was struck with that fact. A mere ten miles.

What team names have these two towns chosen for their high schools? Somerset is, marvelously I think, in light of the occurrences of the past year, the Golden Eagles. Shanksville is much smaller, a hamlet really, of only 245 people. They have a Scandinavian heritage, and their teams are the Vikings. Vikings and Golden Eagles. My Norwegian-born grandmother would have loved that. So do I.

"Let's roll."

Epilogue
A Final Thought

As we have pursued our quest to determine who we are as a nation, we have also discovered a larger truth about the world. Among other factors that bring us together as a nation it is clear that sports is a strong unifying force. It is also a strong force uniting all of us who share the planet. We gather together in our communities on a Friday night or a Saturday afternoon to root for the Tigers, the Railroaders, the Big Green. Later, at dinner on Sunday, around the water cooler on Monday morning, at the barbershop, at the Elks Lodge, over lunch at the local diner, we review last week's games and consider what lies ahead. "He never traveled. That was a lousy call!" "Did you see that catch?" "She got that shot off just before the buzzer!" or "If we can just get a few breaks next weekend, we'll be in the Finals!" Communities become so because of common interests, shared hopes, dreams, and even disappointments. One-time Michigan State football coach Clarence "Biggie" Munn was asked how he felt about all the hype surrounding a big game, perhaps with Notre Dame. He replied with something like, "Eight hundred million Chinese don't care who wins it."

Well, that was perhaps before President Nixon opened relations with China, before American football games were telecast worldwide, before ESPN. I believe millions of Chinese were among the billions of people watching last year's Super Bowl. Yao Ming is a developing superstar in the NBA, and his wonderful smile lights up many a commercial these days. Sports bring us closer as citizens of the only planet we have. Millions of us

Go Huskies! Beat Felix the Cat!

on both sides of the Pacific watched the Chinese women play the Americans in the final game of the 1999 World Cup Soccer Tournament, played in Los Angeles before a live crowd in excess of seventy thousand, spellbound as the issue was finally settled by penalty kicks after the game and overtime period ended in a tie. Just as the towns of Monon and Muncie, Indiana, rallied around their teams and respected the teams from Delphi and Marion who gave them all they wanted on the athletic fields and in gyms, great and small, so too, do nations rally around their teams, be they the South Africa Springboks, the Australian Wallabies, the English Lions, or the American Eagles, and, in the process get to know and respect and like and admire their opponents. I was in the crowd of perhaps seventeen thousand fans watching the championship baseball game between the Americans and the Cubans in the 1991 Pan American Games in Indianapolis. Most of the fans were cheering, of course, for the home team, and I must say we wanted to win it pretty badly. Some saw it as a contest of political systems, not just a baseball game. Well, the Cubans won, and I, for one, will not soon forget their unbridled joy as they took their victory lap around the stadium, leaping and dancing in their powder-blue uniforms with the red numbers, letters, and trim, proudly waving the Cuban flag. And, as they went, I also joined everyone else in the place in rising to our feet and giving our Cuban neighbors the standing ovation they so richly deserved. Thus is the world brought more closely together, as we recognize our common hopes and dreams.

Now you know that there are indeed places where the Appleknockers, Cornjerkers, Spongers, and Syrupmakers play. You know that such teams as Caxys and Obezags exist, and you know what Bonackers, Chitwins, and Sauras are. You know where the Peg Legs, the Sir Bills, the Sweet Potatoes, and the Honey Bears can be found. More important, you know why these teams have these names and what it means to the people who named them and cheer for them. You know where to go to find the Awesome Blossoms, the Boiling Springs Bubblers, the Orphan Annies, or the Poca Dots. You appreciate why strong young men are proud to wear uniforms that say Flaming Hearts, Kewpies, or Alices. You still do not know, however,

A Final Thought

whether the Epsom Salts ever actually played the Pimento Peppers, and that shall remain my secret for the present. Both towns are in west central Indiana. What's your guess?

Some of the names were quite poignant as the story of the Goldbacks certainly attests. Others spoke to our common history and to the value system that ties us together, making one nation of thousands of individual communities. These communities learned together the important lessons of sport: teamwork, self discipline, the rewards of effort, following rules, how to win and lose with grace. They learned these things at much the same time, and that learning helped knit together the fine and cohesive fabric that we are, helped create the culture that we treasure.

We do certainly, all of us, not just those in Austin, Indiana, live "Where Eagles Soar." This, then, is who we are.

Go, Huskies!

Appendix I

A Listing of Most of the Nicknames Appearing in this Book

For those who like reading lists better than reading text or for those in need of a refresher after they have have totally absorbed all the wealth of wisdom previously read.

Boys and Girls Combinations

Orphans and Orphan Annies		Centralia, IL
Chiefs and MissChiefs		Metlakatla, AK
Indians and Squaws	St. Vincent HS	Perryville, MO
Roosters and Chicks		Pleasant Hill, MO
Rajahs and Rajenes		Atwood, IL
Pirates and First Mates		Valmeyer, IL
Pilots and First Mates		Cairo, IL
Rebels and Belles	Southern HS	Stronghurst, IL
Raiders and Ragdolls	Archbishop Ryan HS	Philadelphia, PA
Falcons and Kestrels		Monroe, MI
Bucks and Gazelles		Yankton, SD
Pinelads and Pinegirls		Lanai, HA
Vikings and Viqueens		Lakeview, NB
Blueboys and Bluegirls		Carthage, IL
Chiefs and Maidens		Ronan, MT
Jets and Sugarjets		Enka, NC
Mustangs and Fillies		Casper, WY
Broncos and Fillies		Barrington, IL
Minutemen and Minute Maids		Bunker Hill, IL
Wildcats and Wildkittens		Lovejoy, IL
Princes and Princesses		Princeville, IL
Dukes and Duchesses		Dixon, IL
SeaKings and SeaQueens (*Seaweed?*)	Corona Del Mar HS	Newport Beach, CA
Knights and Lancers (and Pages)		Arthur, IL

Appendix I — A Listing

Foxes and Vixens .... Ft. Sumner, NM
Wolves and Wolfgals .... Flora, IL
Bulls and Belles .... Falfurrias, TX
Titans and Amazons .... Collegiate School .... Louisville, KY
Oredockers and Dockerettes .... Ashland, WI
Golden Eagles and Golden Girls .... Crescent City, IL
Lumberjacks and Jills .... Ladysmith, WI
Sammies and Suzies .... Sutton, MA
Aggies and Agates .... Poteet, TX
Hilltoppers and Angels .... Catholic HS .... Joliet, IL
Spudders and Sweet Potatoes .... Ridgefield, WA

🌀

Patriotic Names

Patriots .... Carlisle HS .... Concord, MA
Minutemen .... Lexington, MA
Patriots .... George Washington HS .... Charleston, WV
Patriots .... Freedom HS .... Bethlehem, PA
Patriots .... Patrick Henry HS .... San Diego, CA
Patriots .... Independence HS .... Charlotte, NC
Patriots .... Valley Forge HS .... Parma Heights, OH
Patriots .... Liberty HS .... Renton, WA
Patriots .... Yorktown HS .... Alexandria, VA
Patriots .... Revere, MA
Presidents .... Quincy, MA
Roughriders .... Theodore Roosevelt HS .... Chicago, IL
Generals .... George Washington HS .... Los Angeles, CA
Generals .... Washington & Lee HS .... Arlington, VA
Railsplitters .... Lincoln, IL
Abes .... Lincoln HS .... Tacoma, WA
Warriors .... Gettysburg, PA
Green Mountain Men .... Ethan Allen HS .... Wales, WI
Continentals .... Washington HS .... Indianapolis, IN
Cavaliers .... Jefferson HS .... Joplin, MO
Gore Rangers .... Vail, CO
Goldbacks .... Newburgh, NY
76ers .... Independence HS .... Columbus, OH

325

Go Huskies! Beat Felix the Cat!

Yankees	Hamilton HS	Los Angeles, CA
Burrs	West Catholic HS	Philadelphia, PA
Minutemen	Marshall HS	Portland, OR
Commandoes	Marshall HS	Chicago, IL
Commodores	Perry HS	Lima, OH
Commodores	Lafayette HS	Oxford, OH
Admirals	Farragut HS	Chicago, IL
Bluejackets	Farragut HS	St. Petersburg, FL
Colonels	Andrew Jackson HS	Chalmette, LA
Volunteers	Andrew Jackson HS	Kershaw, SC
Generals	Stonewall Jackson HS	Quicksburg, VA
Generals	Robert E. Lee HS	Jonesville, VA
Fighting Leemen	Robert E. Lee HS	Staunton, VA
Generals	Sheridan HS	Thornville, OH
Generals	US Grant HS	Oklahoma City, OK
Invaders	Normandy HS	Parma, OH
Desert Shield	Cheyenne HS	North Las Vegas, NV
Yanks		Little America, IN
Rebels	Lee-Davis HS	Mechanicsville, VA
Statesmen	Randolph Henry HS	Charllotte Crthse, VA

All-Girls Schools

SemSirens	Buffalo Seminary	Buffalo, NY
Daisies	Hockaday School	Dallas, TX
Honey Bears	Harpeth Hall	Nashville TN
Bambis	Saint Hubert HS	Philadelphia, PA
Lambs	St. Maria Goretti HS	Philadelphia, PA
Skylarks	St. Francis HS	San Antonio, TX
Pandas	Nazareth Academy HS	Philadelphia, PA
Hearts	Sacred Heart Academy	Waterbury, CN
Jesters	Emma Willard School	Troy, NY
Sundials	Ethel Walker School	Simsbury, CN
Mawrtians	Bryn Mawr School	Baltimore, MD
Bruisers	Girls Prep	Chattanooga, TN
LaPietra (The Diamonds)		Kaimana, HA
Belles		Liberty Center, IA

Appendix I — A Listing

Belles	St. Mary's	Inglewood, CA
Twisters	Oldenburg Academy	Oldenburg, IN
Troubadours	St. Francis	Honolulu, HA
Flippers	Stella Maris HS	Sag Harbor, NY
Mighty Macs	Mother McAuley HS	Chicago, IL
Vivettes	Visitation Academy	St. Louis, MO
Jewels	St. Jean Baptiste HS	New York, NY
Markers	Nerinx Hall	St. Louis, MO
Doves	Western HS	Baltimore, MD
Stingers	St. Scholastica HS	Chicago, IL
Bandits	Resurrection HS	Chicago, IL
Mystics	Maria HS	Chicago, IL
The Lamp	Winsor School	Boston, MA

Just Plain Fun

Awesome Blossoms	Blooming Prairie, MN
Blaze	Burnsville, MN
Blizzard	Winters, TX
Salts	Epsom, IN
Peppers	Pimento, IN
Cutters	Fairlawn, NJ
Flivvers	Kingsford, MI
Dots	Poca, WV
Rifles	Ayr, ND
Rifles	Remington, IN
Super Larks	Grand Meadow, MN
Sparkplugs	Speedway, IN
Whitefaces	Hereford, TX
Little Sulphurs	Trinity Springs, IN
Shiners	Rising Sun, IN
Sir Walters	Raleigh, IN
Hillbillies	Verona, NJ
Hillbillies	Ozark, AR
Hillbillies	Man, WV
Thunderbirds	Edsel Ford HS	Dearborn, MI
Steamers	Fulton, IL

327

Go Huskies! Beat Felix the Cat!

Hatchets		Bad Axe, MI
Hatchets		Washington, IN
Ramblers		Rose Bud, AR
Rollers		Roll City, IN
Happy Hunters		Huntingburg, IN
Rovers		Rootstown, OH
Wooden Shoes		Teutopolis, IL
Twigs		Ft. Branch, IN
Marksmen		Tell City, IN
Marksmen	Sherwood HS	Creighton, MO
Bowmen		Sherwood, OR
Prowlers		Thief River Falls, OR
Nuggets		Klondike, IN
Spuds		Ireland, IN
Hot Dogs		Frankfort, IN
Briar Jumpers		Somerset, KY
Mighty Hoppers	Georgetown Day School	Washington, DC
Billies		Pleasant Hill, OR
Ringers		Scircleville, IN
Bubblers		Boiling Springs, PA
Red Stickers	St. Joseph Academy	Baton Rouge, LA
Feet	Webb School	Bell Buckle, TN
Bats		Belfry, MT
Fighting Frogs	Ribet Academy	Los Angeles, CA
Fighting Planets		Mars, PA
Polos		Marco, IL
Donkeys		Bray, OK
Sailors		Steamboat Sprgs CO
Artists		Laguna Beach, CA
Big Dogs	Carabasset Academy	Kingsfield, ME
Polar Bears		Chili, IN
Polar Bears		Frost, TX
Quips		Aliquippa, PA
Flippers	Stella Maris HS	Sag Harbor, NY
Tories		Britton, MI

APPENDIX I – A LISTING

Takes Some Translation

Whip-Purs		Hampshire, IL
E-Rabs	East HS	Rockford, IL
Orabs		Sheldon, IA
Bonackers		East Hampton, NY
Kares	Rio Hondo Prep	Arcadia, CA
Tologs	Sacred Heart Academy	LaCanada, CA
Obezags	The Key School	Annapolis, MD
Pam-Pack		Washington, NC
Piasa Birds	Southwestern HS	Piasa, IL
COPS		Spencer, IN
Jug Rox		Shoals, IN
Hoggers	Northfield-Mt. Hermon	MA & NH
Hubs		Rochelle, IL
COGS	Genoa-Kingston HS	Genoa, IL
Trevians	New Trier HS	Winnetka, IL
Hyaks	North Beach HS	Ocean Shores, WA
Caxys	Lake Forest Academy	Lake Forest, IL
Hummers	Girard College HS	Philadelphia, PA
Wamps		Braintree, MA
Naps	Holy Name CC	Worcester, MA
Rappites		New Harmony, IN
Little Hoyas	Georgetown Prep	Rockville, MD
Little Noises	Nathan Hale HS	Moodus, CN
Sir Bills		Johnstown, NY
Sprudels		West Baden Sprgs. IN
Little Billikens	St Louis University HS	St Louis, MO
Skibos		Smithville, IN
Bingy Bombers		Williamsport, IN
Kaws		Perry, KA
Hodags		Rhinelander, WI
Kahoks		Collinsville, IL
Spoofhounds		Maryville, MO
Zizzers		West Plains, MO
Wampus Cats		Leesville, LA
Illineks	University HS	Urbana, IL
Buttons	Central Catholic HS	San Antonio, TX

Go Huskies! Beat Felix the Cat!

Voks .... Sidney Lanier Vocational HS .... San Antonio, TX

Animals (Expected and Unexpected)

Panthers .... North Central HS .... Indianapolis, IN
Panthers .... Park Tudor School .... Indianapolis, IN
Lynx .... Diamond HS .... Anchorage, AK
Ocelots .... Baptist Academy .... Hutchinson, TX
Smoky Bears .... Sevierville, TN
Bears .... Berne, IN
Lions .... Luzern, IN
Lions .... Leon HS .... Tallahassee, FL
Mountain Lions .... Altoona, PA
Tenacious Tigers .... Minor, AL
Tigers .... Meek, AL
Bengals .... Belair HS .... Baton Rouge, LA
Chesty Lions .... Lawrence, KN
Glacier Bears .... Haines, AK
Golden Bears .... Upper Arlington, OH
Chitwins (Bears) .... Taholah, WA
Nanooks (Polar Bears) .... Nome, AK
Koalas .... Ursuline Academy .... New Rochelle, NY
Bears .... West Oso HS .... Corpus Christi, TX
Pandas .... St. Pius X HS .... Bronx, N
Porcupines .... Nashua, MT
Chucks .... Punxsutawney, PA
Flickers .... Oriska, ND
Snails .... Madeira School .... McLean, VA
Turtles .... Chatham Hall School .... Chatham, VA
Aardvarks .... Oregon Episcopal School .... Portland, OR
Frogs .... Salome, AZ
Bull Frogs .... Bret Harte HS .... Saltville, CA
Squirrels .... Winslow, AZ
Chipmunks .... Archbishop Chapelle HS .... Metairie, LA
Coons .... Oconomowoc, WI
Raccoons .... Bridgeton, IN
Rabbits .... Wabasso, MN

Appendix I — A Listing

Jack Rabbits		Forney, TX
Armadillos		San Saba, TX
Terrapins	Tampa Prep	Tampa, FL
Toads	Thatcher School	Ojai, CA
Horned Toads		Coalinga, CA
Kangaroos		Kirkland, WA
Zebras		Rochester, IN
Tuskers		Lincolndale, NY
Elephants	Fontbonne Hall	Brooklyn, NY
Red Elephants		Gainesville, GA
Hippos		Hutto, TX
Rhinos	Taft School	Watertown, CN
Wildcats	Wilde Lake HS	Columbia, MD
Wildebeests	Friends School	Sandy Springs, MD
Angoras		Clarkston, GA
Fighting Rams	Kashmere HS	Houston, TX
Winged Beavers	Avon Old Farms	Avon, CN
Wild Boars	Choate-Rosemary Hall	Wallingford, CN
Javelinas		Crystal City, TX
Razorbacks	Arkansas HS	Texarkana, AR
Silver Foxes	Dutch Forks HS	Erma, SC
Red Foxes		Hartsville, SC
Swamp Cats	Manning Academy	Manning, SC
Cats		Catskill, NY
Wildcats		Los Gatos, CA
Tomcats	East HS	Aurora, IL
Martlets	Westminster School	Simsbury, CN
Buffaloes	Smokey Hill HS	Aurora, CO
Buffs	Milby	Houston, TX
Bison		Buffalo, OK
Lobos		Conifer, CO
Wolfpack	Wolfson HS	Jacksonville, FL
Wolverines		Wolf Lake, IN
Wolves		Wolf City, TX
Sea Wolves	Tabor Academy	Marion, MA
Badgers	Badger HS	Lake Geneva, WI
Gorillas		Gregory, SD
Rams		Geddes, SD

331

Go Huskies! Beat Felix the Cat!

Goats		Chelan, WA
Leopards		Colbert, OK
Jaguars	Martin Luther King HS	Chicago, IL
Coyotes		Alice, TX
Camels		Campbell, MO
Muskrats		Algonac, MI

Literary Prizes

Mainstreeters		Sauk Center, MN
Poets	Sidney Lanier HS	Montgomery, AL
Poets	Dunbar HS	Washington DC
Ghosts		Banquo, IN
Oracles		Delphi, IN
Sages		Monticello, IL
Academics	Hillhouse HS	New Haven, CN
Bookers	Booker T. Washington HS	Norfolk, VA
Pied Pipers		Hamlin, TX
Marksmen		Tell City, IN
Chanticleers		Ord, NB
Trojans		Homer, MI
Flying Horses		Troy, NY
Mariners		Homer, AK
Lancers	Tennyson HS	Hayward, CA
Praetorians	Heritage Prep	Orlando, FL
Whirlies	Grimsley HS	Greensboro, NC
Pythians	Lawless HS	New Orleans, LA
Athenians		Crawfordsville, IN

American History

Spy Ponders		Arlington, MA
Peg Legs	Peter Stuyvesant HS	New York City, NY
Doughboys	Pershing HS	Detroit, MI
Cannoneers		Watervliet, NY
Bell Ringers		Easthampton, CT
Clippers		Newburyport, MA

Appendix I — A Listing

Clippers		Portsmouth, NH
Clippers		Sturgeon Bay, WI
Clippers		Columbiana, OH
Ships	Lincoln HS	Manitowoc, WI
Whalers		Nantucket, MA
Whalers		Point Barrow, AK
Whalers		New London, CN
Whalers		New Bedford, MA
Harpooners	Tikigag HS	Point Hope, AK
Windjammers	Camden-Rockport HS	Camden, ME
Jayhawks	Jayhawk Linn HS	Mound City, KA
Presidents		Quincy, MA
Presidents	Black River HS	Ludlow, VT
Cavaliers	LaSalle Peru HS	LaSalle, IL
Crusaders	Marquette HS	Ottawa, IL
Discoverers		Columbus, NB
Explorers	LaSalle HS	Niagara Falls, NY
Admirals	Henry Hudson HS	Highfield, NJ
Explorers	Marquette HS	Alton, IL
Sailors	Hendryk Hudson HS	Montrose, NY
Hambletonians	Chester Union Free School	Chester, NY
Colonials		Morristown, NJ
Colonials	Clay HS	South Bend, IN
Pilgrims (Also Rocks)		Plymouth, IN
Pilgrims		New Plymouth, ID
Pioneers		Lehi, UT
Buckskins	Conestoga Valley HS	Lancaster, PA
Swamp Foxes		Marion, SC
Tomahawks		Battleground, IN
Padres	Fr. Junipero Serra HS	San Mateo, CA
Padres		Carmel, CA
Settlers		Southold, NY
Pioneers	Duchesne HS	St. Charles, MO
Pioneers	Conestoga HS	Berwyn, PA
Quakers		Plainfield, IL
Pathfinders	John Femont HS	Fremont, CA
Generals	John Stark Regional HS	Weare, NH
Boomers		Woodward, OK

333

Go Huskies! Beat Felix the Cat!

Redskins		Manteo, NC
Sentinels		Ticonderoga, NY
Streaks		Saratoga Springs, NY
Rebels	Todd County Central HS	Elkton, KY
Old Abes	Memorial HS	Eau Claire, WI

A Boy Named Sue

Bunnies		Fisher, IL
Bunnies	Benson HS	Omaha, NB
Fighting Kewpies	Hickman HS	Columbia, MO
Posies		Poseyville, IN
Alices	Lincoln HS	Vincennes, IN
Lambkins		Ft. Collins, CO
Tarbabes		Compton, CA
Jesters	St. Joseph HS	Lakewood, CA
Seraphs	St. Bonaventure HS	Ventura, CA
Fighting Chicks		Chicackasha, OK
Thunder Chickens	Doane Stuart School	Albany, NY
Flaming Hearts		Effingham, IL
Roses	Wild Rose HS	Alamo, ND
Brownies		Agawam, MA
Barbs		DeKalb, IL
Kays		Kankakee, IL
Sallies	Salesianum School	Wilmington, DE
Annas		Cynthiana, IN
Posies		Poseyville, IN

Hedonists and Optimists

Sunseekers	Allison Academy	No. Miami Beach, FL
HiTides		Miami Beach, FL
Surfriders		Kailua, HA
Breakers		Pacific Grove, CA
Battling Bathers		Mt. Clemons, MI
Resorters		Elkhart Lakes, WI

Appendix I — A Listing

Resorters		Glen Beulah, WI
Trollers		Bayfield, MI
Skiers		Aspen, CO
Yachtsmen		Falmouth, ME
Millionaires		Lennox, MA
Executives	Jane Addams Career HS	Cleveland, OH
Modeltowners		Gwinn, MN
Crimson Stars	HS of the Arts	Milwaukee, WI
Wonders	Ceredo-Kenova HS	Huntington, VA
Vanguards	Wisconsin Heights HS	Mazomanie, WI
Champions	Cascade HS	Wartrace, TN
Elites		Haubstadt, IN
Highclimbers		Shelton, WA
Aces		Stendal, IN
Immortals	Bloomingdale Academy	Bloomingdale, IN
Preppers	University School	Chagrin Falls, OH

Insects

Earwigs	The Dunn School	Los Olivos, CA
Red Bugs		Fordyce, AR
Gold Bugs		Alva, OK
Red Ants		Progresso, TX
Scarabs	East Technical HS	Cleveland, OH
Wasps		Woodstock, VT
Yellowjackets		Windsor, VT
Hornets		Essex, VT
Bumblebees	Lincoln HS	Port Arthur, TX
VeeBees	Martin Van Buren HS	New York City, NY
CeeBees	Clay-Battelle	Blacksville, WV
ZeeBees	Zion Benton HS	Zion, IL
Battling Bees		Medina, OH
Fighting Bees		Bath, MI
Killer Bees		Bridgehampton, NY
Skeeters		Mesquite, TX
Crickets		Fall Creek, WI

Go Huskies! Beat Felix the Cat!

Vocations

Fishermen		Gloucester, MA
Engineers		Watts, OK
Pistons	Automotive HS	Brooklyn, NY
Express	Transit HS	East New York, NY
Toilers	Manual Training HS	Los Angeles, CA
Oredockers		Ashland, WI
Shipbuilders		Bath, ME
Spongers		Tarpon Springs, FL
Brickies		Hobart, IN
Brickmakers		Hebron, NB
Boilermakers	Bradley-Bourbannais HS	Bradley, IL
Syrupmakers		Cairo, GA
Cheesemakers		Monroe, WI
Cheesemakers		Tillamook, OR
Papermakers		Kimberley, WI
Canners		Ladoga, IN
Canners		Biglerville, PA
Slicers		LaPorte, IN
Konkrete Kids		Northampton, PA
Chemics		Midland, MI
Cobblers		Rapid City, SD
Auctioneers		Mullins, SC
Exporters		Freeport, TX
Packers		Cudahy, WI
Packers		Armour, MT
Packers		Hormel, MN
Sawyers		Saugerties, NY
Craftsmen	Plymouth Regional Tech	Taunton, MA
Windmills		Butler, IN
Hatters		Danbury, CN
Millers		Noblesville, IN
Woolies		Millbury, MA
Prospectors		Apache Jct., AZ
Trappers	Ft. Vancouver HS	Vancouver, WA
Clockers		Ashland, MA

336

Appendix I — A Listing

Agriculture

Irrigators	Newell, SD
Cornjerkers	Hoopeston, IL
Huskers	Serena, IL
Huskers	Holdingford, MN
Apple Knockers	Cobden, IL
Vineyarders	Martha's Vnyd, MA
Grape Pickers	Northeast, PA
Crushers ... Vintage HS	Napa, CA
Apple Boys	Cory, IN
Applemen ... Musselman HS	Inwood, WV
Haymakers	Hayden, IN
Haymakers	Cozad, NB
Haybalers	Hollister, CA
Swathers	Hesston, KA
Tillers	Tustin, CA
Plowboys	Farmersburg, IN
Shockers	Wheatfield, IN
Shockers ... Wheatland HS	Grainfield, KN
Reapers	Plano, IL
Harvesters	Pampa, TX
Blue Jeans	Monroe City, IN
Farmers	Shawswick, IN
Farmers	Wheat Ridge, CO
Farmers	Farmersville, TX
Fighting Farmers	Lewisville, TX
Plowboys	Farmersburg, IN
Aggies	Dana, IN
Beetdiggers	Brush, CO
Meloneers	Rocky Ford, CO
Sugar Beeters	Chinook, MT
Cotton Pickers	Robbstown, TX
Bulldoggers	Dewey, OK
Herders	Glenrock, WY
Sheepherders ... Sweet Grass County HS	Big Timber, MT
Punchers	Big Piney, WY
Spudders	Ridgefield, WA

337

Go Huskies! Beat Felix the Cat!

Kernels		Mitchell, SD
Mule Skinners	St. John's MA	Salinas, KA
Cowboys		Chino, CA
Wranglers		Wickenburg, AZ
Ranchers	White Oak School	Vinita, OK
Diggers		Wilburton, OK
Rangers	Big Pasture HS	Randlett, OK
Grangers		LaGrange, GA
Bull Doggers		Dewey, OK
Mules		Newmarket, NH

Royalty

Kings		Wrightstown, NJ
Kingsmen		Kings Park, NY
Delta Kings	Stagg HS	Stockton, CA
Queesmen	Bishop O'Reilly HS	Kingston, PA
Monarchs	Rex Mundi HS	Evansville, IN
Imperials		Napoleon, ND
Emperors		Dinuba, CA
Ali'i Lani (Royals)		Kahului, HA
Regents		Reseda, CA
Dukes		York, NB
Dukes		Wellington, OH
Dukes		Marlboro, NY
Dukes		Gloucester, VA
Dukes		Essexville, MI
Dukes	Windsor School	New York City, NY
Dukes	Ellington HS	Washington, DC
Barons		Manheim, PA
Knights	Castle HS	Newburgh, IN
Knights	Castlemont HS	Oakland, CA
Black Knights		Windsor, NY
Squires	Calvin Christian School	Grandville, MI
Templars		Manti, UT
Chancellors	St, Thomas More School	Oakdale, CN
Grenadiers		Elk Grove Village, IL

Appendix I — A Listing

Cavaliers	LaSalle-Peru Twp HS	LaSalle, IL
Nobles	LaPuente HS	Nogales, CA
Pharaohs	Raleigh Egypt HS	Memphis, TN
Sultans		Bagdad, AZ
Rajahs		Indio, CA
Sheiks		Hollywood, CA
Marlboros		NewMarlborough, MA

Mining and Quarrying

Quarry Lads		Stinesville, IN
Quarriers		Dell Rapids, SD
Stonecutters		Bedford, IN
Blasters		St. Paul, IN
Copper Kings		Calumet, MI
Miners		Bauxite, AR
Miners		Silverton, CO
Miners		Telluride, CO
Battling Miners		Minersville, PA
Granite Diggers		Mellen, WI
Slaters		Fair Haven, VT
Hematites		Ishpeming, MI
Prospectors	Southwestern HS	Detroit, MI
Gold Diggers		Lead, SD
Scoopers		Sturgis, SD
Sandstoners		Potsdam, NY
Rock Crushers		Knippa, TX
Stone Crushers (formerly, now Lakers)	Danbury HS	Lakeside, OH
Coalers		Coal City, IL

Yummy!

Pretzels		Freeport, IL
Big Macs	Canon McMillan HS	Canonsburg, PA
Berries		Logansport, IN
Berries		Mulberry, IN
Berries	Cranberry HS	Seneca, PA

Go Huskies! Beat Felix the Cat!

Kernels		Mitchell, SD
Honey Bees		Honey Creek, IN
Clams		Tower City, ND
Crabbers		Hampton, VA
Burgers		Warrensburg, NY
Hot Dogs		Frankfort, IN*
Spuds		Moorhead, MN
Russets		Salmon, ID
Redfish	Austwell-Tivoli HS	Tivoli, TX

The Old Country

Spaniards		Cadiz, IN
Aztecs		Montezuma, IN
Cossacks		Russiaville, IN
Arabs		Mecca, IN
Immigrants	Lower East Side HS	New York, NY
Huguenots		New Rochelle, NY
Huguenots		New Paltz, NY
Gondoliers		Venice, CA
Moors		Alhambra, CA
Cossacks	Volga HS	Sioux Valley, ND
Norsemen	Valhalla HS	El Cajon, CA
Norskies		DeForest, WI
Vikings		Valhalla, NY
Swedes		Gothenburg, NB
Dutchmen		Holland, MI
Dutchmen	Erasmus Hall HS	New York, NY
Flying Dutchmen		Oostburg, WI
Gladiators		Roma, TX
Gladiators		Italy, TX
Romans	Latin School	Chicago, IL
Centurions	Broome HS	Spartanburg, SC
Centurions	Century HS	Ullin, IL
Irish		Shamrock, TX
Fighting Irish		Dublin, GA
Gaels	All Hallows HS	New York, NY

Appendix I — A Listing

Gaels	Iona Prep	New Rochelle, NY
Gauls	Webb School	Claremont, CA
Turks		Sultan, WA
Liberators		Bolivar, MO
Scotties		Glasgow, KY
Highlanders		Scotland, ND
Scots	Highland HS	Anderson, IN
Golden Horde		Granville, NY
Moguls		Escalante, UT
Tartars	Torrance HS	Torrance, CA
Saxons	North HS	Torrance, CA
Spartans	South HS	Torrance, CA
Athenians		Crawfordsville, IN
Trojans	Athena HS	Greece, NY
Olympians		Marathon, NY
Blazing Trojans	Bloom Twp HS	Chicago Heights, IL
Normans		Beverly Hills, CA
Armens	Holy Martyr Armenian Sch	Encino, CA
Tuetons		Inman, KA
Cubans		Cuba City, WI
Cajuns	Park Country Day School	Metairie, LA

Anti-Heroes

Outlaws		Rawlins, WY
Criminals		Yuma, AZ
Highwaymen		Teaneck, NJ
Bandits		Pembina, ND
Maniacs		Orofino, ID
Vandals		Vandalia, IL
Villains	Bishop McGuiness HS	Winston-Salem, NC
Rustlers		Ethan, SD
Terrors	Eldred HS	Duke Center, NY
Pugs		Paoli, OK
Renegades		Medford, WY
Urchins		Blue Spring, MS
Hoboes		Laurel Hill, FL

Go Huskies! Beat Felix the Cat!

Muckers	Tonopah, NV
Drifters	Colonial Beach, VA
Hermits ... St. Augustine Prep	Richland, NJ
Riots	Orono, ME
Red Riots	South Portland, ME
Terrors ... Eldred HS	Duke Center, PA
Spoilers	Grafton, ND

Heavy Industry

Oilers	Whiting, IN
Oilers	Wood River, IL
Oilers	Oil City, PA
Shells	Roxanna, IL
Roughnecks	White Oak, TX
Ruf-Nex	Crooked Oak, OK
Roughers	Muskogee, OK
Drillers	Bakersfield, CA
Refiners ... North Toole County HS	Sunburst, MT
Steelmen	Joliet, IL
Steelers	Farrell, PA
Ironmen	Mancelona, MI
Ironheads	Eufala, OK
Ingots ... River Forest HS	Hobart, IN
Chemics	Midland, MI
Tractors ... Fordson HS	Dearborn, MI
Railroaders	Monon, IN
Boilermakers ... Bradley-Bourbannais HS	Bradley, IL
Rails	Proctor, WI
Hi-Liners	Valley City, ND
Tarriers ... Wright Academy	Tacoma, WA
Locomotives	Laurel, MT
Engineers	Harlowton, MT
Silver Streaks	Galesburg, IL
Truckers	Norwalk, OH

Appendix I – A Listing

Lumber

Lumberjacks		Bemidji, MN
Loggers		Butte Falls, OR
Axemen	South HS	Eugene, OR
Logrollers		Wabeno, WI
Woodmen		Greenwood, IN
Timberjacks		Hayfork, CA
Lumberjax		Wright City, OK
Foresters		Forrest City, PA
Oaks		Oakland, IL
Oakers		Coventry, RI
Maples	Seaholm HS	Birmingham, MI
Evergreens	Northwind HS	Minong, WI
Piners		Lakewood, NJ
Chaparrals	Wyatt HS	Ft. Worth, TX
Cedars		Lebanon, PA
Longwood	Longwood Academy	Chicago, IL

Fish and Such

Sharks		Malibu, CA
Sharks	Spanish River HS	Boca Raton, FL
Barracudas		New Smyrna Bch, FL
Marlins	Bayside HS	Virginia Beach, VA
Dolphins		Marathon, FL
Fighting Tarpons	Charlotte HS	Punta Gorda, FL
Muskies		Muscatine, IA
Redfish		Tivoli, TX
Eels		Eminence, IN
Sea Horses		Burlington, VT
Muskrats		Algonac, MI
Beavers		Beaver Falls, NY
Otters		Fergus Falls, PA
Sea Otters		Seldovia, AK
Sand Crabs	Seabreeze HS	Daytona Beach, FL
Seals		Selinsgrove, PA
Gators		Everglades City, FL

Go Huskies! Beat Felix the Cat!

Wild Gators		Lakeview, SC
Fighting Conchs		Key West, FL
Manta Rays	Lemon Bay HS	Englewood, FL
Stingarees	Senior HS	Miami, FL
Seals		Selinsgrove, PA

The Weather Report

KaMakani (The Wind)	Hawaii Prep	Kamuela, HA
Zephyrs		Mahtomedi, MN
Chinooks		Klama, WA
Whirlwinds		Floydada, TX
Golden Gales		Lancaster, OH
Cyclones	Agricultural Science HS	Chicago, IL
Cyclones		Ottawa, KA
Tornados		Griggsville, IL
Twisters	Oldenburg Academy	Oldenburg, IN
Hurricanes		Mt. Dora, FL
Hurricanes	Buxton HS	Cape Hatteras, NC
Hurricanes		Block Island, RI
Purple Hurricanes		Gainesville, FL
Monsoons	Mayfair HS	Lakewood, CA
Storm	Sky View HS	Vancouver, WA
Thunder	Mountain View	Vancouver, WA
Thunder	Out of Door Academy	Tampa, FL
Lightning		Lehigh, FL
Thunderbolts	Andrew HS	Tinley Park, IL
Flashes	Franklin Central HS	Indianapolis, IN
Blue Flashes		Calhoun, SC
Blue Tornado	Tilghman HS	Paducah, KY
Purple Flashes	Lone Oak HS	Paducah, KY
Salt Fork Storm		Caitlin, IL
Red Storm	St. John's Prep	Astoria, NY
Magic Storm		Munich, ND
Blue Storm	Mercersburg Academy	Mercersburg, PA
The Sun	Southwestern Academy	San Merino, CA
Northern Lights		Shismaref, AK

Appendix I — A Listing

Golden Sandstorm		Amarillo, TX
Starfires	South Adams HS	Berne, IN

The Wild Blue Yonder

Blue Angels	Christian School	Aurora, CO
Thunderbirds	Hinckley HS	Aurora, CO
Aces		Mulberry Grove, Il
Bombers		Brownstown, IL
Flying Forts		Ft. Edward, NY
Bombardiers		Attleboro, MA
Blockbusters	Yeshiva Academy	St. Louis, MO
Flyers	Lindbergh HS	St. Louis, MO
Aviators		Alliance, OH
Pilots	St. Joseph-Notre Dame HS	Alameda, CA
Jets	Encinal HS	Alameda, CA
Flying Jets	Adams Central HS	Berne, IN
Sonics	Ursuline Academy	Springfield, IL
Rockets	Broad Ripple HS	Indianapolis, IN
Rockets	Goddard HS	Roswell, NM
Rockets	Moon Valley HS	Phoenix, AZ
Purple Aces		Bristow, IN
Purple Flyers		New Market, IN
Bombers		Richland, WA
Rockets	John Glenn HS	Westland, MI
Astros	Alan Shepard HS	Palos Heights, IL
Space Pioneers	Northwest HS	Indianapolis, IN
Missiles		Milledgeville, IL
Red Barons		Gatesville, NC
Flying Squadron	Home HS	Highland, AL
Zeps		Sarahsville, OH
Flying Flucos	Fluvanna County HS	Palmyra, VA

Heavenly Bodies

Comets	McCluer South	Florissant, MO
Stars	McCluer North	Florissant, MO

Go Huskies! Beat Felix the Cat!

Stars	North HS	Muhlenberg Cty., KY
Suns	South HS	Muhlenberg Cty., KY
North Stars	North Syracuse HS	Cicero, NY
Blue Stars		Port Hope, OH
Komets		Kasson, MN
Stars	Mary Star of the Sea HS	San Pedro, CA
Fighting Planets		Mars, PA
Meteors	DeLaSalle HS	Chicago, IL
Orions		Orion, IL
Quasars	Star Concept HS	Lakefield, MN
Cosmos		Springfield, VT
Lunas	Lahainaluna HS	Lahaina, HA
Satellites	South Central HS	Union Mills, IN

Location

Artesians		Martinsville, IN
Capers		Cape Elizabeth, ME
Fighting Pointers		Point Loma, CA
Portagers		Onekama, MI
Ledgers	St. Mary's Springs HS	Fond Du Lac, WI
Harbormen		Hingham, MA
Baymen		Oyster Bay, NY
Porters		Greenport, NY
Covers		Glen Cove, NY
Dalers		Farmingdale, NY
Pointers		Mineral Point, WI
Fighting Pointers	Point Loma HS	San Diego, CA
Islanders		Beaver Island, MI
Islanders		Mercer Island, WA
Islanders		Coronado Island, CA
Lakers		Skaneateles, NY
Lakers		Des Lacs, ND
Lakers		Sunapee, NH
Divers		Lake Preston, SD
Shorians	Lake Shore HS	St. Clair Shores, MI
Shoremen		Avon Lakes, OH

APPENDIX I — A LISTING

Bays		Dollar Bay, MI
Tars	South Shore HS	Chicago, IL
Tars		Anchor Bay, MI
Rivermen		Alma, MI
River Kings		Clinton, IA
River Rats		Newberry, IN
Rapids	James River HS	Midlothian, VA
Coasters		Tununak, AK
Mountaineers		Iron Mountain, MI
Mountaineers		Rainier, WA
Mountaineers		Andes, NY
Columbians		Rainier, OR
Ridgers		Glen Ridge, NJ
Foothillers	Grossmont HS	LaMesa, CA
Hillers		Haverhill, MA
Hillies	Tower Hill School	Wilmington, DE
Hillmen		Auburn, CA
Hilltoppers	Glenbard West HS	Glen Ellen, IL
Hillclimbers		Urbana, OH
Toppers		Mt. Pulaski, IL
Kavemen		Kuna, ID
Cavemen		Carlsbad, NM
Bushmen		Pine Bush, NY
Pilots		Glenns Ferry, ID
Plainsmen		Bailey, KA
County Seaters		Belvedere, NJ
Stateliners		Phillipsburg, NJ
Border Aces	Border Central HS	Calvin, ND
Borderites		Blaine, WA
Shiretowners		Houlton, ME
Villagers	Our Lady of Mercy HS	Newfield, NJ
Senators		Springfield, IL
Governors	Farrington HS	Honolulu, HA
Caps	Needham Broughton HS	Raleigh, NC
Solons		Montpelier, VT
Salt Hawks		Hutchinson, KA
Vikings	North HS	Denver, CO

347

Go Huskies! Beat Felix the Cat!

Rebels	South HS	Denver, CO
Cowboys	West HS	Denver, CO
Angels	East HS	Denver, CO
Marshmen		Horicon, WI
Bridgemen		Fort Lee, NJ
Canalmen		Bourne, MA
Westerners		Lubbock, TX
Mounders		Elk Mound, WI
Crescents	Cabrini HS	New Orleans, LA

Happy Halloween

Blue Devils	Shortridge HS	Indianapolis, IN
Blue Devils		Quincy, IL
Red Devils	Mt. Diabolo HS	Concord, CA
Green Devils		Friendship, WI
Purple Devils		Franklin, NY
Black Devils		Hettinger, ND
Satans		Devil's Lake, ND
Sun Devils		Rough Rock, AZ
Dust Devils		Mohave Valley, AZ
Devil Dogs		Travelers Rest, SC
Devil Pups	Lejeune Prep	Lejeune, NC
Screaming Devils		Warrenton, GA
Go Devils		Gurdon, AR
Diabolos		Mission Viejo, CA
Imps		Cary, NC
Demons	RJ Reynolds HS	Winston-Salem, NC
Blue Demons		Albia, IA
Green Demons		Manson, LA
Ghosts	Eastside HS	Paterson, NJ
Phantoms		Proctor, VT
Phantoms	Cathedral HS	Los Angeles, CA
Spirits	Notre Dame HS	Salinas, KA
Goblins	Wonderview HS	Hattieville, AR
Horsemen		Sleepy Hollow, NY
Riders	Ichabod Crane HS	Valatie, NY

Appendix I — A Listing

Black Cats .... Goreville, IL
Witches .... Salem, MA

Some Nasties

Scorpions .... Sedona, AZ
Tarantulas .... Gabbs, NV
Sand Lizards .... Dardanelle, AR
Cobras .... Ft. Pierce, FL
Spiders .... Concord, NC
Savages (Cobras) .... Sigourney, IA
Vipers .... Villa Madonna .... Covington, KY
Copperheads .... Anaconda, MT
Rattlers .... Tucumcari, NM
Diamondback Rattlers .... Belleview, FL
Gila Monsters .... Gila Bend, AZ
Pythons .... Pelham, NH
Serpents .... Mineral Cty. HS .... Hawthorne, NV
Sidewinders .... San Luis, AZ

Myths and More

Dragons .... St. George's School .... Newport, RI
Dragon Hunters .... St. Genevieve, MO
Dragon Slayers .... Salt Lake Christian Acad. .... Sandy, UT
Pendragons .... Pender, NB
Wyverns .... St. Francis HS .... Louisville, KY
Chimeras .... Willingboro, NJ
Griffins .... Phillips Academy .... Exeter, NH
Gryphons .... Holy Child Academy .... Rye, NY
Unicorns .... New Braunfels, TX
Centaurs .... Culver City, CA
Phoenix .... Quigley HS .... Chicago, IL
Fighting Phoenix .... McMichael HS .... Mayodan, NC
Firebirds .... Kansas Free State HS .... Lawrence, KA
Firebirds .... Phoenix, NY
Thunderbirds .... Zuni, NM

349

Go Huskies! Beat Felix the Cat!

Vulcans		Vassar, MI
Mercuries		McGregor, MN
Apollos	Sunset HS	Portland, OR
Plutos		French Lick, IN
Titans	Arcadia HS	Greece, NY
Hodags		Rhinelander, WI**
Lava Bears		Bend, OR
Gold Bugs		Alva, OK
Wampus Cats		Conway, AR
Green Hornets	Southside HS	Elmira, NY
Red Riders	Madonna HS	Weirton, WV
Road Runners	Sacred Heart Academy	Stamford, CN
Mickey Mouse	Hallahan Catholic HS	Philadelphia, PA
Jeeps	Northeast Dubois Cty HS	DuBois, IN**
Argonauts	Argo HS	Summit, IL
Juggernauts		Erlanger, KY
Furies	Forsyth Country Day Sch	Lewisville, NC
Nikes		Burlington, ND
Gremlins		Karis, PA
Menehunes		Waimea, HA
Wizards		West Warwick, RI
Magicians		Marblehead, MA
Magic		Barberton, OH
Magi		Colon, MI
Martians		Goodrich, MI
Winged Lions	Rowland Hall-St Marks Sch	Salt Lake City
Valkyries	Sacred Heart Academy	Louisville, KY
Pterodactyls	Marvelwood School	Kent, CN
Dinos	Carbon HS	Price, UT
Saber Tooth Tigers	St. Thomas More Acad	Champaign, IL
Leprechauns	St. Patrick HS	Parsons, KA
Banshees (also Eagles)	Bethlehem HS	Bardstown, KY

Playing with Fire and Electricity

Sparks	South Park HS	Buffalo, NY
Flames		Lodi, CA

Appendix I — A Listing

Blue Flames		Pickens, SC
Blue Blazes		Westbrook, ME
Torches	Tabernacle HS	Gardendale, AL
Blazers	Bush HS	Seattle, WA
Fire	Word of Life HS	Wichita, KS
Blaze		Burnsville, MN*
Flaming Hearts		Effingham, IL*
Volcano		Chester, CA
Dynamos	German School	White Plains, NY
Arcs	Brush HS	Lyndhurst, OH
Electric		Philo, OH
Power Cats		Niagara Falls, NY
Electrons	Franklin HS	Philadelphia, PA
Flashes		Franklin, IL

Clothing

Blazers	Trinity HS	River Forest, IL
Zippers		Monmouth, IL
Saddleites	Regina HS	Harper Woods, MI
Tartans	Stuart Country Day School	Princeton, NJ
Buttons	Central Catholic HS	San Antonio, TX
Blackshirts	South HS	Waukesha, WI
Dusters		Holdredge, NB
Blue Jeans		Wheatland, IN

Other Heroes

Captains	Kettering HS	Waterford, MI
Warriors	Al Smith HS	New York City, NY
Ambassadors	Adlai Stevenson HS	New York City, NY
Patriots	Stevenson HS	Lincolnshire, IL
Governors	DeWitt Clinton HS	New York City, NY
Generals	MacArthur HS	Decatur, IL
Cadets	Eisenhower HS	Yakima, WA
Statesmen	John Marshall HS	Falls Church, VA
Statesmen		Webster Groves, MO

351

Go Huskies! Beat Felix the Cat!

Senators	Sparkman HS	Harvest, AL
Senators	Robert Taft HS	Cincinnati, OH
Volunteers	Bowie HS	Arlington, TX
Texans	Sam Houston HS	Arlington, TX
Presidents	Woodrow Wilson HS	Portsmouth, VA
Presidents	Warren Harding HS	Marion, OH
Presidents	FDR HS	Hyde Park, NY
Presidents	Grover Cleveland HS	Buffalo, NY
Macs	William McKinley HS	Buffalo, NY
Trailblazers	Daniel Boone HS	Gray, TN
Athletics	LaGuardia HS for the Arts	New York City, NY
Inventors	Thomas Edison VT HS	New York City, NY

Pairings

Purple Pounders	Harrison HS	Chattanooga, TN
Yellow Hammers		Rotan, TX
Scrappers	Southside	Memphis, TN
Wreckers	Staples HS	Westport, CN
Kellys		Laona, WI
Caseys	Catholic HS	Red Bank, NJ
Salts		Epsom, IN
Peppers		Pimento, IN
Clovers		Cloverdale, IN
Shamrocks		Dublin, OH
O-At-Kan-Kats		LeRoy, NY
Rock-A-Chaws	St. Stanislaus HS	Bay St. Louis, MS
M-Cats	Maimonides HS	Brookline, MA
Y-Cats	Gardner HS	Topeka, KA
L-Cats		Lake Mills, WI
Purple Roses	St. Rose HS	Belmar, NJ
Ramblers	Carteret School	Carteret, NJ

Appendix I — A Listing

Blugolds	Aquinas HS	LaCrosse, WI
Purgolders	East HS	Madison, WI
Runnin' Reds	Stephen Decatur HS	Decatur, IL
Movin' Maroons		Dieterich, IL
Wheelers		Audobon, IA
Hubs		No. Hagerstown, MD
Steamrollers		Steelton, PA
Iron Heads		Eufala, OK
Boxers		Brocton, MA
Contenders	Faith Baptist HS	Canoga Park, CA
Gents		Crowley, LA
Hillbillies		Man, WV
Poets	Sidney Lanier HS	Montgomery, AL
Generals	Robert E. Lee HS	Montgomery, AL
Tigers	Washington HS	Massillon, OH
Bulldogs	McKinley HS	Canton, OH
Thorpes		Pine Ridge, SD
Olympians		Jim Thorpe, PA
Maple Leafs	Geneseo-Darnall HS	Geneseo, IL
Canucks		North Plainfield, NJ
Sandites		Sand Springs, OK
Golden Sandies		Amarillo, TX
Sons of Thunder	Calvary HS	Youngstown, OH
Lions of Judah	Living Word HS	Syracuse, NY
Eskomos		Esko, MN
Eskymoes		Escanaba, MI
So-Bos		South Beloit, IL
Wa-His		Walla Walla, WA

Go Huskies! Beat Felix the Cat!

Pacers	RB Hayes HS	Delaware, OH
Trotters	Fox Valley HS	Milton, IA
Boomers		Toledo, OR
Dynamiters		Glendale, CA
Purple Flashes	Lone Oak HS	Paducah, KY
Blue Tornadoes	Tilghman HS	Paducah, KY
Magicians		Marblehead, MA
Wizards		Windsor, CA
Shamans		Chefornak, AK
Crescent	Crossroads HS	St. Louis, MO
Rapids	James River HS	Midlothian, VA

The Rule of Law

Jurists	Marshall HS	Rochester, NY
Justices	Marshall HS	Richmond, VA
Barristers	Marshall HS	Los Angeles
Judges	Cardozzo HS	Flushing, NY
Lawmen	Jonathan Law HS	Milford, CN
Wardens		Deer Lodge, MT
Marshals	Marshall County HS	Benton, CN
Canons	Cathedral Prep	Rye, NY

A Girl's Best Friend

Diamonds	Lower Richland HS	Hopkins, SC
Black Diamonds		Sallisaw, OK
Emeralds		Manistique, MI
Blue Stars		Port Hope, MI
Agates		Two Harbors, MN
Garnets		Rye, NY
Jems	Villa Joseph Marie HS	Holland, PA
Jewels	St Jean Baptiste HS	New York City, NY

Appendix I — A Listing

Argents	Bishop Hoban HS	Wilkes-Barre, PA
Rocks		East Rockaway, NY
Rocks		Rock Island, IL
Greenbacks		Pratt, KA

Horses and Cows

Chargers		Chariton, IA
Ponies		Stillwater, MN
Mustangs		Sutton, NB
Pintos		Moriarty, NM
Broncos		Bronxville, NY
Colts		Colton, NY
Stallions	Schlegel HS	Kansas City, KA
Thoroughbreds		Hialeah, FL
Arabians		Pendleton, IN
Warhorses	Peabody HS	Alexandria, LA
Pacers	RB Hayes HS	Delaware, OH
Dark Horses		Clinton, NC
Ponies		Chincoteague, VA
Blue Ponies		Havre, MT
Horses		Schuylerville, NY
Flying Horse		Troy, NY
Burros	South Park HS	Fairplay, CO
Mavericks		Lordsburg, NM
Steers		Magdalena, NM
Brahmas		Diamond Bar, CA
Brahmins		Okechobee, FL
Dogies		Forsyth, MT
Holsteins		New Salem, ND
Longhorns		Aqua Dulce, TX
Shorthorns		Marfa, TX
Thundering Herd		Carlisle, TX

Anchors Aweigh

Dreadnaughts	Lakeland, FL

Go Huskies! Beat Felix the Cat!

Cruisers .... Power, OR
Destroyers .... Dunellen, NJ
Steamers .... Fulton, IL
Clippers .... Putnam, RI
Windjammers .... Camden-Rockport HS .... Camden, ME
Yachtsmen .... Falmouth, ME
Mariners .... Narragansett, RI
Tars .... South Shore HS .... Chicago, IL
Sailors .... Scituate, MA
Harbormen .... Hingham, MA
Skippers .... North Kingstown, RI
Navigators .... Hampton Roads Acad .... Newport News, VA
The Sextant .... Belmont Hill School .... Boston, MA
Middies .... Middlesburg, PA
Anchormen .... St. Clemons HS .... Somerville, MA
Commodores .... Perry County HS .... Hazard, KY
Admirals .... Admiral King HS .... Lorain, OH

◎

Small Packages

Midgets .... Butternut WI
Bantams .... Belfield, ND
Mighty Mites .... Masonic HS .... Ft. Worth, TX
Little Johns .... Danville, AR
Atoms .... Annandale, VA
Atomics .... Graceville HS .... Poplar Springs, FL
Atom Smashers .... Johnson HS .... Savannah, GA

◎

Sharpies

Arrows .... St. Sebastian HS .... Needham, MA
Musketeers .... Ft. Jennings, OH
Swordsmen .... Bayonet Pt Grace Chr Sch .... Hudson, FL
Swords .... Christian Academy .... Garland, TX
Blades .... East Bakersfield, CA
Darts .... Davis HS .... Kaysville, UT
Daggers .... Pahoa, HA

APPENDIX I — A LISTING

Sabers .... Souhegan HS .... Amherst, NH
Lasers .... Southside HS .... Atlanta, GA

How 'Bout Them Dawgs?

Huskies .... Oak Park, IL
Huskies .... Akiachak, AK
Malamutes .... Lathrop HS .... Fairbanks, AK
Whippets .... Shelby, OH
Bloodhounds .... Ft. Madison, IA
Boxers .... Brocton, MA
Houn' Dogs .... Aurora, MO
Bull Dogs .... Winston Churchill HS .... Potomac, MD
Bull Dawgs .... Haddonfield, NJ
Seton Setters .... Mother Seton HS .... Clark, NJ
Scotties .... Glasgow, KY
Hounds .... Huntington School .... Ferriday, LA
Red Hounds .... Corbin, KY
Dawgs .... Ambassador Christian HS .... Fontana, CA
Blue Dogs .... Wilshire West HS .... Santa Monica, CA
Airedales .... Alma, AR
Terriers .... Titusville, FL
St. Bernards .... All Saints Academy .... Winter Haven, FL
Greyhounds .... Carmel, IN
Great Danes .... Maranatha Christian School .... Boise, ID
Mushers .... Camas County HS .... Fairfield, ID
Watchdogs .... Beresford, SD
Wardogs .... Miami, OK
Salukis .... Red Hill HS .... Bridgeport, IL
Police Dogs .... Tippecanoe, IN

Our Feathered Friends

Pelicans .... Klamath Union HS .... Klamath Falls, OR
Cranes .... Cranbrook-Kingswood Sch .... Cranbrook, MI
Golden Cranes .... Crane, TX
Herons .... Gunston Day School .... Centreville, MD

357

Go Huskies! Beat Felix the Cat!

Auks	Afrchmere Academy	Claymont, DE
Ducks	Fontbonne Academy	Milton, MA
Mighty Ducks	Douglass HS	Baltimore, MD
Mallards	Worcester HS	Berlin, MD
Drakes		Blackduck, MN
Ring Necks		Hill City, KA
Flying Geese	Weathersfield HS	Kewanee, IL
Ganders	RE Lee HS	Baytown, TX
Honkers		Lakeview, OR
Gobblers		Broadway, VA
Pheasants		Parker, SD
Roosters		Palco, KA
Bantams		Clarkston, MN
Fighting Cocks	Cocke County HS	Newport, TN
Gamecocks		Sumter, SC
Chix		Zeeland, MI
Kaws		Perry, KA
Ravens		Ravenna, OH
Sea Gulls		Seaside, OR
Garnet Gulls		Pt. Pleasant Bch., NJ
Salt Hawks		Hutchinson, KA
Jayhawks		Mound City, KA
Night Hawks		Nightmute, AK
Seahawks		Seward, AK
Skyhawks		Fairborn, OH
Hawks	Hawken HS	Gates Mills, OH
Thunderhawks	Lakotae HS	Middletown, OH
Fighting Hawks	Prairie HS	Cedar Rapids, IA
J Hawks	Jefferson HS	Cedar Rapids, IA
Tiger Hawks	Colfax-Mingo HS	Colfax, IA
E Hawks		Emmetsburg, IA
Kee Hawks	Kee Hs	Lansing, IA
Go Hawks		Waverly, IA
Red Hawks	Natama County HS	Traer, IA
Wahawks	West HS	Waterloo, IA
Golden Hawks	Mid Prairie Comm HS	Wellman, IA
Blackhawks		Hastings, IA
Silver Hawks	Howell HS	Winter Park, FL

358

Appendix I — A Listing

Red Tail Hawks	Tamalpais HS	Mill Valley, CA
Warhawks		North Chicago, IL
Hawklets	Rockhurst HS	Kansas City, MO
Swifts		Nazareth, TX
Wrens		Wrenshal, MN
Skylarks	St. Francis HS	San Antonio, TX
Canaries	Allen HS	Allentown, PA
Larks		Sublette, KA
Bluebirds	Lake Clifton HS	Baltimore, MD
Blue Jays		Stanley, ND
Jays		Jefferson City, MO
Snowbirds	St. Mary's HS	Gaylord, MI
Ricebirds		Stuttgart, AR
Tanagers		Vermillion, SD
Red Birds		DePere, WI
Red Wings		Hoboken, NJ
Kardinals		Kearney, NJ
Cardinals		Louisville, IL
Scarlet Fliers		Neptune, NJ
Martins		Montpelier, ND
Red Robins		Antigo, WI
Bob Whites	Bellows Free Academy	St. Albans, VT
Owls		Hartford, CN
Roadrunners		Rosamond, CA
Ridgerunners		Grove, OK
Parrots	Poly HS	Sun Valley, CA
Penguins	Cushing Academy	Ashburnam, MA
Raptors	Eaglecrest HS	Aurora, CA
Condors		Whittier, CA
Golden Eagles		Owings Mills, MD
Bald Eagles		Duchesne, VT
Screeching Eagles	Mt. Assisi HS	Lemont, IL
Eagles		Freedom, OK
Eagles		Tuskegee, AL

Go Huskies! Beat Felix the Cat!

Bambi and His Friends

Antelopes		Adrian, OR
Moose		Palmer, AK
Gazelles	Sacred Heart Academy	Bloomfield Hills, MI
Golden Bucks		Bucksport, ME
Bucks		Buchanan, MI
Buckhorns	Wallenpaupack Area HS	Hawley, PA
Stags	Cheverus HS	Portland, ME
Stags	St. Agnes Academy	New York City, NY
Stags		Hartsburg, IL
Antlers		Deer, AR
Reindeer		Clarkton, MO
Impalas	Poudre HS	Ft. Collins, CO
Pronghorns	Farson-Eden HS	Farson, WY
Elks		Elk Rapids, MI
Golden Elks		Elkton, MD
Deer		Deer Park, TX
Bambis	St. Hubert HS	Philadelphia, PA

Spanish Heritage

Conquistadores	El Camino Real HS	Woodland Hills, CA
Toreadors	Taft HS	Woodland Hills, CA
Toros	Mountain View HS	Mesa, AZ
Matadors	Shadow Mountain HS	Phoenix, AZ
Dons	Coronado HS	Scottsdale, AZ
Lobos	Escalante HS	Tierra Amarilla, AZ
Gauchos		El Cerrito, CA
Caballeros	Flowing Wells HS	Tucson, AZ
Vaqueros		Irvine, CA
Padres		Carmel, CA
Torres	Country Day School	LaJolla, CA
Diabolos		Mission Viejo, CA
Dorados	Canyon del Oro HS	Tucson, AZ

Appendix I — A Listing

Miscellaneous

Nimrods		Watersmeet, MI
Magi		Colon, MI
Buckaroos		Smackoveer, AR
Avengers		East Greenwich, RI
Treaders	Chalcedon School	Atlanta, GA
Fighting Episcopalians	Kent School	Kent, CN
Villa Novans		Woonsocket, RI
Valley Cobs		Alexandria, AL
Tarblooders	Glenville HS	Cleveland, OH
Hubbers		Smethport, PA
Links		Lincoln, NB
Jugglers	Notre Dame HS	Utica, NY
Jungaleers	SE Tech HS	Detroit, MI
Big Green Machine		Naples, NY
Green Wave		Ft. Myers, FL
Crimson Tide		Concord, NH
Prophets		Prophetstown, IL
Paladins		South Plantation, FL
Bullets	Brandywine HS	Topton, PA
Unis	United Nations Int'l School	New York City, NY
Ambassadors	Bodine Sch of Int'l Affairs	Philadelphia, PA
Valiants	Valwood HS	Valdosta, GA
Yoemen	Cameron-Yoe HS	Cameron, TX
Fords		Haverford PA
Fordians		Waterford NY
Sandites		Sand Springs OK
Cahillites	Roman Catholic HS	Philadelphia. PA
Treaders	Chalcedon School	Atlanta, GA
Green Giants	Alden-Hebron HS	Hebron, IL
Blue Darters		Apopka, FL
Hustlers	Central Catholic HS	Melbourne, FL
Dashers	Divine Savior-Holy Angel HS	Milwaukee, WI
Speed Kings		Swayzee, IN
Speed Cats		Dunkirk, IN
Speed Boys		Bessemer, MI
Sharpshooters		Milton, IN

Go Huskies! Beat Felix the Cat!

Hotshots		Rosedale, IN
Lightning Five		Warren, IN
Watch City Five (Officially Maroons)		Elgin IL
Porters		Lockport, IL
Flying L's		Ft. Lauderdale, FL
Buccaneers	Caravel Academy	Bear, DE
The Caravan	Mt. Carmel HS	Chicago, IL
Utes	New Utrecht HS	New York City, NY
Lancers	Winston Churchill HS	Eugene, OR
Heralds	Whittier Christian School	La Habra, CA
Ventures	Bishop Foley HS	Madison MI
Footmen	Mattawan Christian HS	Mattawan, MI
Stanners	Archbishop Molloy HS	New York City, NY
Guards	Bellarmine-Jefferson HS	Burbank, CA
Seekers	West Valley Christian Sch.	West Hills, CA
Wildkits		Evanston, IL
Travelers		Gauley Bridge, WV
Victorians	St. Matthias	Downey, CA
Campers	Allegany HS	Cumberlan, MD
Iron Mikes	McCorriston HS	Trenton, NJ
Defenders	Bryan Station HS	Lexington, KY
Orientals	East HS	Akron, OH
Sherman Tanks	Unioto HS	Chillicothe, OH
Dodgers		Ft. Dodge, IA
Pirates		Palatine IL
Buccaneers		Belvedere, IL
Corsairs	Carmel HS	Mundelein, IL
Olympians		Jim Thorpe, PA
Thorpes		Pine Ridge, SD

Appendix II

The Hebron Story (Full Treatment)

We are a nation of people who believe anything is possible. Talent and effort will be rewarded. Presidents can be born in Hodgenville, Kentucky; Plains, Georgia; Dixon, Illinois; or Hope, Arkansas. Basketball championships can be won by teams from Milan, Indiana; Hebron, Illinois; or Cuba, Kentucky; and heroes can come from places like Dana, Indiana; Newburgh, New York; or Somerset, Pennsylvania.

Hebron, Illinois, is a small town of about eight hundred or so in population. It is very close to the Wisconsin line and is surrounded by beautiful farmland as far as the eye can see in any direction. If you approach Hebron from the east you might think you were in the Bible belt. Zion, on the shores of Lake Michigan is followed by Antioch and then Hebron. The town is fairly typical of any Midwestern farming community: a mostly brick building lined Main Street with a hardware store, grocery store, feed store, and several antique stores these days. The marquee of a one-time theater. Nicely groomed smallish homes, grain elevators and a water tower. It is the water tower that immediately catches your eye as you come near Hebron from any direction. The tower is painted an off orange, almost brown color. It has black curved lines on it: It is a basketball! There is a message, too, for all to read: State Champions, 1952.

In 1952 the Illinois State Basketball Tournament was single class, some eight hundred schools starting even at the close of the regular season. But, I get ahead of myself. In Oak Park, about eighty miles to the southeast of Hebron, we first became aware of that little school with its less than fifty boys enrollment when we saw our schedule for the 1951–1952 basketball

Go Huskies! Beat Felix the Cat!

season. They were on it for an early January game at our field house. Now, Oak Park was a school of close to three thousand students. We had gone to Champaign for the state championship Sweet Sixteen the previous March and had only graduated one starter, Ward Ellis, who had gone on to play for Kansas State. We were a genuine contender, we thought, and so did the *Chicago Tribune* and the *Chicago Sun*, for that year's title. How could they want to tangle with us? Just three years ago we had been ranked first in the state with a team that included Charlie Hoag, who, also in 1952, would not only start for a Kansas team that would win the NCAA Championship but would also win a gold medal at the Helsinki Olympics; Keston Deimling, a two-time state tennis champion who would play both basketball and tennis at Duke; Dean Anderson who went on to play for Iowa, I think it was, Ron Huseth who went on to Princeton, and several other fine athletes. They had lost to an Elgin team led by a big center named Peterson and a deadeye guard named Pearsall, and a quick other guard named Leach, plus Survant and Estergard, and we had been forced to watch the Elgin fans snake dance their way out of their gym that night chanting "Champaign, here we come . . ." on their way to wherever they celebrated such glories. Hadn't we returned the favor by beating a perhaps lesser talented Elgin team just last March? Didn't we have an all-stater in our captain, Chuck Mead, later to be baseball captain at Indiana? Wasn't he surrounded by talented players like Jim Sellergren, the best pure shooter I ever saw until Rick Mount; Dick Kolian, who later would quarterback at Wisconsin; and the super all-sport athlete, Chuck Schaefer? We had size. Jim Duncan was six feet eleven inches, said to be the tallest man ever to play in the Sweet Sixteen up until that time. Bill McConnell, who was a dead ringer for Chuck Conners and would later be a stand-in for him on the *Rifleman* and a successful actor in his own right, was six-six. We had depth in junior forwards Ron Fraser and Tom Donahoe, who both later starred at Dartmouth, and in guards Charlie Lewald, Donnie Caputo and Jere Kinnan, also juniors.

So, we tended to forget about Hebron and concentrate on our traditional rivals, Morton, Hinsdale, Proviso, Evanston, New Trier. And we were winning. Also, we began to note, was Hebron. They must have known

Appendix II – The Hebron Story

they had something special coming when they drew up their schedule. They were playing, and beating some pretty good large schools. Schools like Joliet, Waukegan, Lake Forest. Their game with DeKalb was moved into the Northern Illinois University gym to accommodate the many fans who wanted to see it. They won the McHenry County tournament and the Kankakee Holiday tournament, defeating highly regarded Danville in the championship game of the latter. By the time January came around we were both pretty highly rated in the state, and we knew we would have a game on our hands.

The Oak Park Field House was a big old barn of a place, with the basketball court and bleachers installed on a dirt floor used by the indoor track team, with a nine laps to the mile track, shot-put triangle, pole-vault pit, and so forth. It could seat fifty-five hundred, which was about as large as anything in Illinois high school basketball at the time. Our athletic director asked theirs how many tickets they wanted. He said a thousand. A thousand? For a school of less than one hundred in a town of around eight hundred? Yes, he said. They drew from many surrounding farms and had developed a large, faithful following that attended every game and had merged with nearby Alden some three years previously, adding a bit more to their following. Well, it was just like a scene out of *Hoosiers*. Down the highway they came, in a convoy. Cars, trucks, several buses. Into the gym they marched, all in order, and began their cheers. You talk about fun! They were having the time of their lives. As I remember it, there were only six players on their team, not including those who suited up and played in the preceding freshman-sophomore game and returned to sit on the bench for the varsity game. Two of the starters were the Judson twins, Phil and Paul, younger brothers of Howie, the pitcher on the Chicago White Sox. Phil played forward and Paul played guard. They also had a six-foot eleven-inch center named Bill Schultz, who went on to star at Northwestern, as both of the Judson's did at Illinois. They had a speedy guard named Kenley Spooner, who also went on to play for Northwestern, and the other forward spot was held down by Don Wilbrandt who went to Valparaiso and played there. Thus all five went to big time college basketball schools, what we refer to as

365

Go Huskies! Beat Felix the Cat!

"Division I" today. There was nothing fluky about this team. Schultz was more than merely tall: he moved well, had a good shooting touch and could rebound. The other four were superb shooters and ball handlers, and had played together for so long they instinctively knew exactly where all of their teammates were on the floor at any given time and what they each could do. They were tenacious defenders and kept themselves in top physical condition. To make a long story short, Hebron won. They beat us in overtime.

We had hoped to meet them again in Champaign, but for us it was not to be. Although we went on to win our Suburban League championship and were able to beat a Lyons team with a young budding star named Ted Caiazza who would, in fact, be good enough to win the 1953 state championship, we could not beat a tough Thornton team and thus did not go "downstate" for a repeat visit.

Hebron did. And they had only lost one game all season, to county rival Crystal Lake, en route to getting there. Earlier I said every school started out even in the Illinois State Tournament, but that was not quite true. Smaller schools, such as Hebron, had to win a district tournament to get in the main draw. Thus, they had to win another eleven straight games to nail down the state title, including two in one day on the final Saturday when the semifinals were in the afternoon and the finals in the evening. Quite a mountain to climb for a team from a small school like Hebron.

In those days the Sweet Sixteen was a three-day affair played in the old Huff Gymnasium on the campus of the University of Illinois, which would seat only some sixty-eight hundred people. Many more would go into the fieldhouse across the street and hear the amplified radio broadcast. On the wall of Huff Gymnasium they would have a large outline map of Illinois just next to the scoreboard. There would be a bright white light at the location of each school in the tournament with a large red star at Champaign and lines running to the star from each school's light. As a team would lose, its light would be extinguished until only two were left. Then, after the final game, the winner's light, the only one still on, would flash on and off until all the trophies and awards were given. Thus the expression "Shooting the

Appendix II – The Hebron Story

lights out" was what the Champion had done to the other fifteen contenders.

That year, 1952, was also the first year the Finals were televised in Illinois. We all, I and my high school friends, who included most of the players on our team, watched it on the television my father had bought, which was in our study. There weren't a lot of TVs in Oak Park yet and ours was a large screen. Yes, it was twelve inches across, almost round, and covered by a magnifying glass! We all watched as Hebron played a very strong Quincy Blue Devils team in that memorable final game. Quincy is a wonderful town, filled with elegant homes, located on the Mississippi River. It is in that part of the state that, due to the course of the river, bulges out to the west. Quincy is thus further west than St. Louis or a fair bit of Iowa. It is a populous town with a large high school. So you had a tiny school about as far north as you can get in Illinois against a large one about as far west as you can get. The game was close all the way—either team could have won. But it was Hebron who did so, again in overtime, topping off a miraculous season with an amazing, well-earned state championship. No wonder they still remember it up there. No wonder those of us who saw it will never forget that magical season of the Hebron Green Giants.